THE PARTY THAT CHANGED CANADA

Lynn McDonald

THE PARTY THAT CHANGED CANADA

The New Democratic Party,
Then and Now

Macmillan of Canada
A Division of Canada Publishing Corporation
Toronto, Ontario, Canada

Canadian Cataloguing in Publication Data

McDonald, Lynn, date.
  The party that changed Canada

Bibliography: p.
ISBN 0-7715-9559-X

1. New Democratic Party—History. I. Title.

JL197.N4M22 1987   324.27107   C87-093006-0

Design by: Don Fernley

Macmillan of Canada
A Division of Canada Publishing Corporation
Toronto, Ontario, Canada

Printed in Canada

To the memory of
Tommy Douglas

CONTENTS

PREFACE

The Party That Changed Canada was written to answer the kinds of questions that a practising politician, especially of my persuasion, is asked while canvassing door-to-door in elections: "Why should I vote for your party?" and "Is the NDP really different from the other parties?" Sometimes the question is more specific, although I suspect this one is more often thought than asked: "Since you've never been in government, what makes you think you would be any different from the Conservatives or the Liberals? Isn't it just too easy to propose changes in Opposition, when you won't have to implement them?"

These are all thoroughly reasonable questions, although extremely difficult to answer in the brief time an ordinary Canadian is prepared to give an ordinary MP at the door, even during a summer election!

For students of Canadian society and politics, not only must these questions be answered, but some documentation must be provided as well. Hence this book.

I believe my party really is different from the others and has amply demonstrated this *in government*, in three provinces and one territory. European social democratic parties like the NDP have shown that they can both gradually implement their promises and manage their economies to pay for their welfare-state, educational, and health-care programs. I believe that a New Democrat government in Ottawa could do as much and would be a welcome change from the politics of broken promises, patronage, and drift that now so dominates our national life.

Even without being in government federally, the New Democratic Party and its predecessor, the Co-operative Commonwealth Federation, have helped to make Canada a distinctive country. The fact that we have a party unlike any in the United States is a sign of our difference. This party fought for the social programs, civil-liberties measures, equality rights, and cultural sovereignty that make us Canadian. As we become increasingly nationalistic—in the positive sense of desiring to shape our own destiny—the NDP contribution becomes ever more relevant.

Several people deserve special thanks for assistance in the writing of this book. Pauline Jewett, Jo Surich, Eleanor Wright Pelrine, and Lukin Robinson read and commented on an earlier draft. My assistant, Cynthia Callard, helped beyond the call of duty. The many researchers, archivists, librarians, and information officers who provided prompt answers and expertise cannot be thanked by name, but I would like to acknowledge their considerable assistance. It was, indeed, one of the great pleasures of doing this book that I was able to spend some time again reading books, following ideas, and browsing in libraries.

Lynn McDonald, MP
Toronto, Ontario
November 1986

1

WHO, WHAT, WHEN, AND WHERE

In the early 1980s Canada went through what people other than the unemployed called a recession. Official unemployment rates rose to 12 per cent, and the unofficial rates were higher still as many people gave up looking for a job and thus, for statistical purposes, ceased to be part of the labour force. Single-industry towns had unemployment rates in the 30-50 per cent range, and they were even higher in some parts of Newfoundland and Cape Breton. One out of five young people was unemployed. Small businesses went bankrupt in record numbers. Yet, despite all this, the suffering was not remotely on the scale of the Depression of the 1930s, when unemployment was, at least for some years, only marginally higher.

The tragic stories of gaunt men riding the rails, of families losing their homes, of the elderly sick going untreated for lack of money, were not repeated. Canada is a very different country from what it was fifty years ago, thanks largely to the social programs put into place in the intervening years. The purpose of this book is to look at the political party that is largely responsible for this difference: the CCF/NDP. Most of Canada's social legislation was enacted by Liberal, and to a lesser extent Conservative, governments, but the party that first articulated the need and convinced Canadians that reform could be achieved was the CCF/NDP. These social programs are now under attack as being too expensive. "De-indexing" has begun and poses yet another threat. Given the seriousness of these attacks,

1

it is more timely than ever that we consider how they were achieved, and afforded.

On the surface, with its Holiday Inns, Howard Johnsons, and Ford and General Motors plants, Canada does not look all that different from the United States; politically, the differences are enormous. In 1984, in the midst of a Conservative landslide, 2.4 million Canadians voted for the New Democratic Party. In the United States there was also a landslide in 1984, for Ronald Reagan. But there was not even a social democratic candidate on the ballot, for the last one ran in 1956. The highest number of votes ever attained by a social democrat in presidential elections is less than a million, and that in a country with ten times the population of Canada.

Our social programs are at the heart of our distinctiveness from the United States. Yes, we still have the poor with us, but not to the extent of our richer neighbour. Our cities may not be as well planned as they could be, but we are spared the public squalor so obvious in the United States. Our rate of violent crime is only one-fifth theirs, and few Canadians feel the need to carry guns.

Canada's old age pension, unemployment insurance, and family allowance provide a safety net that catches most people before they hit economic bottom. Our medicare system, though not perfect, is arguably the best in the world. All these programs are remarkable accomplishments for a relatively small country only recently industrialized and urbanized.

The Co-operative Commonwealth Federation had its start in the Depression. The Conservative and Liberal parties hoped that the new party that came with the grasshoppers would also leave with them, but they were wrong. In the United States the closest equivalent, the Socialist Party of America, was already in decline by the time the grasshoppers arrived, and it continued to lose support despite their assistance. Canada's CCF/NDP has had its setbacks, but it has continued to be a major force in

Canadian politics, with an articulate presence in Parliament, and substantial public support.

The origins of this most un-American party, its ideology, structure, style, and dreams, are the subject of the rest of this chapter. Its achievements in the legislation of Canada's social programs, human rights, and civil liberties are the subject of Chapter 2. Chapter 3 is an exploration of why, despite this success, the CCF/NDP has never been elected to govern federally, and has never even formed the Official Opposition.

Must virtue be its own reward? Other social democratic parties with the same problems as the New Democratic Party have been elected in Sweden, Norway, West Germany, Britain, Austria, Australia, New Zealand, France, Portugal, Spain, and Greece. In the Netherlands, Belgium, Finland, Switzerland, and Ireland social democratic parties have shared in coalition governments. But nowhere in the world is a social democratic party the favoured party of the media, and everywhere conservative and liberal parties are better-financed, thanks to corporate donations. The question Chapter 4 poses is, How have *they* managed to overcome difficulties the CCF/NDP has not? Is a more highly unionized labour force with close ties to the social democratic party — which is the usual pattern — really essential for victory? Or can some other combination of support be garnered to bring the NDP to power?

For the New Democratic Party ever to attain power requires the solving of several credibility problems. As well as convincing people that its policies are worth supporting — and many are highly popular — the party must also convince voters that it can run the shop. It has, in fact, been the governing party in Saskatchewan, Manitoba, and British Columbia, and its record in social legislation and economic management is examined in Chapter 5. It has also been elected to government in the Yukon, in 1985, but it has not been in office long enough there to be judged. Three European countries serve as useful examples of countries that have social democratic governments similar in their purpose to the NDP: Sweden, Austria, and Greece. In all three we shall see an impressive list of accomplishments, all in countries smaller in population than Canada, and economically far less favoured.

The social programs that are the party's great legacy to Canada now need updating and fine-tuning. The party that proposed solutions for the 1930s Depression now needs a program for the end of this century, the subject of Chapter 6. Specifically, the New Democratic Party must find positive alternatives to free trade, elucidate an incomes policy that is fair, propose ways of reducing the deficit, and come to terms with the nature and role of public ownership. In arguing for alternatives, the party must expose the present government's excuses for not putting more money into job creation and social benefits. Demystification of the federal budget must be part of the New Democrat political agenda.

Chapter 7 argues that the NDP needs a judicious mix of policy issues, adding some "trendy" ones with which to attract new voters, while not discouraging its core members, whom it has won on bread-and-butter issues.

The party that began its life in the Canadian West must now gain support east of the Ottawa River. Its prospects for electing MPs in Québec, where it never has, and in Atlantic Canada, where it has only occasionally, will be considered in Chapter 8. In this last chapter we also go back to several basic questions: Does the vision of a co-operative commonwealth make sense any more? Is equality outmoded as a goal before it has ever been remotely attained? How do the new movements for social justice relate to the old social passion that led to the formation and strength of the CCF? Finally, the NDP's prospects as a Canadian political party and as part of an international movement are considered.

The Ferment and the Passion

By the time of the founding of the CCF, there had been several decades of radical agitation and organization in Canada, amongst farmers and workers, and in various agrarian movements, the Progressive movement, and small labour parties. Reform organizations, with overlapping aims and memberships, worked variously for temperance (meaning prohibition), the vote for women, and workers' education. There were settlement houses, labour churches, and YMCAS and YWCAS. The farmers of that time, many destitute and nearly all exploited by the eastern banks, were socialists in all but name. The American sociologist S. M. Lipset, in *Agrarian Socialism*, said that there were more lay social scientists per acre in Saskatchewan than he had ever seen anywhere else. There were probably also more liberation theologians, as they would now be called. Farmers read economics seriously, and analysed their increasingly desperate situation. Immigrants from countries with stronger labour movements, and parties, saw the need for similar organizations in Canada. The two labour MPs and a handful of the more progressive members of the Progressive Party were collaborating in Parliament as the "Ginger Group".

Canadian social democracy emerged out of this ferment. It was influenced by the Labour Party (especially Keir Hardie), Fabianism, and Christian socialism (notably F. D. Maurice and Charles Kingsley) in Britain. It was also influenced by the social gospel movement in the United States (especially Walter Rauschenbusch and Reinhold Niebuhr). Most of all, it was influenced by the social gospel movement in Canada itself. Called the "social passion" by historian Richard Allen, this movement drew on all of these sources to arrive at its own distinctive analysis of problems, and to fashion its own response to them.

The evangelical movement of the nineteenth century helped prepare the way (present-day revivalists take note). If repen-

5

tance could change persons, so could it change nations. The American revivalists of this time were never rugged individualists, but their preaching reflected a strong social conscience. And we are not long past the abolition of slavery, and the vital role of the churches in that great social movement.

The social gospel preachers rediscovered the Christian parables of the rich young ruler, the narrowness of the gate, the last being first and the first last. Jesus himself was a poor man, and a worker. God as creator worked, and identified with the poor and oppressed. The parable of the good Samaritan answered the question: "Who is my neighbour?" J. S. Woodsworth answered it in similar terms: "Every unjustly-treated man, every defenceless woman, every neglected child has a neighbour somewhere," and "Someone is responsible!"[1] The prophets neither begged for charity nor humoured the powerful. Rather they denounced unjust rulers, believing that if the rights of the poor were not recognized, "we shall all be destroyed, for the moral structure that holds up our community is undermined."[2] The poor in the Old Testament looked for divine deliverance from oppression. Jesus himself did not weep for the poor, but he was anxious for the rich, who required a miracle to enter the kingdom.[3]

The social teachings of the Old Testament were stressed, with their many restrictions on the making of profits and the accumulation of wealth, and their positive measures for the protection of the poor. God's scriptural limitation to private ownership was rediscovered in Leviticus 25:23: "The land shall not be sold for ever: for the land is mine." Jesus' own life and teaching had led his disciples to the sharing of property.

The differences between biblical teaching and the economic practices of the day were plainly evident. William Irvine, a Methodist minister and later a Member of Parliament, wrote a pamphlet entitled *Can a Christian Vote for Capitalism?* His answer was "No", for capitalism was "savage" both in theory and in practice, "the very antithesis of the Christian spirit".[4]

It exalted the lowest impulses of human nature and crushed the noblest and most divine. Where would Jesus lay his head in that "mad, ruthless scramble of the stock exchange"?

The Reverend Salem Bland, another Methodist minister and a teacher at Wesley College in Winnipeg, wrote the foreword to Irvine's pamphlet. In it, he affirmed that "Christianity and the present economic system are as essentially and incurably incompatible as ever were Christianity and slavery." One or the other had to go. In his own influential book *The New Christianity*, Bland asked how it was possible to reconcile servitude and subjection with the inherent dignity of every human soul, and such august titles as "joint heirs with Christ".[5] It was the divine right of every ordinary man and woman to share in the control of church and community.

So the social gospel called for a revival of faith, to persuade people not to lay up treasures on earth. People must take control of the economy, in order to choose a social system in which Christian ideals could fit.[6] *Social* change there had to be, for you could not "pour the new wine of co-operation into the old dried-skin bottle of cutthroat competition." The biblical teaching to all to be servants to one another resulted in the classless society, with no private property to distinguish a few from the many.[7] The overall message was, as of old, to repent and believe. The kingdom was at hand, and increasingly that kingdom was seen to be the co-operative commonwealth.

J. S. Woodsworth urged that Christianity "add its moral force to the social and economic forces making for a nobler organization of society."[8] If it did, it would not only promote the cause of justice, but "regain its own life". He called on Christians to vote as they had for generations prayed: "Thy kingdom come." Unfortunately, Irvine observed, they voted that the kingdom *not* come, and the vote was more potent than the prayer.[9]

The social gospel message had a noticeable impact on the churches themselves. The bearers of the message often suffered for it, and a number of ministers, professors, and teachers lost

7

their jobs. Yet, despite the fact that they continued to be dominated by conservative businessmen, the churches began to take up social justice issues.

By 1914, the Methodists were the most progressive on the social programs, acknowledging the right of all people to adequate maintenance, in spite of unemployment or seasonal employment. By 1918, the Methodist Church had condemned profiteering and *all* unearned wealth. It called for a democratic organization of industry, for labour to be co-partners with management. It also proposed a mixed economy based on substantial public ownership (natural resources, utilities, transportation, and communications) and the establishment of controls over profits. The church's social goals included the raising of wages above a set minimum level and the establishment of a publicly funded old age pension. Committees within the church even recommended unemployment insurance, sickness and disability insurance, widows' pensions, and maternity benefits. At the extreme, the churches condemned capitalism in general as leading to war.[10]

Other churches also called for reform. Even Mackenzie King's own Presbyterian Church was well ahead of his party in its social teaching. The Anglican Church was somewhat less radical than the Methodist and the Presbyterian, and even the Church of England in Britain, but it was still ahead of both the Liberal and the Conservative parties in teaching social responsibility.

The Founding of the CCF

J. S. Woodsworth had not been quick to move to the founding of a national party, believing that Canada needed to find its own way, and not follow the British model too closely. Then, in January 1932, as the Depression worsened, the United Farmers of Alberta issued a call for like-minded people to work together to establish a "co-operative commonwealth". The Ginger Group responded positively. The decision was made in its regular caucus meeting on May 26, 1932, in the sixth-floor Centre Block office of MP William Irvine. Included at that meeting were Canada's first woman MP, Agnes Macphail, a leading member of the Ginger Group, and several other farmer and labour representatives. On July 1, 1932, the United Farmers of Alberta executive met with the labour MPs and MLAs, issued a call for a convention, and set a date. On August 1, 1932, the convention took place at the Calgary Labour Temple. There, the CCF was given its name, a set of eight principles, and a president, J. S. Woodsworth. The organizations represented, with the United Farmers of Alberta and the labour MPs and MLAs, were three small labour parties and the Canadian Brotherhood of Railway Employees. Individually, the delegates comprised a good cross-section of Canadian society: twenty construction workers, nineteen unemployed persons, fifteen farmers, twelve MPs and MLAs, six each of housewives, railway workers, and teachers, three journalists, three accountants, two lawyers, two union executives, one merchant, one professor, one miner, and one moving-picture operator. The unwieldy, untranslatable party name that emerged was a compromise. Louise Lucas had proposed "Socialist Party of Canada", J. S. Woodsworth "Canadian Commonwealth Federation", and several others even more descriptive but bulkier titles. When a French name for the party had to be found, it was "Parti social-démocratique".

The drafting of a comprehensive manifesto was handed over to the League for Social Reconstruction, of which J. S. Woodsworth was honorary president. The LSR had recently produced its own manifesto, which was very close in its philosophy to the eight principles of the CCF. Professor Frank Underhill, who later defected to the Liberals, produced the first full version at his summer cottage in the Muskokas. Other members of the LSR reviewed it with him, and the document was passed back to the CCF executive just before the convention. No one knows, or will admit to knowing, who added the famous last sentence:

9

No C.C.F. government will rest content until it has eradicated capitalism and put into operation the full programme of socialized planning which will lead to the
establishment in Canada of the Co-operative Commonwealth.

Regina: July 1933

The 131 delegates came from across the country, by bus, train,
car pool, Bennett buggy, boxcar, and thumb. They remember
those three days as a time of great excitement and hope. With
unemployment the highest in Canadian history, farms failing,
banks foreclosing, and families losing their homes and businesses, the failure of capitalism seemed imminent. Nor were
they in any doubt as to the alternative, the co-operative
commonwealth. Production to meet people's needs would
replace production for profit. A social security system would
ensure an adequate standard of living to all through old age
pensions, unemployment and disability insurance, and medicare. A high level of education and culture would permit "a
much greater degree of leisure and a much richer individual
life for every citizen". Change would be brought about by
political action "supported by a majority of the people".

The Regina Manifesto roundly condemned the existing
economic system for its "inherent injustice and inhumanity",
its "exploitation of one class by another", the "glaring inequalities of wealth and opportunity", and "chaotic waste and
instability". The present order "in an age of plenty" condemned
"the great mass of the people to poverty and insecurity"; it
was a cancer "eating at the heart of our society". Continuing
the medical metaphor, the Depression was a sign of "the mortal
sickness of the whole capitalist system". Power had become
"more and more concentrated into the hands of a small
irresponsible minority of financiers and industrialists". "To their
predatory interests the majority are habitually sacrificed."

Specific sections dealt with economic planning, ownership, taxation and public finance, agriculture, trade, co-operatives, social justice (meaning criminal justice), the BNA Act, and external relations. The section on the labour code included insurance against unemployment, sickness, disability, and death, as well as measures for equal rewards and opportunities by sex, and health and occupational safety. The section on "socialized health services" proposed publicly organized health, hospital, medical, dental, and preventive services. Freedom of speech and assembly were advocated for all, with equal rights for all races, nationalities, religions, and political beliefs. The Senate, as "a standing obstacle to all progressive legislation", and "one of the most reactionary assemblies in the civilized world", would be abolished. An "emergency programme" was the final item proposed, a temporary measure until the long-term economic planning of the new co-operative commonwealth could be fully worked out. This list included housing, slum clearance, hospitals, libraries, schools, parks, reforestation, and rural electrification.

The manifesto, as adopted, is close to the original draft. It omits only one crucial area of policy: the role of Québec. There was to be protection against discrimination on the basis of nationality, but this would hardly be adequate. The manifesto was also woefully naive in its policy on criminal justice. Otherwise, its chief fault, in retrospect, lies in its over-confidence. In its tone it accurately reflects popular opinion of the day, and indeed that of the preceding generation with its equally confident interpretations of the social gospel and secular socialism. As an indication of this optimism, the manifesto envisaged only a "brief transitional period" between the election of a CCF government and the implementation of a planned economy.

In the party's first federal election, in 1935, the CCF's 118 candidates won 8.9 per cent of the popular vote, and 7 seats out of 245. In 1940 it ran only 87 candidates, and finished with 8.5 per cent of the popular vote and 8 seats. The party had no candidates in Atlantic Canada in its first election, and, with only one candidate in Québec, won precisely 7,326 votes in that province. In 1940 it won a seat in Nova Scotia but was otherwise nearly absent from the election in Québec and the East. The small caucuses elected were far from the breakthrough the party had hoped for, although enough to ensure a vigorous showing in the House of Commons. Provincially, the party formed the Official Opposition for the first time in British Columbia in 1933, with 31 per cent of the popular vote, and in Saskatchewan in 1934, with 25 per cent of the popular vote.

The First Leader, J. S. Woodsworth

The CCF/NDP has been fortunate in its leaders, beginning with J. S. Woodsworth. Woodsworth was born in 1874 on an Ontario farm, called Applewood, in what is now Etobicoke. (The original house has been preserved as an historic monument, and can be visited, and indeed rented for suitable occasions.) The young Woodsworth was educated at McMaster University and at Oxford. He became, as did his father, a Methodist minister. In England he worked at an East London settlement house, and began to read the Fabians and social gospel writers. Back in Canada, he served as superintendent of the All-People's Mission in the North End of Winnipeg. Among his parishioners was the family of Tommy Douglas, who were then recent immigrants from Scotland. Woodsworth also did some early sociological research and worked for a provincial welfare organization, from which he was fired when he publicly opposed the war. He then moved to his last parish in Sechelt, B.C. His books, *Strangers Within Our Gates* (1909) and *My Neighbor* (1911), are early applications of the social gospel message to Canadian society.

Woodsworth resigned from the ministry in 1917 in opposition to the church's active support of the war. His letter of resignation explained that "for me the teachings and spirit of Jesus are absolutely irreconcilable with the advocacy of war. Christianity may be an impossible idealism, but so long as I hold it, ever so unworthily, I must refuse . . . to participate in war." He moved to Vancouver and went to work as a longshoreman.

Woodsworth first came into national prominence through his support of the Winnipeg General Strike of 1919. He spoke at rallies, wrote articles for the *Western Labor News*, and preached at meetings of the "labour churches" that sprang up to support the strike. Woodsworth was charged with sedition, and briefly jailed, for publishing a pamphlet that included, amongst other things, a plea for moderation on both sides of the strike. But the gem of the indictment was count 4 — two quotations from the prophet Isaiah, without comment, and correctly attributed.

> Woe unto them that decree unrighteous decrees, and that write grievousness which they have prescribed; to turn aside the needy from judgment, and take away the right from the poor of my people, that widows may be their prey and that they may rob the fatherless.
>
> (Isaiah 10:1,2)

> And they shall build houses and inhabit them; and they shall plant vineyards, and eat the fruit of them. They shall not build and another inhabit; they shall not plant and another eat; for as the days of a tree are the days of my people, and mine elect shall long enjoy the work of their hands.
>
> (Isaiah 65: 21,22)

The authorities, however, were not so foolish as to put the Bible on trial and stayed the proceedings.

Woodsworth was elected to Parliament in 1921 in Winnipeg, and continued to be re-elected until his death in 1942. As will be clear in the following chapter, he fully used his time in Parliament to put forward the case for the co-operative commonwealth, and specific measures promoting social and economic justice, civil liberties, equality rights, and justice rather than vengeance in international affairs. He travelled widely to promote the party, which he continued to think of as "the movement".

A pacifist since his young-manhood, Woodsworth opposed Canadian entry into the Second World War. He resigned as leader of the party in 1940, when the caucus supported Canada's entry into the war, but remained as honorary president. His health failed soon after, and he died in 1942. It is a signal tribute to him that he won re-election to Parliament in 1940 with an increased vote, and even won the soldiers' vote. Lucy Woodsworth was a worthy companion and co-worker to her husband, and a feminist and peace activist in her own right. Their daughter, Grace MacInnis, was also a distinguished MP, serving indeed as the only woman in the House of Commons after the Trudeaumania election of 1968.

Woodsworth is so often seen as the prophet in politics that his considerable intellectual contribution has often been under-estimated. It is probable that future assessments will give him more credit as an original thinker, and a major source of a distinctively Canadian social democracy.

M. J. Coldwell

Coldwell had a difficult act to follow as Woodsworth's successor. As David Lewis put it: "One respected and loved Coldwell, but one revered and worshipped Woodsworth." M. J. Coldwell was born in Devon, England, and emigrated to Canada in 1910 as a young teacher. He taught briefly in Alberta, then moved to Saskatchewan, where he was a school principal for twenty years. He was a red Tory in England, and a Progressive in Canada in 1921; then the growing Depression completed his education. He was also a practising Anglican, and was influenced by the social gospel tradition. By 1926 he had helped to organize the Independent Labour Party in Saskatchewan, and he ran for alderman on its ticket, topping the polls. In 1929 he helped to organize, and indeed led, the Farmer-Labour Party of Saskatchewan, which was one of the founding groups of the CCF. At the Regina Convention he had the delicate task of chairing the policy research committee, which framed the party's first policy statement. He was elected to Parliament in 1935 for Rosetown-Biggar, which seat he held until the Diefenbaker landslide in 1958.

In the House of Commons, Coldwell's gentlemanly appearance and quiet, courteous manners belied a passionate commitment to social justice. He was a fine speaker, blessed with a rich voice and a gift for the right turn of phrase. He was also an able parliamentarian who knew his points of order. When his wife developed a crippling disease, Coldwell offered to quit politics. She insisted he stay on, which he did, while continuing to look after her at home.

In the House, Coldwell argued for social security measures and a decent labour code, and against war-profiteering and corporate handouts. He followed Woodsworth's practice of setting out comprehensive strategies for reform, yet supporting whatever halfway measures the government would accept. As leader in the post-war period, Coldwell had the unhappy experience of helplessly watching the Liberal theft of his party's policies. He was acutely aware of the votes the stolen reforms attracted to the Liberals, and of the gaps that were left as measures were imperfectly implemented. In a radio speech in 1953, he said:

> We have seldom succeeded in achieving our full objective in any field. The measures we have introduced and campaigned for have been accepted reluctantly and half-heartedly by administrations that didn't really believe in them. In every case there are vast improvements still to be made.

15

On his defeat in 1958, Coldwell left active politics, albeit at the respectable age of seventy. He continued to support the party, and especially its transformation into the NDP in 1961. He was made a privy counsellor in centennial year, and died in 1974.

Hazen Argue

On Coldwell's forced retirement in 1958, Hazen Argue served as parliamentary leader of the CCF until 1960, and then as party leader until the founding convention of the New Democratic Party in 1961. Argue ran second to Tommy Douglas at that convention. A year later, he resigned from the party. He subsequently joined the Liberal Party and accepted an appointment to that reactionary institution he had previously wished to abolish, the Senate.

T. C. Douglas

Tommy Douglas was born in 1905 in Falkirk, Scotland, an industrial area of ancient origins. The family emigrated to Winnipeg when he was six, but returned to Scotland during the First World War, when his father was in the army. As a boy, Tommy nearly lost a leg because his family could not afford a necessary operation. Fortunately, a doctor gave his services, but the lesson was not lost on the patient. Canada's medicare system undoubtedly owes a lot to this bad knee.

Back in Winnipeg in 1919, the fourteen-year-old Tommy went to work as an apprentice printer. Over the next five years he also participated in amateur theatricals — evident in his later speech-making — and became the lightweight boxing champion of Manitoba. He was in Winnipeg during the General Strike, and saw strikers charged by horses and shot at. At the age of nineteen he went back to school, to Brandon College. One of his fellow students was Stanley Knowles.

Douglas was ordained as a Baptist minister in 1930 and was called to his first church in Weyburn, Saskatchewan. He did what he could to relieve the suffering of the Depression, mobilizing the resources of church and community. Volunteers handed out food, clothing, bedding, and the most basic of supplies to destitute families. He organized the Weyburn Labour Association to provide moral support and entertainment to the unemployed, and to supply what local short-term jobs could be found. They also handed out apples and vegetables. At this time Douglas began to speak to farmers, who were coming to understand the need to work together with labour. He went on lobbying expeditions with farm groups to the provincial government, but without success.

Wondering how to get farmers and labour together for political action, Douglas wrote to his old minister, J. S. Woodsworth, then in Parliament. Woodsworth had received a similar letter the same day from Coldwell, and got the two together. (To Mackenzie King this would have been proof of divine intervention!) Coldwell made the trip down to Weyburn one Saturday morning, finding the young minister in his study at the back of the church, preparing his Sunday sermon.

Douglas missed the first round of CCF organizing in the summer of 1932, as he was studying economics at the University of Manitoba. The economics, in turn, was to lead to a master's degree in "Christian Sociology" from McMaster University, a subject that has since disappeared from the curriculum. Douglas was elected to the national council of the CCF, and in that capacity attended the Regina Convention. In 1934 he ran for the Saskatchewan Farmer-Labour Party in the provincial election. Thousands came out to the election meetings and he, optimistic as always, thought he would win. The party won five seats, to form the Official Opposition, but Douglas lost. It was a rough campaign. Once, stopping to fix a flat tire, he discovered that all the nuts on a wheel had been loosened. A few bad eggs and some rotten fruit were thrown at him, but he admits to "creating as much disturbance as he received". The underdog, he would attend his opponent's election meetings, ask questions from the floor, and demand time, which he usually got, to explain *his* views! His own speeches, he admitted, were more like those of a university professor teaching a sociology class, a mistake he was not to repeat.

After the election, Douglas went back to the University of Chicago, where he had already begun to work on a Ph.D. in sociology, studying unemployment in that city. He had not intended to run in the 1935 federal election, but he changed his mind when a church superintendent told him, "If you don't stay out of politics, you'll never get another church in Canada, and I'll see to it." Douglas replied characteristically: "You've just given the CCF a candidate." The superintendent, incidentally, later changed his mind and told Douglas how delighted he was with his work in politics. The Reverend Tommy Douglas in fact remained on the church rolls as a minister for the rest of his life. He preached frequently, but he always opposed using "religion as a gimmick for gaining political support".[11]

Douglas declined the offer of a chair in Christian and social ethics at the University of Chicago to enter Canadian politics. He won his riding in 1935 by 301 votes, crediting the victory to the ineptitude of the Liberal incumbent more than to any brilliance in his own campaign. His opponent had urged Canadians to reconcile themselves to a lower standard of living and recommended army camps for the unemployed, along the lines of Hitler's in Germany. During the campaign, CCF literature was stolen in a break-in at its printers, and was later found in the home of the president of the Liberal society!

In Parliament, as one of the first seven CCF MPs, Douglas was spokesperson for agriculture, youth, and foreign policy. He was a strong advocate of collective security, including military force against the rising fascists in Europe. When Canadian corporations urged a policy of non-intervention in the arms race, he opposed this as a strategy simply to make money. The corporations continued to sell oil, nickel, and other needed war materials to fascist governments. In 1936 he spent three months in Europe, at the League of Nations, in Spain, and in Germany. He heard Hitler speak at Nuremberg. Back in Canada, he devoted an extensive speaking tour to the Nazi threat, predicting with remarkable accuracy the steps leading to the Second World War. As a result he was threatened by pro-Nazi groups. Douglas joined the Second Battalion of the South Saskatchewan Regiment, was commissioned to go to Hong Kong in 1936, but was kept back because of his bad knee. (If he had, he would have, at best, spent the war as a prisoner of war.)

Douglas was invited back to Saskatchewan in 1944 to lead the CCF in the provincial election that the party, correctly at last, expected to win. Sweeping 47 of the 52 seats, he became the first social democratic premier in North America. He went on to set records for progressive, humane government, without a hint of patronage or corruption, always balancing the budget. These feats are described in Chapter 5.

Douglas had been premier seventeen years when he was called back to Ottawa. Elected the first leader of the New Democratic Party in 1961, he led the party for ten years until his resignation in 1971. He remained another eight years in Parliament as the MP for Nanaimo–Cowichan–the Islands. In his last years, he continued to be much sought after as a speaker. His Burns' Night speeches were legendary, for Douglas knew the poet by heart and was always a good story teller.

Douglas was so handsomely eulogized on his death in 1986 that it is easily forgotten how many setbacks and how much abuse he endured in his life. He twice lost his own riding while campaigning as national leader, and had to run again in by-elections. He was called a "stinking skunk" in the Saskatchewan legislature for uncovering graft by the previous Liberal administration. He also received the usual taunts of the short man, but gave back better than most. Said a particularly large, burly opponent: "Tommy, you little squirt, I could eat you whole." Douglas replied, "In that case, you'd have more brains in your stomach than in your head." Said a young Liberal heckler at a university meeting: "Tommy, do you believe in birth control?" "Yes," was the reply. "And in your case, I'd make it retroactive."

Ideology

As in other social democratic parties throughout the world, CCF ideology was moderated over the years. In Saskatchewan, Premier Douglas quickly learned that public ownership was not always affordable. In Europe, social democratic parties were putting welfare-state measures into place, without much public ownership. In the Soviet Union, there was vast public ownership, but with little freedom, and still with great inequalities. By the time the Winnipeg Declaration was adopted in 1956, public ownership had become one measure among others, and not a prerequisite for the achievement of social democracy. The Canadian people needed "effective control over the means by which they live", which could be achieved by government regulation. "Private profit and corporate power must be subordinated to social planning" — evidently they were not to be eliminated entirely. "Equality of opportunity" sometimes replaces equality pure and simple as a goal. "The highest possible living standards for all Canadians" replaces more basic concerns for bread, milk, and fuel. Yet there is still the belief that the co-operative commonwealth is the better way, for "a society motivated by the drive for private gain and special privilege is basically immoral." To its opponents, at least, even the moderated CCF represented radical socialism, to be vigorously fought, and eradicated if possible.

The party's Winnipeg Declaration could correctly claim that Canada was a better place in 1956 than it had been a generation ago, "not least because of the cry for justice sounded in the

Regina Manifesto, and the devoted efforts of the CCF members and supporters since that time." It accurately predicted that technological change would produce even greater concentrations of wealth and power, and could cause great distress through unemployment and displacement of workers. The "eradication of capitalism" aim was replaced by a more cumbersome declaration that concerned the whole world, not just Canada. The party would now not rest content "until every person in this land and in all other lands is able to enjoy equality and freedom, a sense of human dignity and an opportunity to live a rich and meaningful life as a citizen of a free and peaceful world."

Over the years, the CCF lost its sense of the inevitability of its coming to power, originally felt by so many of its members. The Regina Manifesto had refrained from making sure predictions, but other writings and speeches reveal a decided sense that history at least, if not God, was on our side. Thus, in 1943, David Lewis and Frank Scott concluded:

> The C.C.F. . . . . emerges as the inevitable and logical political instrument of the Canadian people and its programme as the inevitable and logical next step in the evolution of our democratic society.[12]

Not only would good things happen, but the undesirable would cease, as monopoly ownership "must and shall disappear". It was true, at the time, that support for the party was growing, but doubtful that "the relentless logic of events is bringing more and more thousands of Canadians to support the policies and objectives of the C.C.F."[13] The party at the same time was distancing itself from its religious origins. The social gospel roots had always been resented by some non-religious members. To show his contempt, B.C. member Ernie Winch sat at executive meetings with his back to his party leader, the Reverend Robert McConnell, an Anglican priest. Frank Underhill gave as a "major part of his disillusionment"

21

with the party the realization "that most of his fellow CCFers were, under a thin secular veneer, essentially bible-bangers."[14] Evidently Bibles were not thumped in the Liberal Party.

Media attacks on the party were especially vicious, and often contradictory, in the early years. For example, according to the *Montreal Star*, the CCF threatened Canada with "the Fascism of Hitler and Mussolini". It had "many of the incipient characteristics of the Nazi Party in its early political existence".[15] In a *Globe and Mail* advertisement, on the other hand, the CCF was called the "National Fake Socialists" and "Communist-controlled".[16] The advertisement warned against voting for William Dennison, later mayor of Toronto, who was then running for the Board of Control. As a CCF candidate, Dennison would be a "Communist rubber stamp", taking instructions from the "Communist-controlled" CCF. The *Montreal Star* refused to cover CCF events, or even to take paid advertisements of public meetings. Letters to the editor replying to attacks went unprinted.[17]

The *Ottawa Journal* attacked the CCF for having given such a "vile", false picture of the supposedly "wretched conditions" of the Depression. "Piffle. The truth of the matter is that Canada has been a vigorously prosperous country, despite brief phases of business depression of which every country has its turn."[18] According to the *Journal*, the CCF aim was no less than "to seize all main activities of a civilized country and administer them . . . with the idea of levelling society so that the intelligent, energetic and industrious people shall get less, and the lazy, the idle, the inefficient and the unintelligent shall get more." With Coldwell as leader, admitted the *Journal*, there would be only "milk and water" socialism. But with the "extremists" of British Columbia, "it is rank communism." Massive mail-outs, paid for by business groups, carried a similar message. The party did what it could to undo the damage, sending out fresh-faced volunteers as election canvassers. But it could not afford to buy advertising to counter the smears or match the mail-outs.

Life in the Party — or Whist Drives Revisited

Life in the old CCF was not life in the fast lane, but it was strong on work, hope, friendship, and talk. There were scarcely any paid organizers. Money was raised through whist drives, bake sales, and socials. Party volunteers called at members' homes to collect subscriptions, sometimes at fifty cents a shot. Speakers and organizers had no money for hotels, so local members billeted them. "Educationals" were held, often weekly, where members together worked through economics and sociology texts. There were summer camps for party families and young people. The negative side of this was a tendency to cliquishness. The party faithful, who sacrificed so much, were sometimes suspicious of newcomers who had not shared the trials with them.

In an election, the CCF had to get out its message and confront the often preposterous accusations levelled against them by the other parties, the press, and business organizations. Without corporate donations, the CCF had far less campaign money to spend, perhaps one-tenth or one-twentieth that of the old-line parties. In 1949, for example, the total expenditure of the CCF national campaign was $33,000. The Liberal Party contract with one advertising agency alone was worth $189,000. There were then no controls on campaign expenditures, or reporting requirements, so precise comparisons cannot be made.

The Decline of the 1950s

The reasons are still debated, but the fact nevertheless remains that the CCF did not break through to office in Canada in the post-war period. The CCF was elected provincially in Saskatchewan in 1944, and formed the Official Opposition in Ontario in 1943. Then its progress was halted. In the federal election of 1945, the party obtained 15.6 per cent of the popular vote — a record high for it — and a noticeable 28 seats. Then it went into decline.

The post-war recession it had predicted did not materialize, thanks in part to government adoption of some of its policies. Canada enjoyed real growth and high rates of employment, wages, and salaries. Inflation was negligible. The welfare-state measures gave considerable new protection to ordinary Canadians against the vicissitudes of unemployment, ill health, disability, and old age. The result was that in 1949 the CCF share of the vote declined to 13.4 per cent and 13 seats. The party could not get as many candidates to run for it (180) as it had had in 1945 (205), although the number of seats had been increased. It failed to find candidates for seven ridings in Ontario and fifty-three in Québec.

In 1953, there was a further decline in the popular vote, to 11.3 per cent, although 23 MPs were elected. Again there was a decline in the number of candidates running, now only 170. In 1957, when Diefenbaker replaced St. Laurent as prime minister, the CCF fell to 10.7 per cent in the popular vote, although winning 25 seats. It lost its one seat in the East, in Cape Breton. The slide in the number of candidates continued: only 162 for the 265 seats. There were only 22 CCF candidates for the 75 Québec seats, 60 for the 85 in Ontario. The party did not have full slates in the Atlantic provinces either, although this was not a new problem. In the Diefenbaker sweep of 1958, the vote fell to 9.5 per cent and 8 seats. Even the much-loved Stanley Knowles lost Woodsworth's old seat. There had not been any further decline in nominated candidates, however; in fact there was a slight increase. Rather, Dief the Chief took votes from the party across the country, including the CCF's traditional areas of strength.

Organizing the New Party

The reorganizing of the CCF into the NDP took place in the three years following the 1958 disaster. New hope was to be found in the alliance with organized labour, for the first time now willing to give its effort and expertise seriously to the building of a political party with which it could work. The founding convention of the NDP, at the Ottawa Coliseum in 1961, was larger and better organized than any ever held by the CCF. Of the 1801 accredited delegates, one-third were union delegates. The whist drives were over.

The provisional name "New Party" almost stuck, but Ontario insisted on adding Democratic to arrive at the present-day New Democratic Party/Nouveau Parti Démocratique. The clubs that had sprung up in support of the new party were part of the regenerative spirit. Oligarchy, however, seems to have been swift in reasserting its prerogatives. The clubs were disbanded for regular constituency associations, where the new members often found they were not accepted by the longer-serving CCFers.

The New Party promptly won a by-election in Peterborough, with Walter Pitman, and increased its vote sharply in Niagara Falls, although the seat was won by Liberal Judy LaMarsh. Pauline Jewett's study "Who Voted New Party and Why" indicated new support for the party in all social classes, and especially among young people.[19]

Yet the first general election, in 1962, brought disappointing results. The downward trend was now reversed, but at 13.5 per cent of the popular vote the NDP was only regaining the 1949 level of the CCF's strength. To some extent the increase reflected better organization: the party ran more candidates — 218 for the 265 seats. The improvement was greatest in Québec, now with 40 candidates for the 75 seats. In the 1963 election, when Pearson replaced Diefenbaker as prime minister, the NDP won a disappointing 13.1 per cent of the vote, still below the 1945 high. Again there was an increase in nominated candidates, up to 232, and including now a record 60 in Québec.

It was not until 1965 that the party ran at least close to a full slate, 255 candidates for the 265 seats that year, and in 1968, for the first time, it achieved an absolutely 265/265 slate. The popular vote rose to 17.9 per cent in 1965, and remained at 17.0 per cent in 1968. In 1972 there was a little slippage in candidacies, to 251; in 1974 they were back up to 262, with full slates again in 1979, 1980, and 1984.

The 1972 campaign marks the first time the federal party could afford a plane for the national leader's campaign. It was promptly named "Bum-Air" in honour of David Lewis's "corporate welfare bums" attack. (A later year the plane would be called "Doctrin-Air".) The 1972 election is best known for the election of the Trudeau minority government. The New Democratic Party won 17.7 per cent of the votes, and 31 seats. In 1974, its vote declined to 15.4 per cent, and 16 seats. The Liberals were returned with a majority. David Lewis lost his own seat. The defeat of so many members was an especially bitter blow, since they had achieved so much in the minority government situation. The concessions won in that period are described in Chapter 2.

In the 1979 election, won by Joe Clark and the Conservative Party, the New Democrats improved their vote, to 17.7 per cent and 26 seats. This minority government was defeated on an NDP motion of non-confidence in the budget. The Liberals were returned in 1980, in Trudeau's last election. The New Democratic Party won 19.8 per cent of the popular vote, and 32 seats, in that election, its best result ever. In 1984 the party dropped slightly to 18.7 per cent, and 30 members, still a remarkable achievement in the face of the Mulroney landslide.

David Lewis

With David Lewis the pattern of teachers and preachers as party leaders was broken. Lewis was a labour lawyer, a secular Jew, and the first of the leaders to be fluent in French. Journalist Charles Lynch judged him the finest political orator of his day, a verdict with which many would agree. David Lewis was born in 1904 in Svisloch, a Polish town then under Czarist occupation, predominantly Jewish in population. His father, a worker, was a committed socialist and young David grew up in a household of lively debate. The family emigrated to Canada, steerage, in 1921, and settled in Montreal. David, then twelve, learned English well enough in three years to win a scholarship for high school, Baron Byng. He was an articulate and brash political fighter by the time he completed his B.A. Still at McGill, he went on to law, and was encouraged, by Frank Scott amongst others, to try for a Rhodes scholarship. He won.

In 1932, with his fiancée, Sophie, he set off for Oxford, travelling through Europe on the way. Lewis's talents were promptly recognized in Britain. He became president of the Oxford Union, and hob-nobbed with the leaders of the British Labour Party. He was even offered a place to run for Parliament in England. At the same time Woodsworth invited him to join the movement in Canada, and he chose toil and trouble over a safe English seat and a likely post in cabinet. Lewis returned to Canada in 1935, married Sophie, and joined a law firm.

In 1936 he established the party's first national office, at 124 Wellington Street, Ottawa, and became the first national secretary. The office, an unheated storeroom at the rear of his law office, was rent-free. Lewis himself was salary-free. Two years later he gave up law practice for a full-time position with the party, at $1,800 a year. New premises were found, now heated, at $30 a month.

Lewis ran for Parliament four times unsuccessfully in the 1940s, in Montreal and Hamilton. He had the humiliation of running fourth out of four candidates in Cartier, in the area where his family had always lived in Montreal. In 1950 he returned to full-time law practice, now in Toronto. He took labour cases largely, often with a civil-liberties bent. He was finally elected in Toronto York South, in 1962. He was defeated again in 1963, but re-elected in 1965, 1968, and 1972.

Lewis led the party for only four years, from 1971 to 1975, including the productive Trudeau minority government of 1972-74. He was defeated again in 1974 and, ill from leukemia, he resigned. He died in 1981.

Lewis's gift for words was not confined to oratory. He wrote, with Frank Scott, a classic defence of Canadian social democracy, *Make This YOUR Canada*, published in 1943. His political memoirs, *The Good Fight*, alas only to 1958, deservedly won the Governor General's Award for non-fiction. The book gives a fine, decidedly partisan, and often sardonic review of three decades of Canadian politics. David and Sophie Lewis also founded a political family. Eldest son Stephen led the NDP in Ontario in the 1970s, and was appointed ambassador to the United Nations in 1984. Michael Lewis was provincial secretary of the NDP in Ontario from 1982 to 1986, and Janet Lewis Solberg has been an active member and staff person.

Ed Broadbent

John Edward Broadbent was born in 1936 in Oshawa, where he grew up. He obtained his B.A. from the University of Toronto and his Ph.D. from the London School of Economics. His specialty was political philosophy, and he continues to read widely in it, an unusual activity for a practising politician. Broadbent was first elected to Parliament in 1968, upsetting Conservative cabinet minister Michael Starr. His margin was only fifteen votes, but he has since been re-elected five times with respectable victories. He is also an RCAF reserve officer.

Broadbent first sought the New Democrat leadership in 1971, running fourth to David Lewis. He had announced that he would not be a candidate in 1975, but great pressure was put on him to run. He did, and has not been seriously threatened as leader since. The only attack on his leadership, and it was brief, occurred in 1983 when the party fell badly in the polls. He was then to be credited personally with the party's recovery in the 1984 campaign.

Broadbent has continued the modernization of the party. He has worked hard to improve relations with organized labour, including the development of parallel campaigns in federal elections. He has paid a great deal of attention to funding for the federal party, specifically to end the practice of provincial units paying their federal dues only after they have first met all their other bills. The federal party is now doing its own independent fund-raising. Mass mail-outs and computers are in, whist drives out. Broadbent's idea of purgatory is a place filled with New Democrats selling raffle tickets to each other.

Broadbent was elected vice-president of the Socialist International in 1978, and has been regularly re-elected since. Since the 1984 federal election he has been closely involved in the development of the party in Québec, touring and speaking there often. He speaks French fluently, if with a strong Oshawa accent. His wife, Lucille, is a Franco-Ontarian, and a decided asset to the campaign everywhere in the country. Throughout his tenure as leader, Ed Broadbent has enjoyed the good opinion of the Canadian public, including those who do not vote for the party. He is seen as intelligent, able, and honest outside the party, as he is in.

Present Structure

Unlike the Liberal and Conservative parties, the New Democratic Party has a democratic structure. It suffers no worse than the usual tendencies of any organization to oligarchy. There is a strong grass-roots organization. Riding associations elect executives, hold meetings, and send delegates to larger provincial and federal councils and conventions. Policy is determined by majority votes at biennial conventions where the debate is remarkably open and civilized. The party leader, caucus members, and ordinary delegates alike present their cases at the microphone. The negative side of this otherwise healthy democracy is that conflicts as well as constructive ideas are aired in the open, and often make good press.

The Conservative and Liberal parties operate quite differently. There is little function for the membership in those parties, for policy is determined by the leader and a small group selected by him.

In 1986 the total individual membership of the New Democratic Party was close to 150,000, with a further 300,000 affiliated through unions. No comparable figures are available for the Liberals and Conservatives. Their membership numbers fluctuate wildly, soaring with nomination and leadership contests, and then declining as there is little reason for members to renew. The Conservatives, especially, use memberships as a fund-raising device, sending them out unsolicited — even to New Democrat MPs — with a plea for financial contributions. The NDP, however, requires for joining that the person not belong to another political party, and that he or she agree with the principles — but not every resolution! — of the party. Members have been expelled for belonging to another party.

Within the NDP there are further groupings, such as the Left Caucus, the Northern Caucus, and the Participation of Women Committee. The Left Caucus regularly sees its resolutions voted down, and takes this with remarkable good grace. There is an ethic of respecting majority decisions, widely honoured. There is an ethic also of at least hearing minority views and permitting them representation on executive bodies. This is not quite as consistently honoured.

International Affiliations — the Socialist International

Membership in this organization allows New Democrats the opportunity to rub shoulders with social democratic prime ministers and cabinet members from other countries, and to find out what it is really like to be in power. Ed Broadbent, a vice-president, served with the late prime minister of Sweden, Olof Palme, while the former chancellor of West Germany, Willy Brandt, was president. Sixty-three countries belong, mainly West European and Third World. The United States has only associate membership, since it has no full-fledged social democratic party but only an interest group within the Democratic Party.

Election Anatomy

In 1984, of the total Canadian population of 25,000,000, 16,800,000 people were registered to vote at the country's 68,481 polling stations. Just over 75 per cent of eligible voters cast a ballot, almost half (49.7 per cent) for the Conservative Party, while 27.8 per cent voted Liberal. Some 2.4 million Canadians, 18.7 per cent, voted New Democrat. Thanks to our single-member riding system, this near majority of votes for the Conservatives became a landslide in seats, 211 of the 282 seats, or 75 per cent of the House of Commons. The Liberals won only 40 seats for their efforts. The New Democrats, with 19 per cent of the vote, obtained only 14 per cent of the seats.

The parties are required by law to make separate returns nationally and by riding on their sources of income and election spending. At the constituency level the spending limits are not high; indeed, the problem is to avoid over-spending. Any party that cannot raise the maximum (roughly $35,000–$50,000, depending on the number of voters) probably does not have a serious chance of winning the riding. The situation is quite different at the national level, where the limits are very high, at $6,391,497. The Conservatives squeaked under at $6,388,941. The Liberals spent marginally less, at $6,292,983, while the NDP was far below both, at $4,730,723. Relative to the number of voters to be reached, the Conservatives and Liberals each spent 37 cents per registered voter on their national campaigns, the NDP only 28 cents. The big difference is in paid advertising,

31

especially television, where both the Conservative and the Liberal parties could afford major campaigns, while the NDP's efforts were far more modest.

The great advantage the Conservatives and, to a lesser extent, the Liberals enjoy over New Democrats is corporate donations. In 1984, the Conservative Party took in $22 million, half of it from corporations. The total income for the New Democratic Party in 1984 was $10.5 million, or less than the amount the Conservatives obtained from corporate donations alone. The Liberals also received more money than the NDP in 1984, $11.6 million, nearly half of it, $5.3 million, from corporations. The donations the NDP received from unions did not remotely make up for this. In 1984 that total was $2.2 million, or one-fifth of the party's revenues.

The parties save up for elections, so it is useful to look at their incomes in the pre-election period as well. Here again the Conservative Party is the strongest of the three. It collected $14.8 million in 1983, or more than the New Democratic Party in the election year itself. Again the Conservatives' great advantage lay in corporate donations. These contributions include considerable sums from the mass media, which are otherwise obliged, of course, to report fairly and impartially on the campaign. In 1984, Southam Newspapers gave $20,000 each to the Conservatives and the Liberals, and had given a further $31,000 to each in the three years preceding. The Liberals also received $18,000 from Global Television (Toronto), while the Conservatives received $17,500 from CFCF (Montreal). As are all corporate donations, these sums are deductible expenses for income tax purposes. They are, therefore, indirect public subsidies to the two parties, a privilege not enjoyed by the NDP.

The tobacco companies wish to continue peddling their wares without advertising bans or restrictions on smoking at work. Imasco gave $72,000 to the Conservatives between 1981 and 1984, while RJR MacDonald gave $13,000, and Rothmans

$12,000. The same companies gave the Liberals $91,000, $12,000, and $9,000 respectively. Liquor and beer companies altogether gave the Liberals $270,000 and the Conservatives $240,000 over the 1981-84 period.

Some major donors are foreign-controlled multinationals. Gulf Canada gave the Liberals $91,000 and the Conservatives $89,000 between 1981 and 1984. Husky Oil gave less, $27,500 to the Liberals and $43,000 to the Conservatives. The largest corporate donor has been Canadian Pacific, most years contributing $50,000 each to the Liberals and the Conservatives. Denison Mines and the Roman Corporation both outdid it in 1984, each with $100,000 donations to the Conservative Party but nothing to the Liberals. The banks and the trust companies, both federally regulated institutions, were major contributors of nearly a million dollars each over the period 1981-84 to both the Liberals and the Conservatives ($941,829 and $878,543 respectively, to be specific).

The corporations also contribute significantly to Conservative and Liberal campaigns at the riding level. Michael Wilson was the most generously provided for, with corporate donations to his Etobicoke Centre campaign of $64,000, which was $24,000 more than he was allowed to spend. Brian Mulroney received $58,000 in corporate donations for his campaign to become the MP for Manicouagan, $14,000 above his spending limit. Many New Democrat candidates receive union donations in their ridings, but not remotely on the same scale.

The Conscience of the Country

For many Canadians the New Democratic Party has been the conscience of the country. Many wish it to continue in this important role but do not want the party itself to form the government. In this book I want to argue that the New Democratic Party has been far more than a conscience, although it has played that role. It has been enormously successful in

33

influencing public policy. In Chapter 2 we shall go on to look at the achievement of Canada's social programs and the gradual recognition of civil liberties and human rights. Next, in Chapter 3, we shall look at countries where parties like the NDP are or have been in office and have been able to implement even more social and economic reforms.

2

THE PARTY OF SUCCESS

The Social Programs

QUESTION: When is unemployment bad enough to be called a depression, and when is it only a recession?

ANSWER: The term used depends more on the amount of suffering there is than on any precise rate.

The unemployment of the early 1980s is called a recession, although the unemployment rates, at 11 per cent and 12 per cent, are as bad as those of much of the Depression of the 1930s. Unemployment in 1982-84 was not as high as it was during the *worst* years of the Depression, 1932-36, when the rates ranged between 14 per cent and 19 per cent, but it was actually higher than it was in several of the Depression years before 1932 and after 1936. The years 1930 and 1937 would look relatively good today, with unemployment at 9 per cent, while in 1938 and 1939 it was 11 per cent. But the differences in suffering are enormous.

In Canada in the 1930s, farm families lost their homes and their livelihoods. In the towns, businesses failed, as people had little money to spend on goods. Unemployed men rode the rails looking for non-existent work, "begging for the chance to toil", as a poet said. Families with severely ill members often lost their life savings paying medical bills. Those without savings had to depend on free services from doctors and clinics or go without. There was no unemployment insurance of any kind. Older laid-off workers could expect only a meagre public pension, at age seventy.

In the recession of the 1980s, far fewer people were affected. Certain regions and single-industry resource towns bore the brunt of the unemployment. Young people looking for first jobs and older workers who were laid off were in difficulty. The new food banks and the same old soup kitchens prove that we are not as far from the bad old days as we should be. Yet the grim destitution of the "dirty thirties" was not repeated. Such "relief" as was available then was meagre in amount and demeaning to apply for.

Now unemployment insurance carries most people through to their next job. Medicare ensures that care is given, including costly treatment and operations formerly the privilege of only the wealthy. The family allowance cheque, although declining in value, continues to come, both before the unemployment insurance cheque arrives and after the coverage period is over. The old age pension and guaranteed income supplement provide at least some independent income to the elderly; in the case of couples it is sufficient to keep them above the poverty line. All these programs need improvement, but even in their present state they show a night-and-day difference between the conditions of the present and those of the Depression.

These social programs had all been introduced earlier in European countries with stronger social democratic parties. None were CCF/NDP inventions, but none would have been instituted in Canada without CCF/NDP agitation. All were fought by the Conservatives and the Liberals before they were eventually instituted. The CCF/NDP has always believed that society could be organized so as to provide jobs for those who can work, and to generate funding for the programs for those who cannot. Poverty in Canada is due not to lack of resources but to bad organization, especially the wrong priorities. The Second World War proved this by showing what could be accomplished with reordered priorities. As Tommy Douglas argued:

> Surely if we can produce in such abundance in order to destroy our enemies, we can produce in equal abundance in order to provide food, clothing and shelter for our children. If we can keep people employed for the purpose of destroying human life, surely we can keep them employed for the purpose of enriching and enhancing human life.[1]

The United States, which has no party equivalent to the NDP, has few social programs, and none as comprehensive as Canada's. The richest country in the world has an estimated three million people homeless. Its modest publicly supported programs provide fewer adequate benefits than Canada's, often with means tests. Food-stamp programs have recently been cut back, a victim of Reaganomic restraint. Americans pay a higher percentage of their GNP for medical care, but many people are left without any care at all. All the relevant indicators of mortality and morbidity show the United States lagging behind Europe as well as Canada. That the United States should ever be treated as a model to be followed by a Canadian prime minister and the Conservative Party is disturbing indeed. The Canadian way is different, and now is threatened by a "free trade" agreement with the United States. That Canada as a country has taken a different path from that of the United States is largely due to the work of the CCF/NDP, its positive proposals, and the threat of its forming a national government.

The Old Age Pension

The old age pension is a key part of Canada's income security system, and was the first victory of the founder of the CCF. Its acceptance by Mackenzie King in 1925 is also an apt illustration of the effect even a small opposition caucus can have in a minority government situation. In this case there were *two* MPs who forced the Liberals to bring in the legislation.

37

The idea of unemployment and health-care insurance had been accepted in principle by all three parties some years before. A National Industrial Conference, sponsored by the federal and provincial governments in 1919, had voted unanimously for an inquiry into a state insurance plan for a broad range of conditions, including sickness, disability, and an old age pension. The Liberal Party had also adopted a resolution during the post-war period of idealism and ferment, but nothing had been done. A Liberal MP had subsequently introduced a motion, which was approved, asking the government to consider ways of establishing old age pensions. Yet, when Woodsworth, a year later, asked if the government intended to bring in legislation in that session, the answer was no. In 1924, King established a committee, on which labour representative William Irvine served, which urged the government to consult with the provinces on the creation of an old age pension. A year later, there was still no action because, it was said, of Québec's declining to participate.

The breakthrough came after the election of 1925, when two labour representatives, J. S. Woodsworth and A. A. Heaps, held the balance of power in Parliament. They wrote to the two major party leaders asking their intentions regarding the introduction, in the current session, of provisions for unemployment insurance and an old age pension. Conservative leader Arthur Meighen's reply was not encouraging, but King, although he sidestepped the unemployment insurance issue, was as straightforward as he ever was. He even added promises of action on several civil-liberties concerns and, off the record, offered Woodsworth a seat in cabinet.

Legislation for the old age pension was passed in 1926, although opposed by the Conservatives and some Québec Liberals. It was then overturned by the Conservative-dominated Senate. The socialist proposal the senators found so offensive was for a means-tested pension at age seventy, at $20 a month. (They themselves at that time were liberally provided with retirement pensions of $4,000 a year.) Senators made much of the harm that would be done to the family, the "nucleus of society". To Senator Beaubien that nucleus was "kept together, healthy and strong, by the obligations of one member towards another — by the children's obligations to maintain and uphold their parents".

> One of the highest privileges we possess is to look after our old people, and it is an even greater privilege that we have been allowed the liberty by means of our civil laws, to increase and strengthen the family tie.[2]

The obligation to elderly parents was said to have "a steadying influence on the people". There was, in any event, "an admirable system organized by charity" for the needy. The finest house in Québec was devoted to the needy.

Senator Sir George Foster was worried that criminals would get the pension. It was neither fair nor just, he felt, to make no distinction between the man who was industrious and the man who was a wastrel and a spendthrift. As Conservatives do today, he looked to the United States for a positive model. That country had no such federal statute.

> Wisely they have left that to the family first, to the municipality second, and to the individual State in the third place. That is the natural source to which to look for the sustenance, help, comfort and providence for old age, and sickness.[3]

The old age pension was condemned as a new form of dole, an innovation that would hurt the family, removing from it "its flavour and the finest of its moral fibre". Beaubien astutely realized the consequences of government's taking on this responsibility. The door once opened, he asked, would we ever be able to close it? "We must take a stand now." Honourable senators indeed took that stand with him and defeated the bill.

The minority government situation led to an early election, in which pensions naturally became an issue, undoubtedly winning the government votes. The Liberals were now returned with a majority. The Conservatives have never since been so bold as to *oppose* the old age pension entirely, although in 1985 they did try to de-index it.[4]

When the second pension bill again reached the Senate, the same senators who were for the family and moral fibre again spoke against the bill, now even more vehemently. To Senator Beaubien the pension was now no less than "an iniquitous measure . . . unhealthy in its basic moral principles. It is going to stunt the growth if it does not altogether blight and wither all incentive for thrift and providence in the land."[5] Sir George Foster again warned that it would give the wrong idea to young and middle-aged men, telling them that "if they are lazy and indifferent and reckless in their expenditure" they will still be provided for at age sixty-five or seventy. The old age pension would injure "the character and stability of family life and nationhood". The thrift theme was taken up by Senator McCormick:

> Burn the candle at both ends; spend all you make, and when you are 65 or 70, and unable to work, go to those people who have been leading well-ordered lives, who have been practicing the good old habit of thrift.[6]

None the less, their party having lost one election on the issue, the Conservative senators knew when to stop. They voted against what they considered to be the best interests of the country and let the bill pass. Improvements in the old age pension, such as lowering the age to sixty-five and eliminating the means test, and increases in amounts, were gradually, if undramatically, won in later years. Woodsworth's successor in the riding of Winnipeg North Centre, Stanley Knowles, led in these fights.

Increasing the amount of the pension and providing for regular indexing were achievements of the NDP in another

Liberal minority government situation in 1972-74. Now with a caucus of thirty-one members, the NDP also won improvements in both the amount of the family allowance and fairness in its implementation. The amount was tripled, but the family allowance now became taxable, so that the increase went largely to those who needed it most. Petro-Canada was established as a national oil company to provide a "window on the industry", and to prevent foreign multinationals from holding Canadians to ransom for their winter fuel. A Food Prices Review Board was also established, in the end to little good result. Important reforms were made regarding the funding of elections with the introduction of a tax credit for political contributions, ceilings on spending, and accountability. The Mackenzie Valley Pipeline Inquiry was started, with Thomas Berger, a former New Democrat leader in British Columbia, as commissioner. For the first time the impact of a pipeline on the environment and native communities was considered. Native people were heard and their concerns were prominently reflected in the report, if less so in subsequent government action. These were significant accomplishments for a Parliament that lasted less than two years. Minority governments have been good for the country, but not necessarily for the NDP, which was reduced to sixteen members in the next election.

Mulroney's plan to de-index the old age pension, announced in his first budget in 1985, demonstrates an age-old Conservative disdain for public pensions (except for senators). Conservatives do not say the same things against pensions that they did in the 1920s, at least not publicly. The rhetoric now revolves around the economic fibre of the nation rather than around its moral fibre. Pensions are no longer condemned as socialistic or totalitarian but as just plain unaffordable. A country that can find $30 to $50 billion in tax give-aways to corporations cannot provide a decent income for its elderly, and this is called economic realism.

The Family Allowance

The story of how the family allowance was won involves no minority-government or balance-of-power tactics. Rather, at the end of the Second World War, Mackenzie King was looking for an attractive election program. The sacrifices demanded by the war had heightened people's sense of social responsibility. Further, a country that could not afford job creation in the Depression had found sufficient money for men and munitions in 1939. Soldiers and their families were no longer prepared to accept the old excuses. By the end of the war, with the CCF win in Saskatchewan in 1944, its near election in Ontario, and favourable poll results, the party was a serious threat to the Liberals. This time King did not need the CCF begging him to act; rather, he was out to win back the Liberals who were deserting to it.

House debate on the family allowance goes back to 1929, on a Liberal MP's motion, when Woodsworth was the only other MP to speak in its support. The subject was studied by a committee, which recommended further consideration, including the question of federal or provincial jurisdiction. A family allowance was later a recommendation of the Marsh report on social security after the war. Marsh was himself an early CCFer and a member of the original League for Social Reconstruction, which had become in effect the research and policy division of the CCF.

In short, King had had plenty of opportunity to bring in a family allowance, but he did not do so until 1944, when the 1945 election was in sight. The legislation then introduced was remarkably generous. The first full benefits, paid in 1947, amounted to 7.7 per cent of federal government expenditures that year. By comparison, the percentage of budget expenditures is now 2.3 per cent. Some families were able to pay their rent with the cheque.

The Conservatives prevaricated. Some MPs spoke in favour

of the family allowance, some against, and some managed to do both. John Diefenbaker, that Conservative too far to the left for Bay Street, hedged. He agreed with the need for the measure but raised constitutional objections. Some Conservatives argued that a large bureaucracy would be needed to administer the allowance, then perversely demanded inspections that would require an additional vast bureaucracy of snoopers. Another frequent argument put forward was that the needy could be looked after adequately at a tenth the cost of family allowances.[7]

A nasty Conservative attack described the family allowance as a Liberal ploy to buy votes in Québec. Decidedly rude remarks were made, in the House and out, about Québec's family size (too large) and its war effort (too small). One Conservative member declared "this measure is a bribe of the most brazen character made chiefly to one province and paid for by the taxes of the rest."[8] The Conservative leader was quoted as asking "when this legal bribery of the electorate is going to be stopped".[9]

After the bill was passed, George Drew, the Conservative premier of Ontario, threatened that his government would do "everything in its power" to see that the family allowance was not put into effect, to save millions of dollars from Ontario going to Québec. He was careful to recognize "the splendid qualities of the people of French stock in Quebec and elsewhere". Yet he incited anti-Québec sentiment by declaiming that "Quebec is not going to receive preferred treatment while it refuses to bear its full share of the burden of war."[10] "Are we going to permit one isolationist province to dominate the destiny of a divided Canada?"

My own predecessor as the member for Broadview, T. L. Church, a former mayor of Toronto, feared that the family allowance would make Canada "a totalitarian socialist state". Citizens would be called upon to exchange "all the liberties that have been won for them through the years and submit to regimentation". No regimentation had actually been proposed in the bill, but this Conservative member called for a means test. None the less, he saw the issue as "a case of liberty and freedom on the one hand versus state control of our lives on the other".

Some forty years later, another Conservative in the same area seems mild by comparison. In the 1982 by-election in Broadview-Greenwood, Peter Worthington opposed the family allowance on the grounds that it would "encourage women to breed". (Men, it would seem, have nothing to do with the matter.) Presumably he would have agreed also with Church that the Second World War was not fought "for certain plans, profiles and blueprints of socialism".[11]

In the 1944 debate Mr. Church also predicted that the family allowance would result in an end to "all subscriptions to charities, churches, and other organizations".[12] "The whole bill will be nothing but a gesture to the left, and I have never yet made any gestures to the left." In any event, as Church philosophized, happiness lay in gainful work and service. "Are we to give up all our liberties and become a totalitarian state?"[13]

Conservative senators were remarkably quiescent, passing the bill with little debate. The same constitutional objections that had been raised in the House were made. Yet only one senator spoke with any conviction against, and even he stressed the unwisdom of adding to the tax burden. A Liberal senator remarked that this lone opposing Conservative senator was the only senator to have been consistent.[14]

King's own inconsistency did not go unnoticed either. A Conservative member recalled his very different stance in the Depression years. When the unemployed "cried out for help, it was none of the Prime Minister's business; but now, when we are on the eve of an election, he suddenly takes an interest in the poor people of the country."[15]

The CCF, in supporting the family allowance, wondered why

its legislation had taken so long.[16] Stanley Knowles argued that there had been growth in the law and it was time for Parliament and the courts to catch up with public opinion. In fact, there was no province opposed to either the old age pension or the family allowance.[17]

Ensuring that the family allowance would be paid directly to the mother was largely Knowles's victory, with behind-the-scenes lobbying by Thérèse Casgrain, later president of the CCF in Québec. In the House, Knowles proposed an amendment to make it clear that the family allowance would normally be paid to the mother, instead of merely listing "mother" as one of the categories of relative to whom it could be paid. He appealed to King, who "knows, despite his bachelorhood, it is the mother who is closer to the children in their younger days. . . . There is a real argument for payment being made to the mother. I suggest that this statute should be looked upon as something new and different in Canadian legislation."[18] Paying the allowance to the mother was not disputed except in Québec, where Premier Duplessis considered that the male "head" of the family should control all the money. Women in Québec had only just gained the vote provincially, after a long struggle, led by Thérèse Casgrain. King hedged on formal amendment but was pushed to accept the principle that Knowles had proposed.

It is interesting to see how little things have changed. The Conservatives have never since attacked the family allowance head on, but while in government they have let payments lag behind increases in the cost of living. Then, on the election of the Mulroney government in 1984, the family allowance was the first universal program to be "de-indexed". Should that de-indexing continue uninterrupted, the monthly payment will dwindle to nearly nothing. In two decades, decreasing at its present rate, it would be worth only $17.54 per month per child in 1985 dollars, or 58 cents a day. Both the New Democrats and the Liberals fought the de-indexing, unsuccessfully. It is also interesting to note that popular support for the family allowance was greatest in Québec, although Québec women no longer have families larger than those of other Canadian women.

Job Creation and Unemployment Insurance

Job creation has always been central to CCF/NDP policy, because people want to work to support themselves and their families, preferably at something useful and satisfying. In addition, without a high level of employment the many measures that make for civilized life cannot be afforded. Given the importance of work, the government must accept the responsibility of organizing the economy so that enough decent jobs are provided. A well-functioning economy then becomes the basis for the support of social programs, education, and the arts.

Unemployment insurance has historically been treated as a desirable, if subsidiary, measure, with the concentration remaining on job creation. The role of the state in facilitating job placement, then, is a logical result. Now taken for granted as Canada Employment Centres, "labour exchanges" were a progressive measure long opposed in Parliament. Perhaps they were feared as an acknowledgment of state responsibility for employment.

The need for federal action on unemployment was obvious to the labour MPs from the beginning. Even in the 1920s, before the Great Depression, there were areas of high unemployment. The First World War had been followed by a recession and high unemployment. Yet the old-line parties persisted in the view that unemployment, like other relief matters, was the responsibility of the provinces. Woodsworth's analysis of the causes of unemployment, and the government's responsibility for job creation, appears as early as 1921, in one of the first issues of *The Canadian Forum*. Most unemployment was involuntary and, when private enterprise fails, "the *state is under obligation to provide work*."[19] If, with all its resources, it is unable to provide suitable work, it should provide "*adequate maintenance*". The message was to be repeated frequently in Parliament.

From time to time Woodsworth proposed resolutions in the House for a comprehensive solution to unemployment in the "co-operative commonwealth". As the occasion arose, he pointed out specific abuses, for example the deplorable conditions in relief camps for the unemployed. When business interests made what he considered to be ludicrous claims, he exposed them. He argued with the general manager of the Bank of Montreal, who held that unemployment was a "natural corrective" to an overheated economy, and one that should be accepted. He was always clear as to the principle at stake in the conflict between welfare and profits.[20]

He noted also the futility of providing federal money for relief, with nothing to show for it. Woodsworth conceded that there had been a time when unemployment was a man's own fault. With free land available and good markets in those days, a man could always move west. That time had now passed, and large corporations controlled the greater part of available work.[21] Job creation should be the "first charge" on the natural resources and credit of the country. Yet governments had allowed our natural resources to be monopolized by private individuals and corporations. Sound familiar?

Long before Brian Mulroney had been thought of in Baie Comeau, Woodsworth was telling the House of Commons that prosperity in Canada could not be had "just for whistling" and could not be had at all without stability in both Europe and the United States.[22] Specifically, our economic future was inextricably bound up with that of the United States. Although advocates of free trade point out that 25-30 per cent of our wealth depends on trade, our ancestors stressed the 70-75 per cent that does not. Woodsworth pointed instead to the potential markets available closer to hand, among the Canadian unemployed. Without jobs or adequate maintenance, workers did not have sufficient buying power.[23]

It is interesting to note that Woodsworth was always sceptical about free trade. He pointed out that unemployment and social problems remained serious in England, where free trade had been tried years before.[24] He was doubtful if free trade could be carried out under existing conditions or if it could solve our problems "except in a very limited degree", for instance eliminating the duplication of some industries in the two countries.[25] Instead, we should be developing our real sources of wealth. Here Woodsworth was very specific indeed. He proposed house construction both to meet the shortage of houses, and to provide jobs. Factories and mills were idle while people lacked necessities. He called on the government to step in to operate the coal mines in the interests of the people.

Both the old-line parties were painfully slow to accept government responsibility for job creation, or any kind of general economic management. Even in the Depression, when Roosevelt began to implement the New Deal in the United States, Canadian Liberals and Conservatives alike were offering excuses for inaction. Both parties were prepared to rely on "trade" as the panacea. Mackenzie King, who liked to think of himself as the workingman's friend, often seemed more Conservative than R. B. Bennett. Replying to Bennett's last speech from the throne, in 1935, King declared that "the Liberal Party believes the aim of every government should be the balancing of its budget." A Liberal government would seek retrenchment of public expenditures and reduced costs of government, while at the same time reducing the public debt and lowering taxes![26] He insisted, quite correctly, that the Liberals were keener on increased trade with the United States; the Conservatives were merely copying their trade policies, trying to look pro-trade for the election. Tommy Douglas, in 1936, the youngest of the newly elected MPs, was appalled by this "stout, elderly gentleman" who would speak for four hours at a time, quoting trade statistics and tariffs at length.

When occasionally conceding the need for reform, King became remarkably cold, abstract, and even more convoluted in his language than usual. The Liberal Party recognized that "the problem of distribution" had become more important "than that of production", and believed that "personality is more sacred than property." It would "devote itself to finding ways and means of effecting a fair and just distribution of wealth with increasing regard to human need, to the furtherance of social justice, and to the promotion of the common good."[27] Conservative R. B. Bennett here rejoined, quite correctly, that the only reform King had achieved so far was the one "forced upon him by the honourable gentlemen to his left", the old age pension.

After five years of the Depression, Bennett finally admitted that there were "grave defects and abuses in the capitalist system", of which "unemployment and want are the proof." Yet, he insisted, great changes *were* taking place; reform would "enable that system more effectively to serve the people." The legislation he brought in, though, was limited and late. He apparently believed that only modest changes were required. His last speech from the throne, in mid-Depression, opened with lyrical optimism:

> I welcome you at a time when our country stands upon the threshold of a new era of prosperity. It will be for you, by your labours, to throw wide the door. During the past year the grip of hard times has been broken.... Employment is increasing. Our trade is expanding.[28]

Bennett noted the signs of recovery. Yet a year later there were still a million unemployed. Tommy Douglas in his maiden speech spoke for these forgotten people, the unemployed, veterans, merchants with failing businesses, and farmers losing their crops. He reported children going to school with gunny sacks wrapped around their feet, babies clothed in flour sacks, and whole families sleeping on rags because they had no money for bedding. There was nothing for these people from either the Liberal or the Conservative governments in the Depression. They asked for bread and were given a stone.

King himself was not moved. He continued to argue that increased trade with the United States was the cure. "We on this side of the house believe that recovery is bound up with the restoration of international trade. Our policies have been based on this conviction."[29] The 1935 election of the Liberals was indeed a mandate for a reciprocal trade agreement with the United States. Accordingly the Liberals eliminated the tariffs, duties, and dumping restrictions put in by the Conservatives. The Liberals had "at last broken the hard crust of economic nationalism and have opened the way to a more extensive trade."[30] As well, the Liberals had ended "the arbitrary and often invisible interference of governmental agencies in the normal course of trade".[31] It was not until 1943, when the CCF was a serious threat to the Liberals, that King became an ardent supporter — and thief — of the party's social programs.

His delays on unemployment insurance, to which we now turn, were especially unconscionable. Until work was provided, people had a right to "adequate maintenance", said the CCF. Yet even this basic principle was resisted in Parliament for years. In *Industry and Humanity*, Mackenzie King conceded that unemployment had a "national significance". As to a national solution, however, King was all qualification, as this speech excerpt demonstrates:

> But I think it is all important that this Parliament should very carefully consider whether the obligation of looking after men who are unemployed should become a federal obligation, rather than it should be ... a matter for individuals in the first instance, between municipalities

and the people living within their bounds, in the second instance, next, between the provinces and the citizens of the respective provinces and only finally a matter of concern in the federal arena.[32]

Yet the Liberal Party had come out in favour of unemployment insurance in 1919, as well as sickness and disability benefits, widows' pensions, and maternity benefits.

A Royal Commission on Industrial Relations, established as a result of the Winnipeg General Strike, had ranked unemployment and the fear of unemployment at the top of the list of the causes of the "unrest". It made a number of progressive recommendations, including the eight-hour day, a minimum wage, public works, industrial councils, and the recognition of unions. Yet major business leaders on the commission disagreed, and it was they who had their way. They argued that the eight-hour day was not needed in all industries, and that an end to piece-work would reduce output. The government would be well advised to consider the effect of such legislation "upon the effort of the individual worker".[33] Unemployment was "not serious", but reflected only a period of readjustment after the war. Touring the country, these business leaders, including the publisher of the Montreal *Gazette*, could see no "real poverty" that was not being properly taken care of by local institutions. They warned that "if a system of old age pension or unemployment insurance were established it might seriously affect the ambition of the worker when he had full enjoyment of his physical and mental capacity."

In 1926, labour MP A. A. Heaps of Winnipeg unsuccessfully moved a motion for the establishment of unemployment insurance at the Committee on Industrial and International Relations. The motion was turned down again the following year, but by 1929 King at least agreed to look at the idea. Still nothing was done. In 1930, King, virtually repeating his earlier point, held that only if the provinces were unable to cope should unemployment properly become a federal problem:

> but until that stage is reached I think that we may well apply ... the old maxim ... for everyone to mind his own business.[34]

In 1931 Heaps again moved that the government consider the immediate establishment of a federal system of insurance for unemployment, sickness, and invalidity. "Of all the primary and important problems which come before this house there is not one of greater importance than unemployment." Further, he argued, "the labourer who happens to find himself out of work is in no way responsible for being in that position. He is merely a victim of circumstances."[35]

In 1932 Bennett, then prime minister, refused even to allow a debate on unemployment insurance, on the grounds that it had been debated within the past year. He noted also that there was insufficient information to proceed; the House should wait for the census results! As to the urgency of the matter, "there is a clear distinction between an extraordinary national condition and what is called, in the language of the law books, a national emergency. Unemployment is not a national emergency."[36] Yet unemployment had tripled from 3 per cent in 1929 to 9 per cent in 1930, and had doubled again to 18 per cent in 1932.

Unemployment insurance was not to be established in Canada until 1940, long after most other industrial nations had legislated it. Britain's plan, the model for Canada's, dates from 1911. Even the Americans beat us, with unemployment insurance adopted in 1935. It was not until that year that Canadian business interests began to soften their opposition. By then, purchasing power had declined drastically and municipalities were being bankrupted by relief costs. High property taxes, to cover relief payments, were hurting real estate. If a little unemployment makes the workers keen, business learned that there could be too much of a good thing.

Just before the 1935 federal election, the Bennett government introduced the Employment and Social Insurance Bill. The Liberals now had the gall to argue that it should have been brought in at a more prosperous time, to build up the fund! The CCF argued that *more* workers should be included; only half the work force was. All parties supported the bill, though, and it was quickly passed.

The Liberals won the 1935 election and King was again prime minister. He referred the act to the Supreme Court of Canada for a ruling on its constitutionality. In 1937 the court struck it down as beyond federal jurisdiction. Further support for a national program was soon to come, though, in a recommendation from the Rowell-Sirois Commission on federal-provincial relations. King finally entered into negotiations with the provinces and obtained unanimous support for the program's implementation by 1940.

By this time there was full war-time employment and business no longer saw the need for unemployment insurance. All the major business groups opposed the bill in some fashion, or asked for an exemption for their particular industry. Yet all agreed that there was a need for some form of insurance. According to the Chamber of Commerce, no one "would attempt to deny the advisability of building up some protection for unemployment when wages are high and a great many persons are employed."[37] Whether this was the best form, they could not be sure. They pleaded for time:

> Irrespective of how worthy unemployment insurance is in principle, it is questionable ... whether the immediate operation of state unemployment insurance will provide the best solution to Canadian unemployment conditions.[38]

Yet the Chamber of Commerce had no other proposal to

make. This was not the time for going into heavy expenditures: taxes were already crippling. Some business representatives purported to be worried that unemployment insurance would divert administrative time and money from the war effort. Although most industrial countries now had unemployment insurance, they argued that Canada would become uncompetitive if the measure were adopted. The Conservatives, however, continued to support unemployment insurance, fearful of a renewed depression after the war.

The long saga is really a tale of the two parties resisting as long as they could, bowing to the reactionary forces of the business community, and hiding behind legalistic and constitutional arguments. Only one party pushed for it in Parliament, working with progressive groups outside. One has to wonder if, left to their own devices, either of the old-line parties would ever have brought in unemployment insurance at all, let alone expanded it over the years.

Political Rights for Workers

Corporations have long exercised their "right" to influence the political process by making contributions to political parties. The comparative right of unions to be active politically was long resisted by Conservatives and Liberals alike. Unions today are still fighting court cases, brought by right-wingers, to preserve this right. In the 1920s, the founders of the CCF began the fight in Parliament for the very basic right of unions to contribute to political parties.[39]

The frequent use of the police to break strikes was denounced by the CCF founders from the beginning. Woodsworth at one point even introduced a motion to abolish the RCMP because of its use in strike-breaking. The Regina Manifesto called for the participation of employees in "works councils", with considerable say in decisions on production and conditions of work. Consistent with the goal of greater democratic control generally was the goal of democracy in the workplace.

Civil Liberties and Equality Rights

The record of the CCF/NDP on Canada's social programs is recognized, if grudgingly, even by its political opponents far to the right. Less well known, by friend and foe alike, is the party's contribution to civil rights. The old CCF's contribution must be seen in light of Canada's dismal record in this area and the weakness of groups that in other countries were active supporters of civil rights. Academics and lawyers now play this role in Canada, but in the days when defending free speech was more costly, they were not prominent among the volunteers. Unions were probably the strongest advocates of legal reform, for their members were victims of investigations, deportation, and the threat of deportation.

One of the blackest marks on Canada's record of civil liberties was section 98 of the Criminal Code. It had been legislated in reaction to the Winnipeg General Strike of 1919. As well as suppressing political opposition, this section had a reverse onus provision: a person could be presumed to be a member of an unlawful association and had to prove the contrary. Further, a person could be prosecuted for membership in an unlawful association even when the association was not unlawful when he or she had joined it.

Woodsworth introduced several motions in the House from 1931 on to have section 98 of the Criminal Code amended or repealed. Some of these bills were passed by the House only to be rejected by the Senate. The section was finally repealed in 1937, on a Liberal government motion. In fairness to the Liberals the record should show that the Conservatives were decidedly worse. Under King's government the motion was passed, to be permitted a decent burial in the Senate.[40]

Under Bennett's governments, however, these amendments were voted down even in the House. "The Tory strangulation of civil liberty in 1919 and during the Bennett regime is a disheartening record," said Woodsworth's biographer, the distinguished historian Kenneth McNaught.[41] Of the CCF, "no party had a more enviable record in the defence of civil liberties," said political scientist Walter Young.[42]

Also in 1931, Woodsworth proposed a bill to prevent the deportation of immigrants who had lived in Canada ten years or more. In fact 2000 people had been deported as public charges. The threat of deportation was a useful means of suppressing trade-union and radical activity. It is still so used, but the scope of the threat has been considerably restricted. Bennett's government was guilty of another suppression of dissent in 1931, this time of the comparatively small group of B.C. Doukhobors. The government's bill, clearly aimed at them, was to prohibit nude protest parades. The B.C. Doukhobors were actually disenfranchised in 1934 by the Bennett government.

It was during the debate on Doukhobor disfranchisement that Woodsworth was asked the critical question if he supported also the vote for Orientals. He said yes. It would be difficult today to find anyone to say no, but at that time racial discrimination was thoroughly respectable, indeed practised by the best people. Those discriminated against, of course, had no political recourse, and their economic options were severely limited by legal exclusion from most professions. The CCF's support for the Oriental vote, and equal citizen rights for Orientals in general, was used against them in British Columbia by the Liberals. Posters showed leering Chinese men (their wives were still excluded from Canada under other discriminatory legislation) threatening the virtue of white women. Liberal election posters declared:

A vote for any CCF candidate is a vote to give the Chinaman

and the Japanese the same voting right you have!

You mothers of young girls, wake up, when some one asks you to vote for a CCF candidate.... Look behind ... and you will see an oriental leering ... with an eye on you and your daughter.[43]

The Woodsworth statement undoubtedly cost the CCF votes, and some members pointed this out, critically, after the election. Woodsworth chastised them for their opportunism, quoting back to them a rhyme:

A merciful Providence
Fashioned us holler
So that we could
Our principles swaller.

Today Conservatives and Liberals vie in flattering all ethnic communities, and no Chinese New Year can be celebrated without them. Congratulatory plaques and messages are *de rigueur* in pursuit of the ethnic vote. It is a perk for back-bench MPs to be allowed to deliver them at ethnic banquets, rallies, and dances. This happy state of harmony owes much to the CCF, which fought for equality before it was a vote-getter.

The story of how this measure of equality was achieved is worth recounting. In 1936 Angus MacInnis forced a debate in the House of Commons on the equality issue. The law barring Orientals from voting was provincial, and hence could not be changed by the federal Parliament. The result was an incongruous resolution to exclude all immigrants who would not be allowed full voting rights. MacInnis then spent ninety-five per cent of his speech arguing *against* discrimination, and *for* equality. The points may seem blatantly obvious today, but they were evidently needed at the time. Orientals were "intellectually and in every other way ... the equal of other races or national groups." Canada should "do everything possible to make them good and loyal citizens, having pride in our institutions, than ... try to create race prejudice against them in the midst of the ignorant."[44] Mackenzie King, characteristically, said nothing against Orientals having the vote, but nothing for, either. He down-played the use of racist slurs in the last federal campaign as a "localized" matter. The decision of the British Columbia legislature to pass the discriminatory law should be respected.[45] King pointed out, correctly, that Conservative and Liberal governments had dealt with the issue in the same way. Both condoned the discrimination.

Other MPs were less measured in their remarks. Orientals were not interested in the vote, one explained, but only in making a living. J. S. Woodsworth here pointed out that not having the vote had limited their economic opportunities as well; Orientals could not hold a municipal or provincial office, sit on a school board or a jury, become lawyers or pharmacists, or bid on a public work. Woodsworth appealed directly to King to end this "violation of the Liberal tradition". His plea was to no avail, and in fact it took more than a decade for the law to be changed.

Defending the Japanese Canadians

In 1942, some 22,000 Japanese Canadians living on the West Coast of British Columbia were interned and relocated, largely in camps in the interior of the province. Their houses, fishing boats, and businesses were confiscated and sold, often at prices well below market values. The compensation they were paid after the war did not remotely make up for the losses incurred. Not until 1947 were the Japanese Canadians permitted to return to the Coast.

The unpopular task of defending these people was taken up by the CCF. Angus MacInnis led the struggle in the House, with courage, dignity, and moderation. He pointed out the hardships caused by the internment, the injustice and stupidity of it. Again the points seem blatantly obvious, but at the time the atmosphere was extremely hostile.

> We must always keep in mind that most of the Japanese in British Columbia — the people of Japanese origin — are not Japanese, they are Canadians.[46]

He accurately understood the problem as racism, "the colour of their skin", not a genuine military threat. Japanese Canadians were entitled to the treatment that would be accorded to a Canadian citizen whose skin was white. It was difficult to see the threat to the British Columbia coast posed by a Canadian-born law graduate of Dalhousie University, top of his class no less, yet denied admission to the Nova Scotia bar.[47]

While racial slurs outnumbered religious ones, there were also occasional disparaging references to "the heathen".[48] There was little recognition of the fact that many of the Japanese Canadians were Christians; novelist Joy Kogawa's father, for example, was an Anglican minister. The relevant drawback of being heathen was that one's oath would signify nothing. The implication was clear that Japanese Canadians could not truly be, or become, citizens, because any oath of allegiance they took would be meaningless.

Meanwhile, Liberal and Conservative MPs were complaining that the Japanese Canadians were being too well treated, at public expense. They were being fed the best canned peaches and pears, while their guards were given only dried fruit.[49] They were over-compensated for their possessions; some had managed to take away stoves and other items from their fishing boats before they were seized. One speech decried

> the lavish hospitality that was shown to these gentlemen. They were put into camps, yes; and they ran the camps — the Japs did, not the government. If the Japs did not like a white foreman, the government fired that foreman. The Japs were not disciplined at all. . . . Not long ago they had

a strike because they were not being supplied with
asparagus tips for breakfast.[50]

The MP concluded with two demands:

> that Parliament shall introduce legislation to prohibit the
> further immigration of Orientals and, second ... at the
> peace table to insist upon the repatriation of all Japanese
> now in Canada, whether of Japanese origin, whether
> naturalized — by a fake naturalization — or native born.[51]

These are extreme statements, of course, but not isolated
examples. Yet the only MPs to counter such remarks were the
CCF. John Diefenbaker, who later claimed to have opposed
the internment, was silent during these debates.

Angus MacInnis followed the "flesh-creeping speech" just
quoted.[52] He insisted that "the population of Japanese origin
in the Dominion of Canada has been just as loyal as any other
section of the people," yet no other had been treated so badly.
They had co-operated in the evacuation, and had committed
no act of sabotage or subversion, then or later. Many had tried
to enlist, but few had been allowed, so as not to strengthen
their claim to citizenship after the war. Someone pointed out
that one Japanese Canadian was serving in the army. "One
too many!" was the brilliant rejoinder by an anonymous
member.

The decision to deport the Japanese Canadians after the war
was made by the King cabinet, under the War Measures Act.
The way was prepared in the House:

> Send them back to Japan. Anything you like.... But they
> are not coming back to British Columbia.[53]

The fight against the deportation was won ultimately in the
courts. It was led by Andrew Brewin, later to become the New
Democrat member for Greenwood. At this stage, too, the
Canadian record is abysmal. The Supreme Court of Canada

failed to disallow the deportation orders-in-council. They were only ruled illegal, and then only partially, by the Privy Council in London. The case made legal history as well, as it was the last case heard by the British Privy Council before appeals to it as Canada's highest court were abolished.

The CCF members were appalled by King's hypocrisy on the use of the orders-in-council, with claims that the government was "doing justly" and "acting with mercy". Said MP Alistair Stewart: "My stomach revolts. If this be Liberalism, then it is no wonder that all over the world Liberalism is failing and declining, because Liberalism has never had the courage to live up to its finest ideals."[54] It is no wonder that New Democrats resent the charge that they are merely "Liberals in a hurry", when the Liberals so seldom are even going in the same direction.

The 1947 extension of the emergency powers, to keep the Japanese Canadians from returning to British Columbia, shows how much racism, and not military threat, was behind the original evacuation. Said a member, "The Japanese race will never do Canada any good. Therefore we, as Canadians, should guard Canadians as long as we have the power to do so."[55] MacInnis, as usual to the defence of the Japanese Canadians, was accused of being in their pay.[56] The very success of the Japanese Canadians in the fishing industry was used against them. They were gaining "control" of it, which should not be allowed to happen again. Howard Green, a leading Conservative and later External Affairs minister, defended the internments and urged the continuation of restraints against the Japanese Canadians. The risk of a fifth column was real; the Japanese Canadians had "an intense loyalty to Japan". He charged that their young people had gone to Japan for military training. Their fishing boats were not ordinary boats, either, but powerful enough to cross the Pacific. Japanese naval men had been trained on the B.C. coast.[57] As to the fact that the Japanese Canadians had not committed any acts of sabotage,

Green pointed out that they lacked the opportunity; the Japanese had not, in fact, landed.[58]

In terms of career success, Howard Green was to beat his CCF opponents, becoming Secretary of State for External Affairs under Diefenbaker. Yet, in terms of policy, winning the minds of Canadians, and eventually legislation, there is no doubt that he lost and the CCF/NDP won. Indeed, it is inconceivable today that someone with Green's views could ever become a minister, let alone of External Affairs. Canada has changed a great deal. The churches helped in the later stages of the struggle, in particular condemning the deportation orders-in-council. The Canadian Jewish Congress, whose members had suffered discrimination, and worse brutality, took a stand on principle. But the CCF was the chief advocate of equality rights and fighter against discrimination, without much other help in the early years.

If there were any people as unpopular in middle Canada as the Asian Canadians and the nude Doukhobors already discussed, they might have been the Jehovah's Witnesses, Communists, and criminals. The CCF, naturally, came to the defence of all three. In 1937 and 1938, J. S. Woodsworth urged the referral of the infamous Québec padlock laws to the Supreme Court of Canada, where, eventually, the laws were declared unconstitutional. Woodsworth in particular and the party in general repeatedly fought the jailing of Communist Party leaders for their political beliefs. Prisoners have never been a popular cause in Canada, Communist prisoners less so. Yet the CCF championed both from the early 1930s on. In case any of these activities be confused with political opportunism, let it be remembered that Jehovah's Witnesses by religious principle do not vote, Communists vote Communist (or Liberal where there is no Communist candidate), and prisoners only began to get the vote in the 1980s.

The Bill of Rights

Given the extent of discrimination just demonstrated, it is understandable that the party would want to bring in legislation against it when it had the opportunity. On the party's election to government in Saskatchewan, Canada's first bill of rights was passed in the CCF's first term of office there. Astonishingly, it was opposed as unnecessary. The bill, as well as guaranteeing freedom of speech and assembly, the right to vote, to hold property, and so forth, prohibited discrimination in education and employment on grounds of race or religion. Fines were levied as penalties.

As with so many other reforms, the Saskatchewan Bill of Rights was fought tooth and nail on its introduction, although at the end no one voted against it. The Attorney General was in no doubt.as to its significance, likening it to the BNA Act and the Saskatchewan Act. Others went further, comparing it with the Magna Carta, the English Bill of Rights, the American Declaration of Independence, and the Factory Acts as milestones in the achievement of human freedom. The government's position was that civil-rights legislation was as important as its measures for economic security. Indeed, the two had to be worked on together. According to the Attorney General, "just as we realize that peace is one and indivisible," so also is liberty:

> It is one and indivisible. The world of ours is too small to live half-slave, half-free. When my neighbour's rights are destroyed, my own rights are threatened. . . . Prosecution and discrimination are as contagious as disease, and no citizen is safe, no matter where he lives in this world, as long as they exist and flourish in other parts of the world.[59]

CCF members proudly understood their Bill of Civil Rights to be a contribution to the world. Saskatchewan was only a small part of that world, but they would at least put their own house in order, and be an example to others. As Woodrow Lloyd, future premier of Saskatchewan, pointed out, communities made the world, not the world communities.[60]

Along with a greater world vision than the Liberals, the CCF members had a better understanding of the need for anti-discrimination measures at home. They raised actual examples of racial and religious discrimination, in jobs, local services, and housing. "The racial and religious minorities of Saskatchewan cannot have any real security until they are free from arbitrary discrimination and arbitrary government action such as the deportation orders-in-council."[61]

Opposition members who spoke on the bill all stated that they were against discrimination, but none saw the need for legislation. None raised any concrete examples of discrimination. Several called for better protection of property rights, which were, in fact, included in the bill. Opposition members chastised the government for having made disparaging remarks about members of the elite Assiniboia Club: that was intolerance! The Leader of the Opposition damned the bill with faint praise. He would not oppose it, but he insisted that it added nothing to the rights Saskatchewan citizens already enjoyed. It was "window dressing" dreamed up by the Attorney General. This Liberal leader also took the opportunity to accuse the Attorney General of planning to "set up courts to try and convict men and women who have consistently voted for the old political parties", a preposterous charge repeated by another Liberal.[62]

This next Liberal called it "just a repetition of platitude".[63] "We have been getting along fairly well without a statute of this nature." He then reversed himself to call the bill "rather dangerous". It "could be made an instrument of oppression." In any event, tolerance was a virtue that could not be legislated.[64]

Other opponents were less polite. Colonel Alan Embury, a Conservative sitting as an armed forces representative, called it "slanderous Communistic nonsense ... a callous piece of socialist whimsy".[65] It was "typical Communist jargon calculated to stir up class hatreds and internal strife".[66] He questioned how long it would remain on the books when the CCF had been "successful in usurping a totalitarian control".[67] The bill was "a sort of general anaesthetic administered to the body politic while the painful operation of socialism is performed on them".[68] This member further accused the government of passing legislation "simply to impose intolerable conditions on the employers". There was no need for it, but the government wanted to liquidate private enterprises so that it could then take them over![69]

The contention that the bill was mere repetition was countered by the government itself. Winding up the debate, the Attorney General noted that "the capitalists" had not found the bill meaningless. "There are already complaints that we are taking away from them their God given rights to hire and fire whom they like and to hire either sex, or to hire only people of certain religious denominations."[70] The bill did more than state the existing law as far as minorities were concerned.

Editorial comment was not much more favourable to the government. The Saskatoon *Star-Phoenix* argued that human-rights legislation would defeat its own purpose, tending "to emphasize differences in race, creed and color".[71] Members of racial and religious minorities were counselled to wait for tolerance to be achieved by education and economic integration, even though access to education and jobs was the object of the bill. The legislature had "performed a disservice to the cause of liberty" by passing the bill. After the bill was approved, the paper predicted that it would serve as "propaganda value for a time", and then be forgotten.[72] Instead, not only has it been imitated in every province and federally, but it was the model used by the British Labour Party for its human-rights legislation. The first version of Diefenbaker's Bill of Rights, incidentally, did not go as far as the Saskatchewan Act, providing only for freedom of religion and speech, and the right to vote, but not banning racial or religious discrimination.

The CCF in the House of Commons continued to call for federal legislation against racial and religious discrimination. Alistair Stewart, for example, soon after his election had put a resolution on the order paper to incorporate a bill of rights in the constitution, which finally happened, some forty years later. His proposed bill of rights was to protect minority rights, civil and religious liberties, and freedom of speech and assembly, and to establish "equal treatment before the law for all citizens, irrespective of race, nationality, or religious or political beliefs".[73] The resolution further called for "the necessary democratic powers to eliminate racial discrimination in all its forms". The Canadian Human Rights Commission, established some thirty years later, is a major means of fulfilling that need. The intermediate step, of course, was the Bill of Rights of 1960. It seems that Diefenbaker was influenced by the CCF members, for his final bill prohibited discrimination by race, religion, national origin, and sex, which his original resolution had not.

CCF MPs frequently raised particular instances of discrimination in the House, documenting the need for legislation, insisting that the problem was serious. When the Canadian citizenship bill was debated in 1946, they called for equality of treatment regardless of national origin. A capacity for democracy was not the prerogative of any one group or nation, and not confined to people from the United Kingdom.[74] This point was also to be won eventually, but again not for decades.

One of the many unhappy ironies in this tale is the defeat in the 1958 election of one of the staunchest advocates of civil-liberties legislation in Parliament, Alistair Stewart. Yet it was Stewart's more radical approach to the issue, with the inclusion of equality rights and an enforcement mechanism, that was to win the day. Diefenbaker beat the CCF badly in the election of 1958, but he learned policy from the party in the course, and subsequent legislation shows this.

Labour Laws

The party's commitment to equality rights was most recently seen in the debate over the Charter of Rights in 1981-82. The NDP pressed hard for adequate protection for women and native people, two groups for whom the government's original drafts were especially weak. New Democrat members were instrumental in obtaining amendments that strengthened rights for both.

The CCF government in Saskatchewan was the instigator also of reforms in labour legislation throughout the country. The urban labour force then comprised only one-third of the province's total labour force, but reforms for it were considered vital enough to be introduced in the first session. Amendments to the Trade Union Act established the first labour relations board in Canada. The right to collective bargaining was recognized. For the first time in Canada, that right was also extended to civil servants. Union organization was facilitated, and indeed the number of organized workers promptly grew. "Unfair labour practices" were specified and prohibited. Reprisals for union activity were forbidden, and later amendments were introduced to increase this protection.

On the request of a union, companies were required to collect the members' dues and remit them. The minimum wage was raised to the highest permitted under federal legislation. Another act stipulated a minimum two-week holiday each year, at that time the most generous provision in Canada. The eight-hour day, forty-four-hour week was legislated. Workers' compensation was established, and health and safety measures were gradually introduced. The legislation was drafted by lawyer Andrew Brewin, who had led the legal fight against the deportation of Japanese Canadians.

The bill establishing the Labour Relations Board was naturally

67

welcomed by the labour movement. The Regina Labour Council called it a step forward towards improving living standards for the whole population after the war.[75] It accurately predicted that this model legislation would promote industrial peace. To employers and the media, on the other hand, the legislation was unnecessary, untried, arbitrary, authoritarian, and potentially damaging to the provincial economy. It was the most contentious, longest-fought bill of the session.

An early draft had been sent to employers' groups and unions, and considerable re-drafting was done as a result of the objections raised. Yet Opposition members, employers, and the press all called for delay to allow further study. There was no need to "rush through" such a "drastic" bill, when there was "sound legislation" already on the books.[76] In the opinion of the Leader of the Opposition there was no need to change the labour laws at all. They were not perfect, he admitted, yet the existing legislation came as near to perfection and practicality as was possible. He noted ominously that no similar legislation had ever been passed by a British Parliament.[77] For the record, the existing legislation, modest as it was, had only been hastily passed just before the 1944 election.

The Liberal leader repeated an accusation originally made in a *Saturday Night* story that the purpose of the bill was to promote the CCF's political welfare in other parts of Canada.[78] It would be a sad day for the future of Saskatchewan if the farmer-members of the legislature allowed themselves "to be used as mere rubber-stamps in the game of political expediency".[79] The Canadian Manufacturers' Association echoed the sentiment that change was not needed. There was "no labor strife in Saskatchewan which requires any new legislation". In a largely agricultural province there was "no reason for imposing the very drastic legislation proposed which had been tried out in no other place".[80]

The very idea of a labour relations bill, or at least one with teeth, was opposed. Liberal and Conservative members protested the "extreme powers" to be given the board. An editorial entitled "The attack on justice" called the bill "objectionable", "arbitrary", and "dangerous". It protested the powers to be given the Labour Relations Board as "so extreme a departure from the basic principle of the British concept of law and justice".[81] Stepping up the attack in a later editorial, the Regina *Leader-Post* condemned the trend "towards authoritarianism and confiscation" of the CCF. The Labour Relations Board would "make rulings without rules for doing so, exercise the power of a court and use the court as its policeman". The board suggested comparison with the "nefarious star chamber" of the seventeenth century:

> The similarity is striking. The provision of the act is, in fact, a turning back of the clock, in the matter of justice and individual liberty, by some centuries. The days of the Stuarts are returning.[82]

The paper sarcastically wondered why, with so many teachers in its ranks, this comparison had not occurred to the CCF government. Elsewhere it warned that "The system can be extended to almost every phase of human activity, to business and to personal conduct and to the furtherance of party fortunes."[83] "Justice will indeed have reached a low ebb."

The government was alternately attacked for including rights for agricultural workers, and for not doing so.[84] In 1947, when the eight-hour day, forty-four-hour week was legislated, the Saskatchewan Employers' Federation protested that disparities with agricultural workers would be increased. Yet when the Trade Union Act included agricultural workers as well as industrial workers, it warned of the adverse consequences for agriculture.[85]

Apart from the loss of liberty predicted, the Regina *Leader-Post* forecast dire economic effects from improved rights for workers. The Trade Union Act was "bound to have the effect of retarding industrial development in Saskatchewan". Employers could be found guilty of ten types of unfair labour practice, and employees of only two. "Under such circumstances it is hard to conceive of any person establishing industry in the province or developing present industry."[86] Exports were threatened, and all citizens, including workingmen themselves, would suffer. In fact, the whole economy improved, agriculture as well as industry, in the next years. In the two years following passage of the act there was a sixty-per-cent increase in union membership. Yet, reported the new Department of Labour, in the calendar year 1946 there were no lock-outs and only four strikes, none with any serious time loss.[87]

Constitutional and International Affairs

The CCF's contribution to Canada's constitutional development is even less well known than its work on civil liberties and equality rights. The Canadian Constitution was patriated in 1982, under a Liberal government. As far back as 1924, J. S. Woodsworth had advocated that Canada have full power over its own affairs, the same as Britain. Woodsworth's motive was more practical than Trudeau's: to permit social legislation such as unemployment insurance and the eight-hour work day. The debate on his motion shows that the Conservatives and Liberals did not recognize Woodsworth's goals, for they suggested that he wanted to abolish provincial governments or that he was anti-British. King pretended that patriation was unnecessary: Canadians did not feel subordinate to Britain and the British Parliament would pass Canadian amendments if asked anyway.[88] The more right-wing Conservatives did not participate in the debate at all, so inconceivable was the idea of Canadian control of its own constitution.

J. S. Woodsworth's pacifist stand is well enough known. Not so well known is the fact that his internationalism embraced a number of practical measures to reduce tensions between countries, to prevent rearmament, and to promote international good will. In a period in which international affairs were little discussed in colonial Canada, such a contribution is even more remarkable.

One of the most radical of Woodsworth's proposals in 1923 was that Canada forgo reparations from an impoverished and embittered Germany. He pointed out that not only could Germany not afford them — they soon stopped paying anyway — but reparations would flood the market with goods and cause a depression. Woodsworth made a Christian, moral argument that Germany was not solely guilty and we were commanded to forgive our trespassers.[89]

He also proposed League of Nations' control of the manufacturing and trade of armaments. Canada could play a key role by banning the export of nickel for purposes of war, which was not in fact done until 1939, when it was too late. As well as supplying the uranium for the first nuclear bomb, Canada bears the responsibility of having provided essential raw materials to both the Japanese and the Germans for arms throughout the 1930s.

Culture

Canada as a country has been slow in developing a sound foundation for its cultural life. All parties can be chastised for not having done more earlier, but the least deserving of blame is the CCF/NDP. Recognition of the importance of culture goes right back to the Regina Manifesto, and there are also occasional glimpses of concern earlier in statements by labour MPs.

Probably the party's most notable cultural success has been the establishment of the CBC, although both the Liberals and the Conservatives take the credit for it when so inclined. It is true that the Liberals appointed the Aird Commission, which recommended the establishment of public broadcasting. The Conservatives brought in the legislation. The CCF's role was in the background, with Graham Spry, a founding member, and Alan Plaunt, through the Canadian Radio League. (Spry, incidentally, was a CCF candidate in Broadview in 1934, losing to the Conservative who led the fight against the family allowance, Tommy Church.)

Similarly, it has been the CCF/NDP which has continued to fight for the CBC over the years against neglect, under-funding, and sometimes outright attacks by the Liberals and Conservatives. A debate on CBC funding in 1947 is illustrative, although nearly any year would do. The CCF protested the "comic strip culture" imported from below the border. "It is obvious that if we are going to produce a Canadian culture we must be prepared to pay for it, and one of the tasks of the CBC is to develop and expand this particular form of service to all the people of Canada."[90] Conservative and Liberal members were less keen. As now, they used debate in the House to raise pet peeves. The member for New Westminster, B.C., for example, complained that the CBC had put on "the weepiest play I have ever heard".[91] He opposed increased funding for the corporation.

Other cultural measures the CCF supported before their time were a National Art Gallery, a National Library, and a National Theatre, all with branch outlets and a travelling capacity. Canada was to have its own Canadian flag and its own national anthem. The NDP, at its founding in 1961, called for increased support for the CBC and the Canada Council. While Mulroney's first budget in 1984 cut arts funding by $300 million, the sole New Democrat province, Manitoba, *increased* arts spending. Both federal Conservatives and Manitoba New Democrats had promised increases: only one performed. The New Democrat government in Manitoba increased support both to the arm's-length agencies and to programs directly under the minister. The federal Conservatives cut the independent agencies and increased their interference in management. Funding under the direct control of the minister has increased, although this is the result not of government generosity but of increased money from lotteries.

Medicare

There are a number of political lessons to be learned from the struggle for publicly funded medicare. The issue surely helped the CCF to win its first election in Saskatchewan in 1944. It was undoubtedly the cause of the party's defeat in 1964 and the loss of its federal members in 1962, including Tommy Douglas, then party leader. What happened in between was the development of a substantial system of services, from hospital insurance, local clinics, improved research facilities, better training of doctors and nurses, dental services for school children, and on to the provision of doctors' services through medicare.

Provision for medical care regardless of ability to pay is an old social democratic commitment. It was a demand of the early labour MPs, and was part of the Regina Manifesto in 1933. It was a particular concern for Tommy Douglas, who as a child had nearly lost a leg for lack of such provisions.

A system of medical care, including physician, dental, and hospital services, was a promise of the CCF in the 1944 provincial election. Plans to implement it began immediately after the party's victory, with Tommy Douglas as premier and his own minister of health. The study commission appointed after the election recommended a series of steps. Implementation was piecemeal, on account of costs. It was not until well into the 1950s that the step of insurance for doctors' services was broached. It has been argued that the government waited too long, for initially the doctors had been favourable to a publicly funded scheme.[92] By the time legislation was introduced, however, the medical profession was vehemently opposed. The infamous doctors' strike of 1961 was the result.

The tactics used by the doctors were much influenced by the American Medical Association. Saskatchewan adopted the "key man" American organization, with designated doctors responsible for organizing the profession in their area. There was a massive assessment of fees for the war chest. Doctors who supported medicare were vulnerable to disciplinary action, for the same body that was fighting medicare had also the authority to license practitioners and to withdraw licences. More physicians resigned or left the province than bucked the college. There were mailings to all citizens and a press advertising campaign. Citizens' groups were formed to "Keep our Doctors".

The tactics used played on people's deepest fears. The method of payment for services was somehow said to affect the nature and quality of the services provided, as if germs would not give up the fight, or tissue heal, without the passing of cash between patient and doctor. Pregnant women were told in this literature that they would be denied counselling services they normally would expect. Catholic women were told that a government-controlled plan was a threat to church dogma on maternity and birth control. Said a paid advertisement by the doctors in the Saskatoon *Star-Phoenix*:

> Compulsory state medicine has led to mediocrity and a poorer quality of care everywhere it has been put into practice. We believe that compulsory state medicine would be a tragic mistake for this province and it would undermine the high quality of medical care which you now enjoy. We will always attend the sick, but we will refuse to support and service a plan which will lead to a poorer type of medical care.[93]

Other newspaper reports were even more graphic, referring to "benevolent dictatorships". Doctors who would come to Saskatchewan to work in such a system were "the garbage of Europe".

> As soon as you get an employer-employee relationship in medicine you have to do what the boss says. The boss may say you're not to use penicillin, because it's too expensive.[94]

Medicare was political interference in the treatment process itself. In closing their offices, doctors explained to their patients that they *could* not practise until the government allowed them to give treatment without political control.

All this was blatantly false, for the proposal concerned only the method of payment for services; treatment itself would be up to the doctor and patient as usual. In fact, medicare would permit decision-making in treatment to be based solely on medical criteria rather than on the patient's finances. For the first time, indeed, doctors were able to prescribe and give treatment entirely in accord with the patient's needs.

Reprehensible as the medical profession's tactics were in fighting medicare, they were at least equalled by the Saskatchewan Liberals'. Leader Ross Thatcher continued to denounce "socialized medicine", often with red scare threats: "We're not in Russia yet." The Saskatchewan CCF had campaigned on the establishment of a medicare system in the provincial election of 1960, which they won. They clearly had a mandate to proceed. Yet as the campaign heated up, the Liberals tried to brand them as undemocratic, not listening to the people. At one point Ross Thatcher asked the lieutenant-governor to dissolve the legislature if the government would not reverse itself and suspend the act.

The success of the CCF is all the more remarkable when the failure of medicare in the United States is considered. No less a president than John F. Kennedy was beaten by a reactionary medical profession. His much more modest bill, for partial medicare for the elderly, was overturned in the United States Senate 52-48. Tommy Douglas, Woodrow Lloyd, and the Saskatchewan CCF succeeded where Kennedy and the Democratic Party failed. Some thirty-five million Americans, as late as the 1980s, live without medical coverage.

But the CCF paid the price of being first, of bearing the brunt of the right-wing attack, in election losses. In the federal election of 1962, Diefenbaker swept Saskatchewan. Douglas, by then national leader of the NDP, was defeated in Regina. In the next provincial election, in 1964, the CCF under Woodrow Lloyd lost to the Thatcher Liberals. Yet both the Conservatives and the Liberals were soon to adopt the CCF/NDP policy on medicare. Diefenbaker appointed a red Tory from Saskatchewan, Justice Emmett Hall, to head a royal commission on medical services. The Hall Report duly recommended the establishment of a jointly funded federal-provincial medicare scheme. In 1965, Liberal Prime Minister Lester Pearson announced the implementation of Canada-wide medicare, along the lines of the Hall Report recommendation. The patient work of the CCF and Woodrow Lloyd, defending the need for medicare and answering irrational attacks on it, bore fruit, for the people of Canada more than for the party.

The federal Liberals still claim credit for medicare, and the vicious opposition of the Saskatchewan Liberals is forgotten. By 1985 a full ninety-seven per cent of Canadians agreed that "people who cannot afford it have a right to medical care."[95] As Premier Douglas claimed, health services are now regarded as "an inalienable right of being a citizen of a Christian country". Unfortunately, more than a few Christians were lost to the lions in the course of the conflict.

Why and When

Now that we have seen how Canadian social programs and civil liberties were won, let us consider the process of change. It seems abundantly clear that rational persuasion had little direct part. In some cases the need had been demonstrated for decades before the reform was enacted. In other cases the Liberal Party had accepted the reform as part of its platform, yet never implemented it. Throughout the desperate years of the Depression, Mackenzie King continued to call for budget restraint and increased trade with the United States as the remedies. He only became serious about the social programs when the CCF had become a threat.

The key period to consider is the end of the Second World War, when plans for "reconstruction" were being formulated. The Conservatives resisted change the most. John Bracken in 1942 insisted on adding "Progressive" to the name, but did not insist on any progressive platform to merit the change. When Leonard Marsh's report on social security was published, the Conservative Party commissioned Charlotte Whitton to write a critical reply to it. The study was progressively named, *Dawn of an Ampler Age*, but its analysis was conservative. Whitton pointed out the impediments to action, and counselled patience and further consultation.

It was Mackenzie King who correctly read the need of the country, plundered CCF policy, and succeeded in ensconcing the Liberals in power for another fifteen years. The chronology is instructive:

February 9, 1942   In York South, CCF candidate Joe Noseworthy, a local school teacher, defeated the national Conservative leader and prime minister, Arthur Meighen.

August 4, 1943   The CCF became the Official Opposition in Ontario, replacing the Liberals and coming very close to winning government. The CCF popular vote had risen from 5 per cent in the previous election to 31 per cent.

August 9, 1943   The CCF won two new seats in four by-elections. The Communist Party, then called Labor-Progressive, won one of the others.

September 3, 1943   A Gallup poll was published showing the CCF, at 29 per cent, slightly ahead of both the Conservatives and the Liberals.

Within days of the September poll, King brought together his caucus for a major brainstorming session, followed by a special meeting of the Advisory Council of the National Liberal

Federation. Ministers and civil servants hammered out a progressive post-war reconstruction policy, which King recorded in his diary as "the one thing that can save the Liberal party".[96] King was adamant that the family allowance should go through, although he did yield to pressure from his ministers to delay on health insurance. The costs, he thought, would be prohibitive. Departments of Veterans Affairs, Reconstruction, and National Health and Welfare were established to implement the new policies. Fearing loss of support from organized labour to the CCF, King hastily consulted the unions on a new Labour Relations Code. In pushing forward reforms, King told his diary, "I was dumbfounded at the reactionary attitudes of some of my colleagues on the question of collective bargaining." On financial matters, it is clear that he also had to push a reluctant Department of Finance.

The Liberal caucus was sharply divided on giving an airline licence to Canadian Pacific. King argued that such a concession could cost the party the government. With two parties in favour of private interests over the publicly owned Trans-Canada Air Lines, large numbers of Liberals would defect to the CCF, which would then "control the government" for the next five years. The popularity of the CCF showed people's dissatisfaction with the government and its war policies, "and a desire of the people that the government should be just".

His diaries show King in this period to have been much preoccupied with the CCF and its growing threat. He was understandably very much concerned with the conduct of the war, but the CCF seems to have been more on his mind than his dog Pat. On September 26, 1943, King recorded that he had been so busy revising a speech against the CCF that he had missed church! He discussed the CCF threat, and the by-elections particularly, with Winston Churchill at the Québec Conference. Churchill, interestingly, who was soon to lose an election to Labour, down-played the threat. King was more worried, explaining the great necessity for fence-mending, "getting my party properly organized and seeing to it that I did not lose any members through the CCF".[97]

King was also concerned with the CCF threat during preparation of the budget in June 1944. The Minister of Finance, James Ilsley, had evidently included nothing in his budget for farmers. King told him to, fearing that the CCF would move an amendment that would be popular: "We might in the end be obliged to support it and the C.C.F. would get the whole credit of being the party that was really giving relief to the primary producers."[98]

It is crystal-clear in the diaries that King considered his post-war reform program, stolen from the CCF, to have been divinely inspired. In the course of the special caucus meetings in September 1943, he referred to "guidance and help from Beyond", which would "help to save the party". The rightness of the reforms was further confirmed in his morning Bible reading. Just as he finished reflecting on the proposed social insurance program, he noticed that the hands of the clock were "exactly in a straight line", at 10:23, a sign, to King, of inspiration. His duty was clear: "to prepare for battle as completely as possible program of social insurance."[99]

The CCF even invaded King's dreams, or visions before waking, as he called them. A row of powerfully built white horses, with decorated chains and breastplates, came up to what appeared to be a Toronto hotel. King was standing in front of it "with Mr. Rockefeller and other wealthy men. They were discussing the significance of the CCF."[100] He observed that Mr. Rockefeller was friendly to him, as usual. Whether or not the white horses were meant to be the CCF is not clear. Elsewhere, King recorded dreams where he was a knight in shining armour, and one can imagine him charging off with those white horses, complete with their breastplates of CCF righteousness!

King had his way. The new reform measures were put into the speech from the throne in January 1944. A draft of that speech which King took to cabinet was criticized as being too "leftist".

Something had to be inserted to prevent "a large section of the country" from saying that the Liberals were "seeking to outdo the CCF. We might as well join the Tories."[101] King was also perturbed that the Conservatives and the CCF were out organizing the Liberals, using "more scientific methods". There was a danger of the Liberal Party's "being eliminated altogether in Canada" through the CCF's "selling our ground".

King had been much influenced by a book called *The Strange Death of Liberal England*. In a lengthy speech to his caucus he pointed out that something of the kind had happened to Liberalism in Ontario. It was the MPs' duty "to see that this did not happen in the Federal field". King was well satisfied with his pep talk. Confirmation as to its inspiration came in the fact that "three times today, the hands of the clock have had a very direct and reassuring message."[102]

This succession of events from the end of the war has, I believe, some lessons for people seeking the equivalent social reforms today. Present-day groups lobby as before for the poor and the disabled, for workers and women, and on new issues of the environment and nuclear disarmament. These public-interest groups are heard, for consultation is government policy. Briefs play an educational role by informing the public. The exercise helps organizations to understand their problem area better and to hone their positions.

Yet fundamental reforms, that is, measures beyond token concessions, are not achieved by those means. The examples described in this chapter show that it was not a rational demonstration of the need, or the popularity, of any program that prompted its enactment. Rather, change occurred when the party in power, most especially its leader, realized that it was losing supporters to the CCF. Reforms have been scarce of late, and indeed past progress has been rolled back, because these conditions no longer hold. Cabinet ministers today listen politely to reformers and peace activists, confident they can send them away empty-handed and still get their votes.

3

VIRTUE IS ITS OWN REWARD?
SPURNED BY THE VOTERS

Despite, or perhaps because of, its success in getting its programs implemented, the CCF/NDP has never formed a government federally, and it has formed governments in only three provinces and one territory. People who might reasonably be thought to vote for it out of self-interest do not. Instead, seniors vote for the party that cuts their pension, as women vote for men, workers for their bosses, peaceniks for generals, and environmentalists for the makers of acid rain.

Although the last Liberal and Conservative leadership conventions were dominated by well-heeled business and professional people, they still attracted more "ordinary Canadians" than any New Democratic Party convention. More union members vote Conservative or Liberal than vote New Democrat in any election. The National Action Committee on the Status of Women vets all the parties for their stands on women's issues, routinely ranking the NDP highest. Yet there is no gender bias in favour of the party. Organizations that promote peace and the environment canvass the parties and publish the results for their members. Any literate person can tell that the NDP is far closer to their positions than either of the other parties. Yet there is never the slightest hint of endorsation, and indeed members of these organizations vote Conservative and Liberal with the executives of Litton Industries and Inco.

The Protest Movement Becalmed?

There are several plausible explanations for the New Democratic Party's failure at the polls, each with its own supporters. We shall begin with the one with the most ardent, if not the most numerous, group of supporters: that the NDP is not far enough to the left.

The party is often described as having lost the vision it once had as a movement. People do not vote for it today, it is said, because they cannot see enough difference between it and the other parties. The "protest movement becalmed" has numbed its own potential supporters. The not-left-enough explanation, not surprisingly, has been advanced by members of the Left Caucus of the party, and by political commentators on the left who are not necessarily party members.

From outside the party there is an excellent example of this criticism in the open letter of political theorist C. B. Macpherson to New Democrat leader Ed Broadbent after the 1981 Ontario provincial election. The lack of difference from the Liberals and Conservatives was stressed, the failure of the party to show real leadership. The NDP should tell voters that only with a thorough rejection of "welfare-state capitalism" and a "rapid move to socialism" can they avoid the "creeping impoverishment" of capitalism. To Macpherson, the rightist move by voters was due to disillusion with "centrist, compromise governments", to a lack of a clear political alternative. Since the other parties were more experienced at running welfare-state capitalism, and therefore presumably more efficient at it, they might as well be allowed to continue to do so. People who should be supporting the NDP, according to this explanation, simply did not bother to vote.

There is plenty to support the not-different-enough contention at the level of party membership, but not at voting. In 1982, in the course of seeking the New Democrat nomination in Broadview-Greenwood, I met numerous disgruntled leftists, including many former party members. Although they were New Democrat voters, they would not join the party, or had quit it precisely because they felt it was not distinctive enough to be worth the effort. However, a few days of canvassing ordinary Canadians at ordinary doorsteps would disabuse anyone of the notion that this view is widely held. For the average voter, the NDP *is* a left party: indeed, for many it is so distinctive as to be menacing. It is seen as being too much for public ownership and extremist on civil liberties, if not altogether outrageous in its support of deviants, criminals, and worse.

Further, according to Walter Young's definitive study of the CCF, *Anatomy of a Party*, 'twas always thus. Young points out how far the party was from understanding the feelings and aspirations of ordinary Canadians. During the war the party damned profiteers, not Hitler. After the Second World War, people wanted to make up for lost time, not turn back and help others to catch up.[1] People did not want to be reminded of the Depression, but the CCF revived unpleasant memories. Campaign cartoons, for example, stressed hard times: "Sorry, Brother, No Jobs Today".

The party attracted deviants, allowing them legitimate space to air their dissent,[2] but these were not the concerns of average Canadians. At various times the party attacked popsicles, processed cheese, and packaged breakfast cereals.

If the ordinary voter could not identify with the CCF in those post-war years, it was for good reason. Outside Saskatchewan at least, CCF members, and more so the activists, were not representative of their communities. At a time when most Canadians were still church-goers, a high proportion of CCF members were atheists and agnostics.[3] Voters felt closer to the kinds of candidates the Conservatives and Liberals ran: local community leaders, and church members, without all those funny ideas on human rights and capital punishment.

Let us be perfectly clear that the Conservatives and Liberals were not running your average Canadian as candidates either. Certainly their party memberships have been highly skewed to the wealthy and business classes, under-representing women, natives, and ethnic minorities. But their candidates have reflected what Canadians *hoped* to be more than the CCF or NDP has. The local mayor/hardware store owner/Rotary Club president has been a positive model for Canadians in a way that the NDP's teachers, preachers, and social workers have not been.

The explanation that the CCF/NDP has not been far enough to the left to attract voters fails as an excuse in terms of long-term trends as well. We need only look back to the good old days of the 1930s and 1940s, when the CCF was more radical in its policies, more a movement than a party, to see that the explanation does not wash. The party has increased its strength since moderating its message. Inspired as J. S. Woodsworth was as a leader, it must be remembered that the CCF never rose above 8.9 per cent of the popular vote under his leadership. The worst the NDP has ever done is noticeably better, at 13.1 per cent. Those who consider David Lewis and Ed Broadbent too right-wing as leaders must note that support has grown under their direction. With the more radical Tommy Douglas as leader, the NDP ranged between 13.1 per cent and 17.9 per cent of the popular vote. Under Lewis, the party ranged between 15.4 per cent and 17.7 per cent, while under the supposedly tamest of all, Ed Broadbent, it has attracted between 17.8 per cent and 19.8 per cent of voters. The Regina Manifesto of 1933 was the most radical document in party history. Yet under its standard the CCF attracted on average only 11.1 per cent of the popular vote, while the less radical NDP has averaged 16.5 per cent. In its last five most becalmed years the party has won the support of a fifth of the voters, compared with scarcely a tenth in its most radical period.

Like the CCF, the NDP has a membership different in many respects from ordinary Canadians. For party activists, the differences are stronger still. Activists veer even more to the left than the average party member does. A small majority of these activists would like the party to move further to the left (55.6 per cent in 1983), and more say it should not present a more moderate image to the general public (76.8 per cent). By a two-to-one ratio, activists would seek closer ties with labour and do not share the commonly held view that unions have too much power. New Democrat activists are concerned with the size of government, but not with the principle of public ownership. As many as 98 per cent of NDP convention delegates in 1983 disagreed that there was currently too much government ownership.

In foreign policy, NDP activists advocate less military expenditure and more development aid than do the majority of the population. Most agree with the party position that Canada should get out of NATO and NORAD, and a substantial number (59 per cent) believe that Canada should disarm unilaterally. Nearly two-thirds (65 per cent) of federal convention delegates in 1983 viewed the two superpowers as equal threats to world peace. Of those who blamed one superpower more than the other, New Democrats were five times more likely to choose the United States as the greater threat to world peace. New Democratic activists are far off the Canadian norm also in opposing a return to capital punishment (77.8 per cent), compared with a strong majority of Canadians who support it.[4]

Too Far to the Left?

The argument that the New Democratic Party has failed to win elections because it is too far to the left cannot be examined in the same way, for there is no golden right-wing past with which to compare it. Discussion has to be hypothetical, and it will accordingly be brief. However far to the right the party may move, as long as it remains critical of the private sector it will be attacked. As long as it is not prepared to say that the market itself can best solve our economic problems, and that the only real jobs are in the private sector, it will be suspect. Silence was Trudeau's great offence to the business community. His tax give-aways to the corporations were prodigal, but he would not *praise* them and business leaders always felt he was not with them.

There are, of course, those well-meaning souls who admire the NDP leader or individual candidates but think they are in the wrong party. "If only Ed Broadbent were leader of the Liberal Party, I'd vote for him" is not uncommonly heard. Canvassers patiently explain that if Broadbent were leader of the Liberal Party he would not be the same Ed they like. Voters similarly will say they are attracted to the kind of people the party runs, but they do not like New Democrat policies. The party must obviously learn from, and respond to, these feelings, short of changing those policies that draw such attractive people to it. In so far as these views reflect mistaken perspectives there is a remedy, but I suspect there are not many New Democrat votes in this crowd.

Any general move to the right, or loss of distinctiveness of New Democrat programs, would weaken party members' commitment to work for it. A party without corporate donors depends heavily on its members, both for money and for voluntary work. The NDP depends utterly on these salt-of-the-earth people who do have a different vision of what Canada can be. They are more civil-libertarian than the population at large and it is due to their efforts that we have come as far as we have in the recognition of such rights. They give leadership on equality rights and development-aid issues, and provoke real debate on the usefulness of our military alliances. These New Democrats act as the leaven in the Canadian loaf. If they have distanced themselves from their neighbours, it is because they are more critical and demanding and less complacent than most Canadians. There are exceptions, to be sure, but for most of the differences in opinions and attitudes New Democrats are setting the trends. The preceding chapter shows just how far Canadians have come in accepting New Democrat ideas. Yet often it took decades, and party members appeared to be eccentrics and were called scoundrels in the meantime.

The Union Connection

Perhaps as common as not-far-enough-left as an explanation for the NDP's electoral failure is its link with unions. The connection with organized labour, it is said, is what prevents the party's election to government, putting off many people who would otherwise vote for it.[5] Yet the party, while not obtaining majority support from union members, gets a higher percentage of votes from unionized than from non-unionized voters. Throughout the country, it receives roughly twice as many votes from union members as from non-members, a substantial difference. The New Democrat vote is higher still among members of locals affiliated with the party, now three times the non-union rate.

Further, the vote for the CCF/NDP increased after formal links with organized labour were established. The highest vote the CCF ever got federally was 15.6 per cent in 1945. Support declined throughout the 1950s until the disastrous Diefenbaker election of 1958, with the NDP popular vote at 9.5 per cent and only eight seats. This is what prompted the reorganization and the alliance with labour that resulted in the "New Party". The vote for the New Democratic Party has varied from a low of 13.1 per cent in 1963 up to 19.8 per cent in 1980, results clearly better than before the labour affiliation.

The extent and nature of labour's links with the NDP are exaggerated in the public mind, to the detriment of the party. Only 20 per cent of the national party's funding comes from unions, and union funding at the riding level is considerably less. (By comparison, the Liberal and Conservative parties receive *half* their national funding from corporations, and local contributions by corporations are also substantial.) There is no bloc voting by union affiliates in the New Democratic Party as there is in the British Labour Party. The "inordinate influence" accusation, in short, is a bum rap.

Labour's own image problems are worse yet, since unions are seen as narrowly self-seeking in a way that business is not viewed. Of the great reforms that have made Canada a humane country, like medicare, the old age pension, and unemployment insurance, it was the unions who were the strong advocates, while business consistently opposed the programs. And these were reforms for the benefit of *all* Canadians, not just for union members. The same holds for the advances made in civil liberties, equality rights, affirmative action, international aid, cultural sovereignty, and nuclear disarmament, where unions have been active in promoting reform, while business was either opposed or silent. The image is far from the reality, and this is a problem for both the NDP and the unions. That there is anything to gain by severing the link is, in my view, without foundation. Changes in the relationship can and should be entertained, for the sake of both.

As to the failure of the New Democratic Party to win more votes from union members and other workers, there are standard sociological hypotheses. I am most partial to the explanation of weak social-class identification. My own voting studies from the 1960s showed social-class identification to have a modest but certainly not a strong influence on voting intentions. Young's analysis of the CCF in elections stresses this.

Objectively, a working class exists in Canada, but its members largely do not accept their position as such. Their aspirations and attitudes are middle class. They are not prepared to support a party that is not identified with the status to which they aspire.[6] For many members, the union is just a means of getting ahead in a capitalist society. Since this rather discouraging analysis was made, the size of the working class, and union membership, have declined with the loss of manufacturing jobs.

The tendency to assume a fundamental rationality behind a voter's support, another contention of Young's *Anatomy of a Party*, still holds remarkably well today for the NDP. The CCF was based on pre-Freudian assumptions. "It was assumed that people voted for the CCF because they had been won over to the cause of socialism; this was seldom the case."[7] From years of experience of talking with voters at the door, I would have to concur. Along with the sober assessment of party platforms, there are personal reactions to the party leaders, family voting traditions, identifications of religion, ethnicity, language, and class, and quite inexplicable notions of "it's time for a change". There is a core group of devoted, well-informed CCF/NDP voters, but whether this is greater in the New Democratic Party than in other parties has never been demonstrated. Other than this group, there is considerable shifting from election to election.

The swings in Canadian elections are greater than in many other countries. People come to the New Democratic Party because they like its policies, or they are fed up with the Liberals or the Conservatives, or they like the local candidate for other reasons. Similarly, they will desert the party for any number of reasons that have nothing to do with its policy or its ideology. They will go the party that is the Official Opposition when they very badly want to get rid of the party in power. New Democrats like to think that their voters are more loyal than other voters, but, apart from that small dedicated core, this belief is either wishful thinking or sloppy sentimentality.

One difference that voting studies show on the transmission of party identification works to the disadvantage of the New Democrats. While 62 per cent of Liberal and 48 per cent of Conservative fathers passed on their party identification to their children, only 36.5 per cent of CCF/NDP fathers did. This may suggest a greater rationality among NDP supporters, who must be convinced, but it also means that the party must work harder to retain its support.[8] That this is not impossible is demonstrated by the same analysis. Canadian voters are more volatile than their British or American counterparts, for example, and party identification is not a guarantee of a vote for any party.

The fluctuations in voter support *between* elections, as demonstrated by opinion polls, show this ebb and flow. The response that someone would vote New Democrat if an election were held today may indicate only how well or how badly the party in power is doing. All parties fare better in the polls when getting a lot of news coverage, as during a leadership race. As to how much a politician can rely on this support, ask John Turner.

These fluctuations in support are much greater between elections than at elections, not only for the NDP but for all parties. At election time, disgruntled supporters come back into the fold, every fold. Differences in media coverage narrow during the election campaign. The advantage a party may have had during a leadership campaign declines. For the New Democratic Party, no election result has been as bad as the low of 11 per cent the party hit in the opinion polls in 1984, nor any result as good as the peak of 29 per cent reached in 1986.

For the CCF the range was even greater in the opinion polls, although narrower in actual election results. Not counting the 1930s, when little polling was done, the party ran between a low of 8 per cent in 1958 and a high of 29 per cent in 1943, when it beat both the Conservatives and the Liberals. Yet the CCF never did that well in any election, although in its first election it managed 8.9 per cent of the popular vote. If New Democrat leaders seem phlegmatic in discussing opinion poll results with insistent reporters, they have good reason.

The Peace Vote

The irrationality of voting becomes ever more apparent as we examine particular groups that might be expected to vote New

Democrat in large numbers but do not. Perhaps the most flagrant contradiction is the peace movement's relation to the party. People concerned with peace and disarmament issues vote largely for the parties whose policies they oppose. Peace journals, newsletters, and bulletins routinely give the NDP bad press, or none at all. In election campaigns, peace groups sponsor all-candidates meetings giving every party an equal chance to present itself as their friend. MPs who voted for cruise testing, for example, suddenly appeared in 1984 as opposed to it. At peace rallies, all parties are invited to send representatives. The Conservative and Liberal representatives may echo the sentiments of the New Democrats, but without the support of their parties. The uninformed onlooker may have the impression that all three parties are equally committed to working towards peace and nuclear disarmament.

Canadian peace groups in the early 1980s were working on such issues as nuclear non-proliferation, a world disarmament referendum, Canada as a nuclear-weapons-free zone, and industrial conversion of weapons-manufacturing to consumer goods. When Canada was asked to sign a framework agreement that would include cruise testing, the major peace organizations joined together to oppose it. Massive demonstrations, marches, public meetings, and vigils were held. Write-in campaigns and petitions were organized. Within a short time, *half* of all Canadians agreed that cruise testing should not be permitted on Canadian territory. Yet in 1984 80 per cent of Canadians voted for the parties that supported the tests, and indeed the manufacture of guidance system components and other like weaponry. Even many of the leaders of the peace movement supported Liberal and Conservative candidates. One major peace group, Operation Dismantle, awarded a special prize to the president of the Liberal Party for personally taking a position in favour of a nuclear freeze, although the party opposed it.

By the 1984 election there had been considerable institutional movement on the issue. Major unions and labour federations had come out against the cruise and for a freeze and conversion projects. The major churches in Canada, as elsewhere, had taken stands on the immorality of a first strike, the dangers of nuclear escalation, and the desirability of a freeze followed by a gradual reduction in nuclear weapons. Important women's organizations like the National Action Committee took up peace as an issue. Professional groups formed caucuses, such as Scientists for Peace and Psychologists for Social Responsibility. Parents for Peace emerged across the country. In short, major respectable organizations began to make pronouncements on nuclear disarmament very similar to the NDP's position and far from those of the other parties. Yet, it seems most of the bishops and the presidents, leaders, and members of these groups voted for the parties whose position they were opposing.

Trudeau's peace initiative of 1983 was diabolically clever as a public-relations exercise. It was not, unfortunately, successful in achieving any of its ostensible aims. But how could it? After selling Candu reactors to unsavoury customers, making Canada a major world arms exporter, and then accepting cruise testing, Trudeau had no credibility. He was politely sent on his way after non-committal conversations in the world's great capitals. At home, though, the "peace initiative" was an adman's dream. The Liberals began to pick up at the polls, largely at the expense of the New Democrats. Editorials praised Trudeau's statesmanship, the first kind words said about the man by some papers for several years.

Since then, Mulroney has shown a similar adroitness, but whether he will be as successful in manipulating the peace movement remains to be seen. For the moment, he deserves full marks for trying. The appointment of New Democrat Stephen Lewis as ambassador to the United Nations was brilliant. The appointment of Douglas Roche, the major Conservative peace advocate, was even more so. Roche, a former Conservative MP, had become so identified with the peace movement that large numbers of his own party were out to get him. He chose not to seek re-nomination in 1984, having only narrowly won his re-nomination in 1980. One of the first duties Ambassador Roche had at the United Nations was to vote *against* a nuclear freeze.

Another Conservative gesture to the peace movement was the appointment of representatives from major peace organizations as "advisors" to the Canadian delegation at the United Nations. These advisors attend United Nations meetings with the delegation, but obviously their advice is not taken.

The Conservative government's decision on "Star Wars" is another example of currying favour with the peace movement, while keeping Reagan happy as well. Mulroney surprised many people with his announcement that Canada would not officially take part in Star Wars research. A few clarifications later and the initial "no" had become a partial "yes". Private firms, universities, and research institutes could take part, with public money in fact. According to External Affairs secretary Joe Clark, applications will be judged on a case-by-case basis. The "no" decision means only that there will be no new programs *so called*, but approved projects will be funded through existing military agreements.

By the time of the second "shamrock summit", in March 1986, it had become clear that there would be substantial Canadian involvement in Star Wars research. The NORAD renewal agreement Mulroney signed with Reagan excludes mention of the anti-ballistic-missile treaty, which would prohibit a Star Wars-type system. No new money as such has been designated for Star Wars research, but military spending *in toto* has been increased by the Mulroney government. Throughout, Mulroney has continued to endorse the "Strategic Defense Initiative" as a necessary measure for the United States. Yet peace activists have praised the Prime Minister for his decision. It could have been worse, to be sure, but Mulroney must deserve praise more for his sleight of hand than for his contribution to world peace.

The peace movement's tactics of lobbying individual MPs, especially those of the party in power, evokes a sense of *déjà vu*. For decades the founders of the CCF used the conventional citizens' methods of writing letters to the editor, or explaining a particular need to responsible authorities and asking for action. J. S. Woodsworth actually succeeded in having some new park space developed in North Winnipeg for his efforts. It was precisely because these methods were so ineffectual that Woodsworth, Douglas, et al. took the next step, that of entering politics themselves. Again the method was one of rational persuasion, backed up with well-documented speeches and specific practical proposals.

It is interesting to note that many of these early reformers had to go through a political, but non-partisan, stage before they came to the conclusion that a political party must be the main instrument for social change. Many of the early CCFers worked for the Non-Partisan League, and others were in the non-party Progressive movement. The Progressives actually could have become the Official Opposition in 1922 because of the number of seats they won, but they declined to become a party. They are now a footnote in history, while the two labour representatives elected at the same time went on to get the old age pension for Canada, and formed the CCF/NDP.

Since the 1984 election, the peace movement has been noticeably quieter. To some extent this reflects a change in the movement's tactics. Activists consider demonstrations and marches to have been proven ineffective. They are concentrating now more on education and long-term changes in attitudes. Useful work is being done in curriculum development for schools. Yet one wonders if the silence might reflect a more profound rethinking. The peace movement has been had, and perhaps members are beginning to realize it.

The CCF/NDP may be dove-like in its psychology of what makes people vote as they do, but it has a serpent's understanding of social institutions, interests, and systems. Advocates

94

of peace and justice such as the churches are still largely oriented to individual sin and individual repentance. But how does a corporation repent or a social system lead a new life? If the president of Litton Industries were actually converted by the peace activists who met with him, what could he do but resign? Even if the entire management, work force, and board of directors of Litton had been convinced, they would yet have had to persuade a majority of shareholders. Had the shareholders all been willing to give up the cruise missile contract, the government would simply have given it to another company. Peace advocates working in the New Democratic Party know that the changing of even thousands of hearts and minds would not be enough. They understand that it will only be with the election of a *government* committed to a different kind of foreign and defence policy that the manufacture of nuclear-weapons components will be ended in Canada.

The Abortion Issue in Elections

Some New Democrats consider that the party's pro-choice abortion policy loses it votes. Usually, but not always, these are people who personally oppose that position. Since the 1970s, abortion has been an issue in elections, and the extent to which it wins or loses votes for the NDP is a matter to consider here. For some New Democrat sympathizers, especially Catholics, the party's perceived stand is a real stumbling-block.

Yet access to abortion was legislated under a Liberal government, with a Catholic prime minister, Pierre Elliott Trudeau, and a Catholic minister of Justice, John Turner. The Conservatives as well as the NDP voted for the current Criminal Code provisions, permitting abortion when approved by a therapeutic-abortion committee. The current laws are enforced by provincial governments which are mainly Conservative. A Liberal minister, Francis Fox, had to resign when it was discovered he had helped procure an abortion by fraudulently signing a hospital form. Trudeau brought him back into cabinet a short time later. Three provincial governments have prosecuted Dr. Morgentaler: the Liberal government in Québec, the Conservative in Ontario, and the New Democrat in Manitoba. The only party to have refrained from prosecuting him was the Parti Québécois.

In fact all three major parties have a majority of members who are pro-choice on abortion, reflecting the views of the population at large. All three parties have a vociferous minority that would abolish abortion completely, or restrict it to the rarest of circumstances. The NDP's position is middle-of-the-road, and has never been pro-abortion in any reasonable sense of the word. Pro-choice activists have castigated the NDP for prosecuting Morgentaler, and generally for not being pro-choice enough.

The differences between the parties lie in their different party structures and rules of operating rather than in policy. The New Democratic Party determines its decisions on policy by votes at national conventions. Spokespeople are required to respect those decisions, although they may work internally to have them changed. In the other two parties policies are decided by cabinet and/or senior leaders. Dissension is permitted on this issue. Thus both the Liberals and the Conservatives can play both sides of the issue. Back-bench Conservatives present private member's bills to abolish abortion, when they are not too busy organizing petitions to bring back capital punishment. These bills are routinely talked out by the Conservative government itself, just as the Liberals stopped attempts by back-benchers to change the law when they were in power. It is extremely unlikely that a Conservative or a Liberal government would abolish access to abortion in Canada, but both parties have managed to appear as more "pro-life" than the NDP. Persons opposed to any access to abortion must condemn all three parties.

The New Democratic Party is decidedly pro-life on issues

from nuclear weapons and capital punishment to the positive means of supporting families with family allowances, parental leave, and child care. If people were genuinely concerned about these "life issues", they would support the party that promotes these policies.

I give my own campaign experience as concrete evidence of how the life issue can be twisted to suit another political agenda. In the 1982 by-election in Broadview-Greenwood I was the only woman, the only feminist, and, apart from the Liberal, the only one of the nine candidates much to the left of George III. My strongest opponent was Peter Worthington, who is pro-choice on abortion, as well as pro-nuclear arms, pro-capital punishment, and anti-family allowance. Yet I was "targeted" by a pro-life organization with a massive pamphlet distribution implicating me in the deaths of millions. Not a word was said about Worthington. In the 1984 election Worthington ran again and even publicized his pro-choice position in his literature, yet still he was not criticized. There are, of course, principled and consistent members of the pro-life movement, whose convictions on abortion, as on other life issues, I respect. For some organizations, however, "pro-conservative" might be a more honest name than "pro-life".

Targeting as a tactic seems to be ineffectual against particular candidates. Other New Democrats targeted during the 1984 election were re-elected with increased margins. Several anti-choice members were defeated, although probably for unrelated reasons. Yet I suspect that there is some spill-over effect that hurts the party. The abortion issue, carefully managed by right-wing interests, associates a party of do-gooders with selfishness. As the party of the social gospel became "godless materialism" in the 1930s, so the NDP today is seen by some as immoral and heartless.

The Gender Gap

Until recently, a lower proportion of women than men supported the New Democratic Party. The women's vote has since caught up with the men's, but it should be higher still, and not just on account of the NDP's stand on women's issues such as equal pay and maternity benefits. More women should be New Democrat supporters because of a common concern for the universal social programs.

Simply put, women need the social programs more than men do. Far fewer women than men receive private pensions; therefore, far more depend on public pensions. Given their family responsibilities, women are keener supporters of medicare than are men, and they are far less able to afford "extra billing". Women have also fared worse than men in salary and benefits in the private sector. Consequently, they have had to turn to state intervention for justice, or at least to reduce the inequities between the sexes. Women aggressively call for increased social services even when governments are calling for restraint. Women expect the government to work for them, and do not accept excuses they are given for inaction. If day care is needed — and it is — and the private sector does not supply it — and it doesn't — women want government to respond. In all these respects they behave exactly like New Democrats. But they do not vote accordingly.

To some extent the lower-than-it-ought-to-be NDP voting by women reflects past conditions. In the bad old days before the women's movement, the NDP was a more macho organization. The union link, in that period, did not help to attract women voters. A "union" hall that is a beer parlour/pool hall may not unite all its members. If the brothers eye the sisters with incestuous glances, the women will quite naturally feel ill at ease. All that, of course, has changed in recent years. The unions now support equal pay for work of equal value, affirmative action, child care, maternity benefits, parental leave, and protection against sexual harassment. Women's issues have become union issues, and the NDP and the unions work together on them. Ironically, the NDP has become so identified with the struggle for workingwomen's rights that it has sometimes been accused of not caring about those women who work full time in the home!

If the NDP's faults here are more imagined than real, there are still areas where blame can properly be laid. New Democrats have not been as effective as the Liberals and Conservatives in practising tokenism. As the deliberate appointment of women to senior positions for public-relations purposes, tokenism is to be encouraged and not decried. Ideally, women would routinely get half the appointments as governor general, judge, CRTC board member, ambassador to France, etc., where their abilities and expertise merited them. Until that day, it is arguably better that women be appointed for the wrong reasons rather than not appointed at all. Performing well in these roles will help to make such appointments more natural. In the meantime, the Conservatives and Liberals have used prestigious appointments to their own advantage. Not only have the women done creditably on the job, they have made those parties look more pro-woman than they in fact are.

The New Democratic Party has an affirmative-action policy to ensure that women are equally represented on federal council and party committees, but women are still badly represented in caucus. Well-qualified women have promptly materialized for these positions, and the policy has been a great success. The affirmative-action policy has not, however, been implemented for the nomination of women in winnable ridings. According to the policy, the leader, caucus, and staff are supposed to seek out women for winnable seats. Both the Liberal and the Conservative leaders have done such recruitment, but the NDP leader so far has not. The representation of women in the House of Commons is no worse, at ten per cent of NDP members, than for the other parties. More, however, is expected of the NDP. In fact, the party's practice of running so many women as sacrificial lambs — far more than the other parties — is resented by feminists inside the party and out.

Finally, and again because more is expected of those who espouse equality, the NDP has not provided the leadership on women's concerns that it should. That its policies are better than those of the other parties is an achievement. But the party is not associated with women's issues in the same way that it is with the old age pension or medicare. As shown in Chapter 2, the CCF/NDP has an impressive record of articulating a need, proposing a remedy, and fighting for it inside and outside of Parliament until the point is won. On women's issues the New Democratic Party has been less tenacious, and still has to be lobbied. Feminists within the party must remain vigilant lest the brothers backslide. Happily, women lobbyists are well received and the brothers usually do come through, increasingly with good grace. Yet that is not the same thing as leading the way.

The Media

Blaming the press is so over-used an explanation for lack of popularity — by all parties — that I have deliberately left it as a last resort. Liberal and Conservative prime ministers have blamed the media for their various falls from glory, and Conservative back-benchers cite CBC bias as sufficient reason for closing down the corporation. Most people take this with a grain of salt. The media, however, have treated the NDP differently. Some of the crude attacks on the party in its earlier years have been described in Chapter 1. This kind of journalism is not in style any more, but more sophisticated dismissals and scant coverage generally remain as problems. It is an historic fact that no newspaper, magazine, or television or radio station has ever waged a media campaign for the New Democratic Party or any of its candidates, or ever positively endorsed the

CCF or CCF candidates. Many newspapers do endorse the Conservative or the Liberal Party and are indeed known as Conservative or Liberal papers. Endorsation may include editorial support, columnists' personal remarks, and simply more and better coverage in news and feature stories. The enormous value of this need not be included as an election expense.

Election coverage is only the tip of the iceberg. A more serious disadvantage is the lesser coverage the party receives between elections. The NDP simply does not get the one-fifth of coverage that its support in the electorate should earn it. When coverage is carefully measured and allocated according to formula, as in election campaigns, the New Democratic Party gets closer to its share. In 1984, it received 18.6 per cent of national free broadcast time, only a percentage point lower than its popular vote in the preceding election. For the NDP, coverage improves markedly in election periods. There is more coverage, and great efforts are made at fairness.

In Canada, deliberate bias is now rare, whether in election periods or not. Extent and depth of coverage, however, are another issue. The media should indeed focus on government initiatives and the Official Opposition should get the next crack at coverage, if it has something to say on the issue. Often, however, the story goes no further, even when the New Democrat spokesperson in the area concerned has both criticized the government and provided an alternative. In some cases the NDP critic has made every reasonable effort to communicate his or her position, in question period, speeches, perhaps a private member's bill, media conferences, news releases, and so on. What is most often omitted is the party's alternative solution, so that the NDP appears to be more negative than it is, "opposing for the sake of opposing". Critics appear in stories commenting on the foibles of their minister, while their constructive proposals for a different way to handle the matter are ignored.

The constraints of the electronic media are partly responsible for inadequate coverage. The problem is less acute in the print media. New Democrat solutions tend to be more complicated than Conservative or Liberal ones and harder to report. Free trade is a simpler concept to communicate than industrial strategy, capital punishment is more easily grasped than reconciliation or prevention, welfare for the needy is more quickly understood than a system of unemployment insurance, retraining, and job creation. None of this, of course, is the fault of the individual reporter. The Minister of Finance normally takes close to two hours to read the budget, and officials are given several hours more to explain it to the media in the information "lock-up". Yet the response time allocated the NDP on television may be as little as forty seconds. This obviously does not permit either a comprehensive critique or any exploration of alternatives, let alone both. It is not surprising that opposition coverage should focus on wisecracks or slogans.

The major daily newspapers in Canada are owned by newspaper chains that are as committed to big business as any other corporation. Papers obtain most of their revenue from advertising, only 15-20 per cent from subscriptions and sales. In the pursuit of profit, the daily press "presents an almost insoluble problem to the radical reformer," concluded media expert Neil Compton. "Radical criticisms ... are invariably ignored, parodied, or distorted to the point where serious discussion of them becomes impossible."[9]

The privately owned television and radio stations are also owned by big business interests, and are even more dependent on advertising revenues than the other media. The CBC and the provincial channels have no such business connections, but even they do not escape the pressure to attract big audiences. Arguably, then, "the systematic pressure to produce profitable audiences" is responsible for "a de facto form of political censorship".[10] Newspapers, private radio, and CBC television, wherever advertising is sold, are all affected by this subtle bias. "Ultimately, the most fundamental constraint on news ... may well be the necessity of telling stories in a way which attracts an audience to adopt a consumerist lifestyle."[11]

The situation is different but no better for the New Democratic Party with regard to the small-circulation weekly papers and the growing number of publications by professional, voluntary, and church organizations. The weeklies are as dependent on advertising as are the large dailies. The professional and voluntary organization papers are less so, but with their rising professionalism and gloss, they tend to be non-partisan in the sense of not formally endorsing any party. In election campaigns, some put questions to all parties, and publish the results without comment. Between elections they scarcely mention the NDP; somehow it is considered non-partisan to cover only the government and possibly also the Official Opposition. Some will denounce the government in no uncertain terms for its policy failures, yet not mention the New Democrat position. So even where the organization has a similar outlook to the NDP's, and may be advancing similar policy, there is no mention of a common cause.

I followed the reporting of two small, progressive publications for five years, the *Catholic New Times* of Toronto and *Catalyst*, the publication of Citizens for Public Justice. Both took similar editorial positions to the NDP on economic policy, job creation, the social programs, justice for natives, equality rights, pornography, Japanese-Canadian redress, nuclear disarmament, cruise testing, Latin America, Star Wars, capital punishment, and prisons, not to exhaust the list. Neither paper at any time gave *any* coverage to the NDP's position on *any* of these matters. Both papers routinely criticized Liberal and Conservative governments for their failings in policy, without ever mentioning that there was a third option. And these are progressive papers, with no financial dependence on the corporations, and no philosophical commitment to them. Otherwise, they do high-quality analysis.

However, flagrant bias is never more than a rare occurrence

for either the mass media or these smaller, more specialized publications. Among the Canadian journalists who admit to a party preference, about one in five are New Democrat, the same ratio as the general population. For reporters of every political persuasion, fairness and objectivity are professional goals, and professional standards are high in Canada.

The New Democratic Party is disadvantaged also by a general mind-set that operates subtly. Media people accept many debatable political positions as unquestioned facts of life. Many journalists, like many other Canadians, have swallowed the line that New Democrats in federal government would be irresponsible spendthrifts, although the party's record of balancing the budget in several provinces is better than the Conservatives'. The corporate view of oil as a resource that must be "developed" is a received truth for many Canadians, journalists included. Environmentalists and New Democrats alike have to begin any analysis by redefining the very terminology associated with their subjects. It is difficult to be against *development*, although in this case the word is a euphemism for the using up of a non-renewable resource. Leading media commentators were conned by British Columbia's "restraint" program in 1983, in which total government expenditure actually increased. That foreign-owned multinationals "create" jobs in Canada is often uncritically accepted, although the best evidence shows a substantial net loss of jobs in the branch-plant country. None of this is bias, and all of it is probably harder to fight than bias.

The media help shape people's views of life/society/reality. By voting age, a young Canadian has seen an estimated 20,000 hours of television, 80 per cent of it American. The world portrayed on the screen is largely middle and upper class. While service and manual workers constitute 65 per cent of the population, on television they appear to be a mere 10 per cent. Poverty and unemployment are not the subjects of *Dallas* or *Dynasty*, or of much television programming at all. If class identification is weak for workers in Canada and the

United States, the near invisibility of that class and its problems on television may be part of the reason. According to television expert George Gerbner, the very depiction of a sex, age, and social hierarchy in television drama may help to cultivate the assumptions and behaviour that maintain that same hierarchy.[12]

The prevalence of violence in American programming, and thus on Canadian screens, has important political consequences. On American prime-time television there are on average six acts of violence per hour. On children's weekend television there are eighteen acts of violence per hour, two of them deaths. By age ten, a heavy viewer in the United States will have seen 7,000 screen deaths. Perversely, this violence is trivialized. Only 6 per cent of the victims are hurt badly enough to require treatment. Television violence desensitizes people to the real and painful consequences of violence, legitimizing it as a way of dealing with problems.

In the United States, .41 crimes are committed per 100 people, while on American television, 64 per cent of characters are involved in violence. In the United States, in real life, only 10 per cent of homicides are between strangers, while in television drama, 58 per cent are. Television thus not only grossly exaggerates the amount of violent crime, but the threat of it from the general public. Not surprisingly, heavy viewers are more likely than light viewers to overestimate the number of people involved in violent and serious crime, and consequently to fear walking alone at night. Heavy viewers more than light believe that the police frequently use their guns, and that they "must" use force at the scene of a violent crime.

Heavy viewers are more likely than light to believe that the world is getting worse, not better, that it is not fair to bring a child into it, and that public officials are not really interested in the problems of the average man. While heavy viewers are more prone than light to state that the United States should stay out of world affairs, they are more likely to believe that the United States will be in another war in the next ten years.

105

As a result of this exposure to so much violence, "the large majority of people ... become more fearful, insecure and dependent on authority." There is a "heightened sense of danger and risk in a mean and selfish world" and an increased likelihood of "demanding protection and even welcoming repression in the name of security".[13] This dark view of humanity corresponds all too well with the threatening images people see in their darkened living rooms.

In Canada we are never so extreme. Canadians spend on average one hour less per day in front of the television set. Further, they spend 20 per cent of their viewing time watching Canadian shows, which are less violent. Our rate of violent crime is only one-fifth the American rate, although we imprison people at half the American rate. Canadians routinely over-estimate the crime rate fivefold. The average Canadian believes that half the crimes committed are violent, while in fact only 8 per cent are. Two-thirds of Canadians believe the murder rate is increasing, which it is not.[14]

A study of a small B.C. community that did not have television reception until the 1970s reveals some of the medium's effects on viewers. After two years of receiving only one channel, the relatively non-violent CBC, children had become more aggressive and sexist, and less creative. Adults became less patient in problem-solving tasks. And this study reflects television viewing in 1972, before punk rock and soft-core porn.[15]

No Canadian studies so far have examined the connection between television viewing and political attitudes, but there is evidence of such a relationship to be found in American studies. Heavy television viewers in Canada are more likely than light to overestimate the number of murders, to be fearful of strangers, and to approve of ordinary citizens' carrying weapons and keeping them at home.[16] Conservative politicians may indeed be wrong in considering the CBC a subversive organization!

Canadian-made television and film is quite different from

American in subject matter, mood, feeling, and tone. There are fewer "jolts per minute" of any kind, and there is less violence and more realism. If fewer people are beaten or killed per hour, those who are hurt feel more pain and their assailants suffer more anguish after the fact. Canadian television and films win awards in public affairs, documentaries, and serious drama. We are better at instructing, informing, and reflecting than we are at entertaining. American television is more idealistic, and the violence in it is also idealized. According to Morris Wolfe in his book *Jolts*, American television proselytizes the American dream. It tells beautiful lies, shows the world not as it is but as we wish it to be. Canadian television, by comparison, is far more realistic, dealing in the grey world as we find it. The other side of the American dream, however, is cynicism and despair. In Canada, realism leads to satire rather than cynicism,[17] and always to more ambiguity and reflection.

Should Canadians switch off their sets and pick up a Canadian book instead, there would be other problems. If Margaret Atwood is correct that the dominant theme of Canadian literature is survival, then there is little encouragement to participate in political, or other, activity. Canadian stories, unlike American, tend not to be about people who have made it, but about people who have made it *back* from some awful experience. Says Atwood, "Canadian authors spend a disproportionate amount of time making sure that their heroes die or fail."[18] If there is hope to be found here, it is that any map is better than none at all. Atwood's *Survival* itself ends on a somewhat hopeful note, arguing for the stance of "creative non-victim" as an option.

In developing the "jolts" concept, Wolfe suggests another barrier to social democracy, although he discusses this in the context of more general implications for democracy. The part of the brain that processes television, the paleocortex, likes loudness, even crudeness, and positively thrives on high jolts per minute. Yet a functioning democracy requires a high tolerance for boredom, the capacity to sit through lengthy meetings and read tedious reports. Paradoxically, the more complex a society becomes, the greater the need for this capacity to endure but the less it is fostered.[19] Yet the B.C. television study showed that a mere two years of watching the CBC reduced people's problem-solving ability and their creativity, while making them more aggressive.

Studies have shown that the side of the brain that processes technical information is not used while watching television. Knowing that the left brain switches off, effective television communicators do not attempt to cover complex points but merely leave an impression. For Canadian social democrats the switching off of the left brain is a decided problem, for the message to be communicated is complex and requires active thought. The paleocortex/high jolts combination is a menace not susceptible of solution. Paleotomies are not likely to be any more popular than lobotomies, and jamming would cause noise pollution. Should the NDP then ask people to take the teetotallers' pledge not to take another drop of demon jolts? In fact, it has concentrated on more positive, and practicable, measures, like increased Canadian production through the CBC, the NFB, Telefilm, and Canadian-content regulations by the CRTC.

It is not that there is any provable connection between social democratic views, let alone voting New Democrat, and Canadian culture. It is simply that without a view of Canada as a distinctive country, with its own problems to solve, the party's political agenda makes no sense. Without the belief that people *can* solve their problems, that next step to action will not be taken. The NDP political program thus requires a fundamental conviction that people *can* change the society in which they live. In so far as the media contribute to a sense of powerlessness, they are undermining the New Democratic Party's case.

There is already a strong sense of powerlessness in the Canadian electorate, and voting studies suggest that it is increasing. A major 1979 survey found that only one-third of Canadian voters felt that politicians help to solve problems; some 28 per cent thought not, and a cynical 5 per cent felt that politics makes situations worse. Further, of those who thought that political action did help, one-fifth could not mention a single positive example! Of the examples mentioned, few were in the economic area, although unemployment and inflation were major concerns. Or, while people overwhelmingly thought that government *ought* to be intervening in the economy, they had little confidence that anything it might do would help.

Canadian political leaders were seen as ineffectual, and wasteful, although not dishonest. A full 95 per cent of respondents considered that politicians wasted a lot of the taxpayers' money, and this was while Joe Clark was losing his luggage, long before Brian Mulroney's more splendiferous hotel bills were rung up.

I suspect that this sense of helplessness is a major barrier to greater voting support for the New Democratic Party. Understanding the problem, of course, may also be the first step towards solving it. In the meantime, let us turn to the countries where social democratic parties have broken through the despair, formed governments, and proven in practice that the social programs are indeed affordable, as are high standards in education, culture, and political liberties. By managing the economy well, they have shown that the goals of social democracy are not idle dreams but eminently practicable public policy.

4

THE PARTY OF GOVERNMENT—
IN OTHER COUNTRIES

Social democratic parties in other countries have had to face the same problems as the CCF/NDP in Canada. They are nowhere endorsed by commercial newspapers, nor do television and radio stations give them greater or better coverage. Threats of the collapse of the economy are uttered by chambers of commerce and federations of employers wherever a social democratic party has a real crack at being elected. Yet social democratic parties have been elected in Norway, Sweden, Denmark, Britain, Austria, West Germany, Australia, New Zealand, France, Greece, Portugal, and Spain. Social democratic parties have taken part in coalition governments in the Netherlands, Belgium, Finland, Ireland, and Switzerland.

Instead of wringing our hands at the injustice of it all, let us consider how these other parties with the same obstacles have yet managed to make it. Several key factors will be examined, beginning with the level of unionization in the country and the nature of the link between union and party. Party unity, stability of leadership, and radicalism of position will also be considered. We will briefly look at the role of the media and the nature of the electoral system, and see how Canada compares.

The Northern Pattern

To follow chronological order, the social democratic success tour must begin in the north, with Norway, Sweden, and

110

Denmark, and move south. Southern Europeans have not been any slower to see the social democratic vision, but right-wing resistance has been fiercer in the south. Or Montesquieu's theory on the influence of intemperate climates on the passions is again vindicated. Striking workers and labour organizers were also shot in the north, but in more isolated instances; in the south fascist regimes ruled long and late.

Norway

The social democratic breakthrough came early in Norway, as with many other reforms, including the vote for women. The Norwegian Labour Party was founded in 1887 and began electing members to Parliament early. In 1928 it actually formed a government for eighteen days. By 1933 it had won 46 per cent of the seats, and by 1935 it had become a junior partner in a coalition government. It formed a majority government in 1945 and was re-elected until 1963. Since then it has alternated with the right-wing parties as the government, several times running minority governments. It has long been, and still is, the largest party in the country. The link with the unions is strong and the labour force itself is highly organized. By the mid-1960s over 60 per cent of the labour force was unionized.[1]

The early attempts at unionization in the mid-nineteenth century included small farmers and farm labourers. There was a political component as well in the early labour movement in the struggle for universal suffrage. The first coalition the Norwegian Labour Party had was with the Agrarian Party, an alliance also to be seen in Sweden. Doubtless, difficulties of labour-farm co-operation should not be minimized, but the fact that the groups could work together is significant. Compare this with West Germany, where the sharp divisions between the conservative rural areas and the social democratic urban areas in West Germany have kept the Social Democrats there out of government for most of this century. Similarly, in Nova Scotia, where the farmers and labour gained seven and four seats respectively in 1920, there was no co-operation between the two. Both were defeated by the Conservatives in the next election.

Norway is a smaller country than Canada, with a population of only four million people. Like Canada, it depends on its resource industries far more than on manufacturing. The standard of living is high, the welfare state well organized; education is free to the end of university and there are no nuclear plants. Equality between the sexes is promoted, for example, with provisions for at least 40 per cent of appointments made by government to each sex. In the 1985 election, women obtained nearly a third of the seats. They hold half the positions in the Labour cabinet formed in 1986 by Prime Minister Gro Harlem Brundtland. For those who think that Canada has too small a population to achieve social democracy, Norway is an excellent counter-example.

Denmark

In Denmark, the Social Democratic Party, the trade union movement, and a socialist weekly, *Socialisten*, were all formed at the same time, in 1871.[2] The paper was established initially to call people to a public meeting in support of a strike. The paper, strike, and ensuing political organization were all put down by the police at this stage, although all three re-emerged a few years later. The party elected its first members in 1884, and soon broadened its base to include rural workers. By 1913 it was winning the most votes in national elections, and it still is. It was included in a government as early as 1924, and led a coalition in 1926. Not counting the all-party war-time coalition, the Social Democrats have been in government in some capacity for over forty-three years. They were in power throughout the

1930s, when they put in place Denmark's major social-welfare legislation.

The Danish labour force is even more highly unionized than the Norwegian.[3] By 1921 the unionization rate was as high as 35 per cent, and the Social Democratic Party made its first entry into government in the first election after that, in 1924. The unionization rate reached the 50 per cent mark by 1950, and continued to rise, peaking at 59 per cent in 1976. By comparison, Canada reached Denmark's 1921 level only in 1965. That extensive and increasing unionization is no guarantee of political success can also be seen in Denmark. The popular vote for the Social Democrats peaked at 46 per cent in 1935, although unionization continued to grow considerably after that. The links between party and union are strong, with union leaders sitting on the party executive.

Sweden

Sweden's labour force has been highly unionized for a long time, and the links between the unions and the Social Democratic Party are strong. The party's first, and short-lived, break into government occurred in the First World War.[4] Then the Social Democrats were part of a war-time coalition, when unionization was still only at the level of 17 per cent. The party was in minority governments in the 1920s, when union organization had reached about 25 per cent. The unionization level had risen to 38 per cent when the Social Democratic Party reached the crucial step of forming a government, albeit with a coalition partner, in 1932. Organization proceeded, reaching 60 per cent by the end of the Second World War, and on up to 80 per cent by 1970 and a record 93 per cent in 1977. Even the ambassadors have a union, as foreign-service officers.

Formed in 1889, the Social Democratic Party is the oldest

party of continuous existence in Sweden. Its intellectual origins go back to as early as 1845 with the Stockholm Education Circle. It began to elect members early, becoming the largest party in Parliament by 1914. Canada, by way of comparison, in 1914 had only a few small socialist parties in the West, and the occasional "labour representative" in Parliament. The first elected members went through the apparently universal phase of advocating social security measures for years in opposition. The first such programs were brought in on a local basis by mutual-aid societies organized by workers themselves. Gradually the municipalities began to contribute support.

The decisive turn came in 1932 when, with massive unemployment, five workers were shot during a peaceful demonstration. The first Social Democratic government was elected that same year. Job creation through special government projects was begun immediately.

Party membership in Sweden, through union affiliation, is enormous. There are over a million members, nearly a member for every two votes. Even if three-quarters of the party membership is of union affiliates, that still makes for more than a quarter of a million individual members, out of a population of about 8 million. By comparison, New Democrat membership in Canada, with a population of 25 million, is only about 150,000.

The Netherlands

When we turn to the Netherlands, we begin to see conditions more similar to those in Canada. The available data show a peak of 43 per cent unionization in 1958, with declines after that to 25 per cent in 1983. Political divisions in the Netherlands, as in Canada, follow religious and ethnic lines more than class. The Labour Party itself is a respectable age, founded in 1881 as the Social Democratic League.[5] It first elected a member in 1888. Links with labour, however, were slow to be developed. In 1935, the party and the Federation of Trade Unions issued a socialist plan for combating the Depression. Yet it was not until after the war, when the current party was formed, that formal links were established. The Dutch Labour Party has never formed a government of its own, but it has been a member of most coalitions in the post-war period. It has been a major force in the building of the extensive Dutch welfare state.

Belgium

In Belgium, as in the Netherlands, political divisions based on class are less important than those based on language. Even the Social Democratic Party, which had long been a unitary party, is now technically two parties, albeit allied in elections and Parliament. Founded as the Belgian Workers Party in 1885, the party first entered government as part of a coalition government in exile in the First World War. It was the third-largest party in 1919 and the second-largest by the beginning of the Second World War, when it was dissolved on the Nazi occupation. The party was part of roughly half the coalition governments in the inter-war period. Since 1945, it has been in most coalition governments, three times as senior partner and holding the prime minister's position.

Belgium is a highly industrialized country and the labour force is commensurately organized.[6] In 1971, a high of 67 per cent of the population was unionized. Yet the social democratic union is only the second-largest union in the country, following the Catholic. Thus, this potentially great force for social democracy is divided. Further, the party-union links have weakened in recent years. The original Belgian Workers Party in 1898 founded a trade union committee, from which the present Federation of Labour is descended. For many years there was a provision for indirect party membership through the unions. This link was abolished in the 1960s for a purely individual form of membership.

West Germany

Historically, Germany has had the strongest social democratic party in the world, to the great consternation of Lenin and the Bolsheviks as much as to the German conservatives. The Social Democratic Party in West Germany carries on that tradition. It is the government in a number of the German states, but it has not been as successful at the national level as the Nordic parties. The Social Democratic Party is the only major party in West Germany to have direct continuity with the pre-Nazi past, indeed going back to its formation in 1875, in Imperial Germany, and back to 1869 for one of its constituent parts.[7] Banned by Chancellor Otto von Bismarck, it continued to grow as an underground party. Like the other social democratic parties of Europe, its origins are Marxist. The Communists split off after the Russian Revolution, and the Social Democratic Party continued to evolve as a parliamentary democratic party. Germany is the birthplace not only of Karl Marx, but of the leading revisionists of Marxism, Edouard Bernstein and Karl Kautsky.

The party had the largest number of seats in the Reichstag by 1912. In the early Weimar years it had the unenviable task of winding up the German Empire. It took on the defence of law and order, putting down workers' rebellions at home. It remained the largest party until the Nazi victory in 1932.

The pattern of union growth in Germany was quite different before and after the Nazis. Union growth early in the century was rapid, making up for lost time under Bismarck. Ten per cent of the labour force was organized by 1905, 20 per cent by 1911, and 50 per cent by 1921.[8] After a decline in the First World War, numbers again rose sharply from 38 per cent in 1920 to 53 per cent in 1921. With the unemployment and inflation of the Weimar period, numbers declined again. Hitler promptly abolished the unions on coming into power. After the war, there was modest growth in unionization but never

116

again to those early peaks. The first post-war statistics show a unionization level of 23 per cent in 1947 and slow growth to 42 per cent by 1980.

Post-war German politics were dominated by Konrad Adenauer and his Christian Democratic Party. The Social Democrats then entered the unlikely "grand coalition" of 1966-69 with the conservative Christian Democratic/Christian Socialist Union. They finally formed a government in 1969, with the Free Democrats as junior coalition partner. This Social Democrat/Free Democrat coalition lasted throughout the 1970s, for three governments. When the Free Democrats switched back to the CDU/CSU, the Social Democrats lost power.

The strength of party-union links makes the current unionization level seem low, only slightly higher than Canada's. The SPD (Sozialdemokratische Partei Deutschlands) depends strongly on the union vote, and has accordingly made union concerns a high legislative priority. It has, for example, instituted the strongest "co-determination" policy in Europe, with 50 per cent labour representation on company boards of directors. Yet West Germany did not follow the pattern of Sweden and Denmark with a rapid rise in unionization when a Social Democratic government was formed. In Sweden, for example, unionization rose sharply from 38 per cent to 56 per cent in the first decade of Social Democratic government. In Denmark, the initial increase was not as steep but was still more rapid than in West Germany. Moreover, in both these Nordic countries the gains were continued through the 1940s and 1950s, until the majority of the labour force was unionized. Whether or not this failure to promote unionization was responsible for the party's failure to hold onto government, or to soon return to office, remains a matter of conjecture. Whatever the case, the party's concern more recently has been to attract greater middle-class support.

Great Britain

There are a number of similarities between Britain and West Germany in the degree of success, or lack of it, in their social democratic/labour parties, despite their more considerable differences in ideology and party history. The British Labour Party, so named, goes back to 1906, with older roots in the Independent Labour Party from 1893, and the Social Democratic Federation of 1881.[9] The socialist movement itself goes back much earlier, to Chartism, the Fabian Society, and a host of non-party organizations, Marxist, Methodist, and even Anglican. Yet in Britain, as in West Germany, the Labour Party has been in opposition for more years than it has been in government, even in the post-war period. Labour members began to be elected around the turn of the century. The party reached Official Opposition status in 1922, with 30 per cent of the popular vote. Labour's first incursions into government, under Ramsay MacDonald, left little mark in terms of social legislation, and split the party. There were minority governments in 1924 and 1929. The critical split occurred in 1930 with Ramsay Mac-Donald's proposal for a "National Government" coalition with the other parties.

It was not until after the Second World War that Labour formed a majority government, with a substantial jump — 10 per cent — in the popular vote. That government laid the basis of the modern welfare state, nationalized some industries, and began de-colonization. It lost the general election of 1951, and did not return to government until 1964. Labour and the Conservatives have alternated in government throughout the post-war period, with the Conservatives lasting longer in office. The recent splitting of the Social Democratic Party from Labour saved the Conservative government in 1983. Margaret Thatcher lost votes in her second election as party leader, but thanks to this splitting of the non-Conservative vote, she was returned to office.

The labour force in Britain began to organize early compared with other European countries, but never rose to the high levels of the Nordic social democracies. Nor has Labour voting been as high at similar levels of organization. When Ramsay MacDonald formed his first minority government in 1924, union organizing had passed the 32 per cent mark. With the massive unemployment of the Depression, there was also a decline in union membership. Membership again began to climb in the late 1930s and the war period. It was around 40 per cent when Labour won its first majority government. Membership did not rise significantly after that, unlike the case for the successful continental social democracies. When Labour came back into power in 1964, the level of unionization was still only in the low 40 per cent range. There were further gains in the late 1960s and the 1970s to a peak of 53 per cent in 1979.

Unions in Britain make the news far more often than unions in the Nordic countries and Austria, with British strikes known for their length, bitterness, and violence. Yet Austria's level of unionization is higher and the power of the unions much greater in these continental social democracies. Party membership in Britain is high by Canadian standards, but again not so by Swedish or Austrian standards. There were four million Labour Party members by 1921, rising to a peak of 6.6 million in 1957. There were then some declines, but membership grew again to 6.5 million in 1975. Only about 10 per cent of this consists of voluntary "constituency" memberships, however, the rest being bloc union members.

Finland

Finland does not follow the Nordic pattern for obvious reasons of geography and history, its place on the Russian/Soviet border, and memories of both Russian and Soviet occupation. Yet there are similarities in the rapid early rise of social democracy. The

119

party was founded in 1899 and reached largest-party status in 1907.[10] It won an absolute majority of seats in the shortest time of any European social democratic party, in 1916, only thirty-four years after its inception. This precipitate victory, however, was short-lived. The government was promptly overthrown and civil war followed. The party went underground. It did not come back into government until 1937, and then only as a junior coalition member.

The Finnish labour force is highly unionized, with roughly three-quarters of all manual workers belonging to it. Yet a third of the executive positions on the union central are held by Communists, so that union strength does not necessarily mean social democratic support.

Finnish politics are coalition politics. Governments seldom last more than a year, and coalitions are broadly based, often spread among three or four parties. The Social Democrats were in coalition governments in the 1944-48 period, and were then out for eighteen years. They have been in most cabinets since 1966. In 1982, the first social democratic president, Mauno Kovisto, was elected.

Iceland

Canadians may be dismayed to learn that the country we most resemble, apropos of social democratic success, is Iceland. There the Social Democratic Party is young, founded in 1916, or just two years before Iceland achieved status as a sovereign state.[11] Voting support is weak by European standards, and peaked at the 20 per cent level in the 1930s, declining slightly in subsequent years. Union organization is also weak in Iceland by European — though not by Canadian or American — standards. The Iceland Federation of Labour was formed only in 1916. Suffering internal splits, it has never developed strength anywhere near the level of the other Nordic countries.

France

Alternatively, Canadians might look to their French connection for comparison. There the level of unionization is lower still. Only an estimated 22 per cent of the labour force is unionized, and that proportion is thought to be declining. France is quite exceptional as the only western country to have elected a social democratic government with so low a rate of unionization. Moreover, of the 5.4 million union members, only about a fifth belong to the socialist central. The Catholic trade union federation is equally large, and the Communist more than twice the size.[12]

The first socialist party in France was formed in Marseilles in 1879, in the momentum of a labour union congress.[13] From then on, its pattern of development has been quite different from that in other European countries. The splits and mergers of French socialism are far too complicated to relate here, but suffice it to say that they have been very different from their northern neighbours.

The Socialist Party, with Léon Blum as prime minister, headed the Popular Front coalition in 1936-38. The party went underground during the war. It played an important part in the fourth republic, frequently in coalition governments, occasionally heading them. There was a socialist president from 1947 to 1951. Major nationalizations and welfare-state measures were legislated in this period. Voting strength declined gradually, from 23.4 per cent in 1945, when the Socialist Party was the second-strongest party, to only 5 per cent in 1969. There was a rapid recovery when François Mitterrand joined, bringing with him another small party. By 1978, the PSF (Parti Socialist Français) had regained its old position, and it then went on to surpass the Communists. Mitterrand was elected president in 1981 and the party subsequently won an absolute majority in the National Assembly, for one term. The right was returned with a majority in 1986. The French Socialist Party's route to power was altogether quite different from that taken by the Nordic parties. It did make it without a significant union link, but it did not manage to stay.

Italy

The left is even more crowded in Italy than in France. There are two social democratic/socialist parties, which united briefly in the 1960s, only to split again. The differences between them are substantial. The Communist Party in Italy remains strong as well. As the leader of Euro-communism, and pro-NATO and reformist, it crowds into what is social democratic space in other countries.[14]

Unionization is stronger in Italy than in France, but is probably less so than popularly thought.[15] The data are probably less reliable than for other countries, exaggerated according to experts. Available only for the post-war period, they show rapid unionization growth to a peak of 60 per cent in 1970. The reported levels have since dropped to 48 per cent in 1979 and to 40 per cent in 1983. The current levels thus are only slightly higher than in Canada. The big difference is in the strength of the Communist unions relative to that of the socialist unions. The result of such division on the left is that right-wing parties have run Italy for the entire post-war period.

Social Democrats have had minor posts in a few governments, but no significant influence. There has been a slight change in the mid-1980s with coalitions led by a Social Democratic prime minister, Bettino Craxi. Still, the total voting strength of the two social democratic parties has been too low for there to have been any policy change.

The pattern emerges that social democratic success may be impeded either by progressive religious parties, as in the Netherlands, or by competition from the far left, by a strong Communist Party. Note that the French Socialist Party's victory took place only *after* a weakening of Communist Party strength, even though there have been "union of the left" electoral alliances for years. The countries where social democratic parties have been most successful have been those with both a high level of unionization *and* weak Communist parties. In Sweden, for example, the Communist vote is only about 5 per cent, and in Austria it is slightly less. In Italy, the country with the least social democratic success in Europe, unionization is only moderate, and Communist Party voting is high.

Austria

The great success story of social democracy in central Europe is Austria, which we shall be examining in more detail in Chapter 5. The great Social Democrat governments, however, are a feature of the post-war period. In its early years, under the Austro-Hungarian Empire, the Social Democrats were prolific writers, respected theoreticians, and academic lawyers, but never more than a parliamentary minority.

The Social Democratic Party was founded by Victor Adler in 1889 and won its first representation — fourteen members — in the Reichstag in 1897.[16] By 1914 it was the largest party. It was in an uneasy coalition with the conservative Christian Social Party in 1918-20. The Social Democratic constitutional lawyer Karl Renner was chancellor in 1919-20. Under attack by Conservative thugs, organized as the Home Defence League, the Social Democrats created their own private army. Christian Socialist chancellor Engelbert Dollfuss sought to disband it in 1933, but he did not attempt to dissolve the private army of the right. Street fighting escalated into civil war in 1934 and a fascist victory. The Social Democratic Party was declared illegal, and its leaders variously went into exile, underground, prison, or concentration camps. Following the Allied occupation of Austria in 1945 the former president, Karl Renner, was brought out of his country retirement to head a provisional government.

Party-union links have been the key to the electoral success of the Social Democratic Party in post-war Austria. The level of unionization is high, peaking at 67 per cent in 1961. The proportion declined to 58 per cent in 1979, still a level to be envied by social democrats this side of the Atlantic. There is no closed shop in Austria, so that these numbers represent a real choice by employees, who evidently feel they are better off with a union. Nearly all unions are affiliated with the Social Democratic Party, and union executives are 80 per cent Social Democrat in membership. The one important exception is the civil service union, which is controlled by the conservative People's Party. Party membership is extremely high, for both major parties. With a total population of only 7.5 million people, there are some 720,000 Social Democratic Party members, mainly from the unions.

The Social Democratic Party also has a strong base in municipal politics. Social Democrats have controlled the city council of Vienna for some seventy years, long enough indeed to be involved in graft and scandal. The Canadian arts community may be interested to learn that arts expenditures are a major civic expenditure. The city expects to "lose" money on its city opera and other cultural enterprises, considering them a service to the people and a tourist attraction. The party has also sought in recent years to broaden its appeal to the middle class and farmers. In its early Austro-Marxist years it received little support outside the major cities. Now it has encroached quite successfully into previous conservative strongholds, the reverse tendency to conservative poaching on old socialist preserves. If the Social Democratic Party receives 56 per cent of its support from blue-collar workers, it obtains no less than 44 per cent from those who are not.

Portugal

Social democracy in Portugal dates back to the 1870s as an intellectual movement, but no organized connection with actual workers was made at that time.[17] Nor were there political parties of any kind in this period of constitutional monarchy. A short republic followed, but it was overturned by Antonio de Oliveira Salazar in 1928. He then ruled the country for forty years until his death. A military coup followed soon after, and then the restoration of civilian government.

The present Socialist Party was formed in 1973 in Bonn, by socialist leaders in exile. The Socialist Party won 37.8 per cent of the popular vote in the first elections for a constituent assembly, and 34.9 per cent in the first Assembly elections, in both cases leading the other parties. The Socialists formed the first post-Salazar government, facing all the problems of a sharply divided country, with little experience of democratic government and a weak economy. The standard of living was the lowest in Europe, and illiteracy was at 50 per cent. That a social democratic government lasted sixteen months creates a record in a country where only dictatorships had lasted more than a few months. In 1986 the first socialist prime minister was elected as president of the country, the first civilian in that office.

It would be easy but premature to point to the failings of the short period of socialist government in Portugal. Inflation and unemployment remain high, and with them the national debt. The nationalization of banks and insurance companies has not stopped major capital outflows. Other nationalizations have been mixed successes. Yet there are impressive achievements in the transition to a modern democratic state: the establishment of civil liberties and a literacy program, and the elimination of censorship and fascist institutions. Civil divorce, birth control, and access to legal abortions have all been legislated. The process of integration into the European Economic Community has begun. The enormously successful social democracies of Europe were, let us not forget, decades in the making.

Spain

For Spain as well it would be premature to declaim on the success or failure of social democracy. The Socialist Party of Spain was founded in 1879, and the chief socialist union a short time later, in 1888.[18] Early growth of the party was slow, owing in part to rigged elections. The Socialist Party was the only large political force when the republic was declared in 1931. Several socialists were ministers, as was the prime minister, when the civil war began. Repression by the victorious fascists was brutal. Socialists and Communists fled the country, many of them to face Hitler's fascism only a few years later. In the long years of dictator Francisco Franco's rule, the Socialist Party had no legal existence, and was less organized than the Communist Party underground.

In the first elections after the restoration of the monarchy, and democracy, in 1974, the Socialist Party won 29 per cent of the popular vote, coming second. The socialist trade union grew rapidly in this period, overtaking the Communist union. The party reversed its initial stands on nationalization (pro) and NATO (con). In the 1982 elections, it won 46 per cent of the popular vote to form a majority government. In 1986, the Socialist Party was re-elected to government with a reduced majority.

Social democratic accomplishments in Spain to date include a start on a modern social security system. Compulsory schooling to age fifteen has been legislated, in a country where more than a quarter of the population have never been to school. Conditions for the large farming population have been improved. Reforestation is under way. Trade barriers were promptly reduced, in the spirit of integration with Europe. Civil marriages and divorce were permitted and abortion was legalized. Yet unemployment, at 20 per cent of the labour force, is the highest in Europe, despite concerted efforts by the government to create jobs. This failure, of course, impedes progress in every other policy area as well, for lack of funds.

The Spanish Socialist government has not only decades of economic backwardness to overcome, but more recent mismanagement of the economy by the Conservatives. The government has managed to cut the deficit inherited from the Conservatives, and turned a balance-of-payments deficit into a surplus. Fifty years after the unleashing of the civil war, the Spanish people voted to keep the Socialist government in office.

Australia

The Australian Labour Party, formed in 1888 in Queensland, is the oldest party in the country.[19] In the election for the first federal Parliament, in 1901, it won 8.6 per cent of the popular vote and 11 seats. In 1904 it formed its first, minority, government, which lasted only one year. Its first majority government was won in 1910. It has continued to be a major party ever since, sometimes winning 49-50 per cent of the popular vote. Splits within the party, however, have been followed by electoral defeat, and long years in the wilderness. Labour has also suffered from an inequitable distribution of seats favouring the more conservative rural areas. Thus it has in several elections won more votes than the Liberal Party, but lost in seats. As a result, the party has been in power only about a quarter of this century, despite its considerable base of support and strong union links, ingredients for success in Europe. Further, it has been hampered in the implementation of its program by a hostile upper house. Again, this is the result of over-representation of the more conservative, rural areas.

The trade unions in Australia are formally linked to the party, with representation on executive bodies. They comprise the bulk of the party's membership, and contribute substantially to party funds. The labour force in Australia is highly unionized.[20] The earliest available data show a unionization rate of 9 per cent in 1901, which grew to a quarter of the labour force by 1911. There were strong increases in union membership in the years of Labour governments, and more modest increases, no growth, or slight declines when Labour was not in power. The peak rate of 59 per cent was attained in 1954. There was then a slight decline, to 51 per cent in 1968, and growth again to 56 per cent in 1982, the latest year for which data are available.

No Labour government in Australia so far has lasted more than two terms. An unrelated point, perhaps: the party does better in poor economic times than in good. Australians apparently consider that if times are going to be tough, Labour at least will be fair. Thus, the Labour Party under Bob Hawke was brought back into government in 1983, in response to the recession.

New Zealand

The Labour Party of New Zealand was formed only in 1916, but political organization by the Trades and Labour Congress dates back to 1884.[21] The first national conference of the "parliamentary committees" of the TLC was held in 1885. "Labour representatives" were elected as early as 1891, but in Parliament these members supported the reformist Liberal government. In 1904 the TLC moved to form an Independent Labour Party, which joined with several other organizations to form the present Labour Party.

The New Zealand Labour Party became the Official Opposition in 1925 and formed its first, majority, government in 1935. After two re-elections it went back into opposition. In the period 1935-86, Labour had been in power for twenty-three years, and out for twenty-nine. In its years in office it built the extensive social security system New Zealand enjoys. Most of the measures instituted have survived other governments.

New Zealand has an aggressively egalitarian ethos. It was

one of the first countries to legislate the vote for women, in 1893, and their right to hold office, in 1919. It abolished double voting, essentially the privilege of property owners, in 1889. Legislation favourable to labour was adopted much earlier in New Zealand than in other comparable countries. Also in the nineteenth century, large estates were compulsorily sub-divided, and small independent holdings promoted through favourable loan rates.

The country made international news when the Labour Party won the 1984 election with a policy of not permitting American ships and submarines armed with nuclear weapons to enter its ports. Other social democratic governments — for example, Norway — have a similar policy, but New Zealand is exceptional in enforcing it.

Since it is a highly agricultural country, with little industry, New Zealand's unionization rate seems high in the circumstances. The first available data on unionization show a rate of 8 per cent in 1901, growing to 19 per cent by 1911.[22] (Because of peculiarities in collection, these data understate the rate.) Labour organization grew during both world wars, and declined in the intervening Depression. The peak rate of 48 per cent was reached in 1945. There was then a slight decline in the 1960s, which was reversed in the 1970s. The 48 per cent rate was reached again in 1981. New Zealand thus follows very much the pattern of social democracy in northern Europe, especially Norway.

The Canadian Situation

On return to Canada from our trip abroad we find that the same patterns apply. The relative lack of success of social democracy in Canada parallels the relatively low level of unionization. Canada was slower in industrializing than Europe, and remains less unionized.[23] When the first national data on unionization were collected, for 1921, the level of unionization was only 15 per cent. The proportion rose to 30 per cent by 1946, to peak at 37 per cent in 1958. There has since been a decline to 35 per cent in 1978. The numbers unionized have increased somewhat since then, but the non-unionized labour force is growing at a greater rate. Further, in the recession of the 1980s, the jobs that were lost were mainly industrial, hence jobs where the work force was unionized and affiliated with the NDP.

Unionization rates are lower in Canada than in almost all European countries, Australia, and New Zealand. Yet the proportions are higher than in the United States, where social democratic parties/movements have all collapsed so far. The level of union organization was similar between Canada and the United States in the early years of organization. In 1920, the proportion of the American labour force unionized was 17 per cent, only a fraction above the Canadian percentage. There was then a decline in the United States in the Second World War. The American peak, at 32 per cent in 1953, was lower than the Canadian peak, and the subsequent decline greater, to 28 per cent in 1976. Estimates are that unionization under Reagan's administration has fallen further, to 19 per cent. American unions chose to follow labour leader Sam Gompers' strategy of lobbying the major parties but of affiliating with neither, nor any social democratic party. The results of that choice are all too obvious — a weak union movement and the disappearance of a social democratic alternative in the United States. Under the influence of American unions, Gompers' strategy of "brokerage politics" was a force also in Canada, slowing down the development of a social democratic party-union alliance.

The errors of that choice have only become more and more obvious with Republican Ronald Reagan in the White House. The president who held a union card, and was even president of his local, presided over a massive decline in unionization in the 1980s. Reagan insisted on non-union musicians at his inauguration, and the tune they played proved to be catching. Canadian unions have also lost members as the economy has de-industrialized, but there has also been new labour organization in the clerical and service sectors. Serious as their problems are, Canadian unions are in a far stronger position than the American ones to fight the new battle of government de-regulation. Their greater strength undoubtedly comes from their different political choice. That lesson was learned by trial and error over more than a century.

"Cap in hand" lobbying of government by Canadian unions began as early as 1873, and by 1874 independent labour candidates were running for election. By the end of the century "labour representatives" were being elected to all levels of legislature. The only substantial success was in Ontario, when eleven labour MPPs were elected in 1919, to join with the United Farmers of Ontario to form an administration. In all other cases, only isolated individuals were elected, and most made some accommodation with the major parties.

In 1900 the Trades and Labor Congress (TLC) passed a resolution in favour of the formation of an independent labour party,[24] the same year as the Trades Union Congress (TUC) did so in Britain. In Britain, however, the resolution was acted on, and the British Labour Party is the result. In Canada it was to be another thirty years before the CCF was formed, and fifty-eight years before the NDP. There was only one union representative, A. R. Mosher, at the 1932 meeting in Calgary that led to the formation of the CCF. There were no union representatives as such at the Regina Convention in 1933, although the labour MPs were instrumental in forming the party. J. S. Woodsworth, for example, ran as an Independent Labour Party member in Winnipeg for twelve years before the formation of the CCF. Even after the CCF's formation, there was little affiliation. A Cape Breton local of the United Mineworkers union was the first to affiliate with the CCF, in 1938.

The 1940 merger of the CIO unions into the Canadian

Congress of Labour (CCL) resulted in the formation of a Political Action Committee and CCF endorsation. Yet there was little practical result. It was not until the formation of the New Democratic Party, after the 1958 election, and the substantial setback the CCF incurred, that a real, working alliance was forged. The unions were prominent in the organization of the founding convention, and sent roughly a third of the delegates to it.

The party-union link is needed on both sides. Unions obviously cannot count on a Conservative or a Liberal government for more than occasional gestures, but need a party in government committed to social and economic justice. To a social democratic party, the support and advice of the union movement is crucial. A social democratic government needs understanding as it tries to sell its policies to a substantial cross-section of the public. Advice from unions as policies are refined may prevent a government from making serious mistakes. Who better than the unions can tell a government — in time — that a measure it is proposing is unpopular? What other large organization desires the success of a social democratic government as much as its union supporters? It is probably no coincidence that the most durable and accomplished social democratic parties have been those with good working links with organized labour.

The other European trends apply also to Canada, with divisions along ethnic and religious lines, and competition from the far left, lessening social democratic support. Thus, even with fairly strong levels of unionization, the social democratic vote has not been high enough for a majority government, or even strong coalition status. The weakness of the CCF/NDP in Québec parallels the weakness of social democratic parties in the Netherlands and Switzerland. The French, Finnish, and Italian situations, with strong Communist parties and unions, have their Canadian parallel in British Columbia. Indeed, this competition from the Communists explains an otherwise striking anomaly, why the CCF breakthrough happened not in British Columbia but in Saskatchewan.

The labour force in British Columbia has always been more highly organized than in any other province. The first social democratic party was formed in B.C. Yet the first electoral success of the CCF took place in agricultural Saskatchewan, in 1944, while in British Columbia it was another twenty-eight years before an NDP government was formed. The plausible explanation is the strength of the Communist unions at that critical time in the 1940s. Ten of the twenty-three industrial unions in B.C. either were Communist-controlled or had a strong Communist influence. Only two unions were actually affiliated with the CCF.[25] Communist leaders in the unions prevented them from giving real support to the CCF. CCF members of the unions spent more time and energy fighting the Communists than fighting the Liberals or Conservatives. By the time the CCF had won the union battle, the critical moment had passed and the party itself was in decline.

The effect is most noticeable in British Columbia, but it also can be seen in Ontario, where the CCF formed the Official Opposition in 1943 and came close to forming the government. There, an alliance between the Liberals and the Communists worked against the CCF. In Windsor, for example, all three seats had gone CCF in 1943. In 1945, thanks to this Liberal/Labour alliance, the left vote was split, and all three seats were lost. The Conservatives took two, and in the third the Communist candidate won, only to defect promptly to the Liberals. In this critical period the Communists controlled major unions in St. Catharines, Hamilton, Toronto, Peterborough, and Sudbury as well as in the West. Again, by the time the Communists lost control it was too late, at least for that round, for the CCF to recover.

Along with the strength of the union-party relationship there are patterns to be seen in the length of time the party has had to organize. If Canadians wonder why the New Democratic Party has not made it to government federally in fifty years, they must realize that few other social democratic parties have. The speediest European example is Sweden, where it took 28 years from party formation in 1889 to the first, and short-lived, minority government in 1917. It was *43 years* to its first government as a senior partner, in 1932, and no less than *79 years* from party formation to majority government in 1968. Given that Canada does not have a proportional-representation system or any inclination to coalition governments, the 79-year figure is the relevant comparison.

Australia and New Zealand are relatively speedy examples, with 22 years and 51 years respectively to majority government status. For Norway, also, the time lapse between formation of a social democratic party and its holding office was comparatively short. The party took 41 years to make it to power in a coalition, 48 years to senior coalition status, and 58 years to a majority government. In Britain, the first breakthrough, with Ramsay MacDonald, came 43 years after H. M. Hyndman's formation of the Social Democratic Federation. To majority government it was a full 64 years. For West Germany the time required was 50 years from formation in 1869 to first government in 1919, and the party has yet to form a majority government. For the Netherlands, it was 58 years to junior coalition status, 91 years to senior coalition. The Dutch Labour Party has never formed a majority government. In Austria, the Social Democrats finally made it to majority government *82 years* after formation of the party. The party had reached junior coalition status relatively quickly, in 29 years. To senior coalition status it was 52 years from party formation. For Portugal the road, through exile and prison terms, was even longer, 101 years from party formation to coalition government status. For Spain it was 103 years altogether from party formation to a majority government.

The fact that Canada has not yet elected a federal social democratic government is no proof that it never will. At the

1984 federal election, the CCF/NDP had been in existence as a national party a relatively modest 52 years. Counting the first regional party formation, with the Socialist Party of British Columbia, in 1902, there had been some form of social democratic organization for 82 years to the 1984 election. Other factors give far more cause for distress than sheer length of time: the level of unionization, the size of party membership, the single-member constituency system, and the lack of a social democratic press.

Few social democratic parties have made it to government without a system giving them some proportional representation while they build their forces. The only clear exceptions are Britain, Australia, and New Zealand, all of them countries with a more radical political culture and stronger labour organization. In the case of France, the Socialist Party achieved coalition status under proportional representation, then spent years outside government under the Gaullist system of single-member constituencies. When Mitterrand saw that the Socialist Party would lose the 1986 legislative elections, he had proportional representation reinstated. A single-member system can help a party go over the top, to form a majority government, with 44-50 per cent of the popular vote. With less than this percentage of the popular vote, a party is better off with proportional representation.

In Canada, the lack of proportional representation has cost the New Democrats representation in Québec and Atlantic Canada. In the 1982 and 1984 federal elections, with proportional representation the party would have had 56 and 54 seats, respectively, instead of the 32 and 30 actually won under the present system. Provincially, of course, the CCF/NDP has benefited from the "winner take all" system, in forming majority governments in Saskatchewan, British Columbia, and Manitoba with popular votes as low as 41 per cent. In only one election, in Saskatchewan, has the party won an absolute majority of votes cast.

The pattern of electoral success following moderation of party policy is quite clear in Europe. This is absolutely consistent from Sweden's solidarity negotiations through Austria's social partnership to Spain's recent and rapid toning down of its radicalism. Social democratic parties typically had radical, and usually Marxist, origins. The timing varies considerably, but all parties that have been elected to office have gone through a deliberate process of re-thinking and revision. The Commonwealth countries and Britain are exceptions, as their social democratic parties do not have Marxist origins, but they none the less have become less radical over the years. In some countries there have been direct, personal, links with revolutionary leaders. Lenin lived in Zürich in exile and Trotsky in Vienna. The German Social Democrats were prominent world leaders of socialism before it split into parliamentary and revolutionary parties. Yet everywhere accommodation was made for the growing middle class, and for workers who increasingly had a stake in the system as it was.

No one will be surprised to learn that the most successful parties electorally have been those with large memberships. The extreme case is Sweden, where, with a population of only eight million, the Swedish Social Democratic Party has more than a million members. Even if only individual members are counted, there are over 300,000, twice Canada's number although with one-third the population. Austria, with a population of seven million, similarly has over 700,000 members in its social democratic party, although most of these are affiliated through unions. Norway, with only four million people, one-sixth of Canada's population, has the same party size, 150,000 members, nearly 100,000 of whom are individual members. Other small countries as well have much higher per-capita party memberships than Canada: Finland (population 5,000,000) had over 100,000 members in 1975; Denmark (population 5,000,000) had 123,000 members also in 1975; the Netherlands (population 15,000,000) had 145,000 members in 1970; Belgium (population 10,000,000) had 250,000 members in 1977; France, a larger country, had only 200,000 members in the Parti Socialiste in 1977, but then the party did not last long in office.

The Media

Social democratic parties in Europe are disadvantaged in media coverage compared with the parties of big business, but not as much as in Canada. It is true that the golden past of radical publishing is over, in Europe as well as in North America. Economic changes have made the newspaper a vehicle for selling advertising more than an article purchased for its content. By 1920 newspapers were more dependent on advertising than on sales or subscriptions for their revenues. Left-wing papers, unable to attract the advertising, or unwilling to take it, folded. Still, the situation is better in Europe.

In some countries the party itself publishes a mass-circulation daily, for example *Die Arbeiter Zeitung* (The Workers' Newspaper) in Austria. In other countries there is at least one major paper sympathetic to social democracy, if without any formal connection to the party. In Sweden there are twenty-one social democratic dailies across the country, with a combined circulation of roughly 20 per cent of the national total. (Examples are *Afton Bladet* in Stockholm and *Arbete* in Malmö.) That leaves a preponderance of influence to the conservative papers, but it is 20 per cent more social democratic coverage than in Canada or the United States.

In Britain, the Labour Party had the mass-circulation *Daily Herald* to carry its message for decades. It reached a peak circulation of 1.5 million before expiring. After that paper's demise the party could, for some time, rely on the *Daily Mirror* and the tabloid *Sun* (no relation to any Canadian paper) for sympathetic coverage. The present *Guardian* has no party connection, but it can be counted on to give a civilized hearing

137

to Labour politics. Historically a Liberal paper, as the *Manchester Guardian*, it is now the most left-leaning of the mass-circulation papers. There are also smaller and regional papers, as in Western Scotland, which take a pro-Labour stand.

Le Monde in Paris has no party connections, and certainly does not endorse the Socialist Party, yet it gives relatively sympathetic and thorough coverage to socialist positions and perceptions. The Communist *l'Humanité* is reliably anti-conservative, although not sympathetic to social democracy. In West Germany the party paper *Vorwärts* (Forward) was originally a mass-circulation paper. It is now an internal party bulletin. Clara Zetkin's paper, *Die Gleichheit* (Equality), for social democratic women had a circulation of over 100,000. Yet even with the disappearance of left papers there are regional papers that remain, such as the *Freie Presse* in Bielefeld. Further, serious attention is paid to social democratic positions in the major papers, such as the *Frankfurter Allgemeine Zeitung* and the weekly *Die Zeit*. Other European examples are *Le Peuple* in Brussels; *Aktuelet* in Copenhagen; *Snomen Sosialidemokratii* in Helsinki; *Het Vrije Volk* in Amsterdam; *Avanti* in Milan; *Republica* in Portugal; *Berner Tagwacht* in Berne; and *Ta Nea* and *Ethnos* in Athens.

Every country of Western Europe has some paper at least sympathetic to, if not actually supportive of, its social democratic party. Neither Canada nor the United States has one. The result is that social democratic politicians in Europe can count on reasonable coverage of their views in some papers. Problems they consider serious will somewhere be treated seriously. Simplistic conservative positions will be exposed as such in some, if not most, papers. The peremptory putdowns and mindless dismissals so familiar in the conservative press in Canada still occur in Europe, but alternative coverage is also available there.

Television coverage of social democratic parties is also probably better in Europe. In many countries there is only state television. This presents its own difficulties, but they are fewer than with the commercial networks and their greater dependence on advertising. French state television, for example, has been notoriously conservative, yet the Mitterrand government did not interfere or fire staff. As discussed earlier in Chapter 3, it is not just news and public affairs that have an influence, but entertainment and the commercials also affect people's attitudes. Thus the Thatcher government's pressure to make the BBC take commercials is not merely another case of restraint. The BBC is funded by a special tax on television sets, and not through general revenues. Yet a BBC with commercials would necessarily be promulgating another message: that the market is all, that if something cannot be bought or sold it does not exist. No country has yet elected a social democratic government that watches hours of American television a day.

The factor of leadership is a perilous subject for brief coverage, but it is too important to be left completely unaddressed. When governments may hang or fall on a percentage point, even the staunchest believer in collective forces must consider the personality and gifts of the competing party leaders. The Swedish success is arguably due to exceptionally good leaders whose popularity kept them in office a long time. Olof Palme was only the fourth leader of his party. Austria's success is similarly credited to an impressive line of social democratic leaders from Victor Adler through Karl Renner to Bruno Kreisky. The lateness of success in West Germany, by contrast, might have been due to the redoubtable Christian Democrat Konrad Adenauer. Certainly the Social Democratic breakthrough at the federal level was not made until Adenauer's demise. Willy Brandt then became chancellor, but the party suffered another setback with his early departure from office.

Let us, however, turn from what might have been to discuss what actually did happen. The New Democratic Party has formed governments in three provinces and one territory. Its sister parties have run some of the most successful governments in

Europe. That these governments have served their people well will be seen in the next chapter. What these social democratic governments did to make that difference is a matter of record, which we will now examine.

5

CAN THE NDP *GOVERN*, AS OPPOSED TO OPPOSE?

For the New Democratic Party to be elected to government federally it must convince voters both that it has a valid program and that it is capable of running the shop. The more difficult task, I suspect, is the latter. Voters have been told too often that a New Democrat government is unthinkable, and there is no direct proof to the contrary. Yet evidence is available from the party's record in running governments in British Columbia, Saskatchewan, and Manitoba. Where the NDP has governed, it has governed well; where it has governed longest, Saskatchewan, it has governed best.

Saskatchewan

Why does the NDP not blow its own horn over Saskatchewan? Why does it seem to be ashamed of the government of the scrappy Baptist minister from Weyburn? Certainly it cannot be for lack of accomplishments, for the record is truly impressive. The CCF/NDP in Saskatchewan pioneered the most important social reforms in the country, and it did so on the basis of extremely effective economic management.[1] A major "have not" province, Saskatchewan soon led the way in the provision of services. What's more, it did all this without incurring debt. Indeed, it gradually eliminated the deficit left by the previous Liberal government, the highest per capita of any province.

Its reforms in three major areas — medicare, civil rights, and labour law — have already been described in Chapter

2. These are all matters on which the whole country was eventually to adopt similar legislation. For the rest of the reforms described here, the pattern of imitation or catching up has been more varied.

Since Saskatchewan is a farm province, the CCF's first reforms were to give farmers some protection against bank foreclosures. The Farm Security Act was passed in 1944, prohibiting foreclosure on the quarter section of land (160 acres) on which the family house stood. There were further provisions allowing for mediation on other foreclosures, preventing them in certain cases.

Saskatchewan was the first, and so far the only, province to establish a ministry to encourage producer and sales co-operatives. Co-op development, as a means of diversifying the economy, was both rapid and successful. In 1941 only 6 per cent of the population were members of co-ops. By 1971 the proportion had grown to 32 per cent. Co-operative enterprises themselves range from retail sales outlets, restaurants, and marketing agencies for fish and furs, to an oil refinery and the Wheat Pool.

The province was slower, for lack of capital, in developing its Crown corporations. Premier Douglas sought federal money to begin potash exploitation but was initially unsuccessful. It was the CCF that saw the possibilities of the potash industry when deposits were discovered in 1943. The Liberals, and the local press, scoffed. The major Crown corporation development in resources is an achievement of the later, Blakeney, government. In potash, for example, the province came to control 40 per cent of the industry. Saskoil has been another later Crown corporation success, with profits going into general revenues and helping to fund the extensive social programs. The NDP under Blakeney also continued the CCF's protection and promotion of the family farm. A land bank was set up and a "Farmstart" program initiated. Legislation was passed to keep out the American farm corporations by forbidding absentee ownership of farm land.

The first CCF government improved transportation services enormously by taking over the bus companies, developing northern airways, and building an extensive modern highway system. It developed rural electrification, and reduced power rates across the province. Water and sewer services were also extended to many farm areas for the first time.

Saskatchewan's public insurance corporation, set up in 1946, has been such an unmitigated success that no subsequent Liberal or Conservative government has dared to touch it. The rates for car insurance — Canada's first no-fault insurance plan — dropped to the lowest in the country. For other forms of insurance, private companies had to lower their rates to compete. NDP governments in Manitoba and British Columbia were quick to follow Saskatchewan's example.

The CCF's management and administrative skills were prodigious.[2] The government sought out the best consulting advice for its economic and social programs. It hired and promoted well, so much so that the federal government regularly raided Saskatchewan talent. Patronage was eliminated. Civil servants, following Australian and New Zealand practice, were given the right to political activity on their own time. Under the previous regime, by contrast, political activity was theoretically forbidden but in practice encouraged, for the party in power.

The welfare system was reformed. Not only were assistance rates raised, but the humiliation of recipients' having to prove themselves good supporters of the government was ended. A central government purchasing agency was established and it effected enormous savings. Teacher-training and teachers' salaries were markedly improved. A new university was built in Regina. The first provisions in Canada for student loans were made in 1949. A later education reform, at the end of its term in government in 1964, was to extend full funding for Catholic secondary schools.

It is characteristic of the Saskatchewan CCF that purity of economic policy was sacrificed for concrete reforms when necessary. When the government could not put money into social programs *and* economic development, it chose "humanity first", and let the private sector do more than it would have preferred. Thus the old age pension, mothers' allowance, and welfare rates were all increased in the first budget. Money for expanded community health clinics was immediately found. The tax on food was removed in 1946. The private sector, though, was well taxed for its privileges. Somehow CCF/NDP governments in Saskatchewan have managed to collect more from the corporations proportionately than has Tory Ontario. As a result, individual taxes have been lower in Saskatchewan, and there are no premiums to pay for medicare. Ontario, by contrast, has high personal income taxes and high premiums for its Ontario Health Insurance Plan. Yet Saskatchewan obviously was not taxing corporations beyond their capacity to pay, for private investment also increased throughout this time.

Not the least of the achievements of the CCF in Saskatchewan was its budget management. It pioneered medicare, improved education and social services, built roads, and greatly extended electrification, all while *reducing* the previous government's deficit. The provincial deficit in Saskatchewan in 1944, $178 million, was the highest per capita in the country. By 1960 it was down to $18 million, and it was paid off completely the following year. The method? The government set aside 10 per cent of its budget every year for debt reduction. In terms of its own expenditures it practised balanced budgeting, averaged over several years. In better years a surplus would be collected, in worse years minor deficits were permitted.

One of the few mistakes in economic management made by the CCF government arose from a provision of the Trade Union Act. Later dropped, this clause authorized the government to appoint a controller of an enterprise that "wilfully disobeyed" an order of the Labour Relations Board. In due course a box factory refused to bargain collectively with its employees, fired them, and was itself taken over. The government, however, soon discovered that taking over enterprises with financial or management problems was not the way to ensure permanent jobs. It learned fast, so its record overall in economic management — the collective bottom line of its enterprises — was positive. An impressive 95 per cent succeeded.

In 1944, when the CCF came into government in Saskatchewan, non-agricultural production accounted for a mere $280 million a year. By the time it left government, manufacturing had tripled. Per-capita income rose to third in the country under the CCF. The rate of growth — a 140 per cent increase — for private and public investment was the highest per capita of any province of Canada. In that haven of private enterprise, British Columbia, the rate for the same period was only half that. Even with subsequent Liberal and Conservative governments in Saskatchewan, the province has remained relatively strong economically. Its unemployment rate continues to be lower than British Columbia's.

Perhaps the final point to be made in the Saskatchewan example concerns the durability of the reforms. Almost all the new programs survived subsequent Liberal and Conservative governments. These other governments were reluctant to cancel popular measures, even if they had opposed them at the time they were legislated. No new advances were made, though, and clearly the Liberals and Conservatives were less effective managers. Deficits were accumulated under these governments even without new programs being added, while the CCF achieved pay-as-you-go socialism, and even reduced a previous deficit. Further, Saskatchewan's medicare, labour legislation, and bill of rights were taken up by Liberal and Conservative governments in other provinces, and federally.

British Columbia

In British Columbia, the NDP under Dave Barrett held office for only three years after its election in 1972. Nevertheless, it managed to accomplish a great deal. In retrospect some would say that it accomplished too much, that its frenzy of activity was the cause of its defeat, inciting too many of its enemies to heroic feats of resistance. It was so busy doing good works it had no time to explain them even to its friends. In defence of the Barrett government, though, it must be remembered that more people voted for it in 1975 than in 1972. It lost office because the anti-NDP vote both increased, and coalesced around, Social Credit, traditional Liberal and Conservative voters abandoning those parties.

The social reforms the NDP brought in were broadly popular.[3] "Mincome" was a guaranteed minimum income for the elderly and the disabled, considerably improving their standard of living. For the first time disabled persons were provided support above the general welfare level. "Pharmacare" for seniors was enacted, covering all prescribed drugs and vitamins, free of charge. Paramedical and emergency "trauma" services were greatly improved, raising standards to the best on the continent. A province-wide ambulance service was instituted, again increasing both the availability of the service and standards. Free dental care for children was established. There was massive de-institutionalization of psychiatric patients, with community care programs set up to give support. Women's health centres were opened to provide a range of services. Transition houses for victims of domestic violence were funded, and so were rape relief centres for counselling and police liaison. The B.C. Housing Corporation was established to fund affordable new housing and co-ops. A tenant's bill of rights was enacted. Urban rapid transit was developed. Labour law was reformed. A petroleum corporation was established to ensure supplies in the wake of American threats to cut them off. Human Resources Councils were established across the province, for de-centralization and local control in the welfare area.

The agricultural land reserve was the reform that aroused

the most opposition in British Columbia. The need for the protection of this scarce resource was not disputed. With only 5 per cent of the province's land suitable for agriculture, and only 1 per cent rated as prime agricultural land, a freeze is good public policy. Particular owners hoping to make a bundle by selling prime farm land for other more lucrative uses like real estate development were, however, naturally upset. They organized with great zeal to exercise their democratic right to say so. If they engaged in "rent-a-crowd" tactics, well, these too are legal.

A generally popular measure in British Columbia was the institution of public car insurance, which reduced rates considerably. The B.C. Insurance Corporation also provided household insurance for people unable to obtain it through private companies. (Rural residents, for example, with no fire department near by could not get regular coverage.) Social Credit has since cut back on the public insurance available, and private companies have since discovered they could cover rural residents as well. Yet people were too discontented with the old system, and rates, to go back to it entirely.

Education reforms by the B.C. New Democrats were relatively minor. Classroom size was decreased and the strap abolished. The "training schools" for delinquent children were closed down in favour of community care. Textbooks were vetted for their inclusion of positive role models for girls.

The women's movement has always been strong in British Columbia. This strength is reflected in a number of special measures. Women's centres and advocacy groups were given provincial funding for the first time under a New Democrat government. Day-care places were increased sevenfold. A women's economic rights branch was opened in the Ministry of Economic and Industrial Development, to promote employment opportunities for women. The B.C. Human Rights Commission was responsible for the biggest and best awards in the country for equal pay. The commission has since been disbanded, the victim of "restraint", as were most of the programs for women.

Justice councils were established across the province to enable community representatives to have some say in policing and the administration of criminal justice. An inexpensive program, the councils are a good example of a social democratic principle at work. Citizens' rights were extended while the system received an infusion of community expertise and concern. For the first time women were significantly involved in decision-making in this important area. The justice councils were abolished by Social Credit after their re-election in 1975.

The New Democratic Party showed excellent skills in government in the short time they had. There was the occasional case of a ministry underestimating its expenditures for the year, but no more often than under Social Credit governments. During their three years in office, the NDP balanced the budget while extending the social programs. Since then, Social Credit has run up a massive deficit of $18 billion, all the while cutting social programs. Social Credit, similarly, is responsible for serious neglect of the resource base of the economy, especially of the forests. Such damage will limit British Columbia's economic opportunities for decades to come.

The New Democrat government made a tactical error in calling an election in 1975 with three months of the fiscal year to go. In the campaign, Social Credit accused the party of overspending. On taking over as the new government, Social Credit then spent wildly in that last quarter of the fiscal year, to try to make good its overspending charge.

The New Democrat government had a Disclosure Act passed, requiring the declaration of financial assets by all candidates as well as by elected members. The need for such a measure became particularly apparent with subsequent revelations of Social Credit ministers' approving special concessions to companies in which they held an interest. Conflict-of-interest guidelines for ministers have become routine federally and in other provinces, but the Social Credit Party has persisted in denying B.C. citizens protection from this abuse of office.

What makes the social democratic experience in British Columbia so different from that in other provinces and countries is the transience of the reforms it achieved. Social democratic governments in office longer have time to iron out the wrinkles in their programs, and win themselves strong supporters. Feasibility is not an issue in the next election; indeed, there are large numbers of voters who realize they have a lot to lose on the program's demise. In British Columbia, *most* of the New Democrat reforms were killed: three years, evidently, is not enough.

Not only were the programs the party had brought in cut, but other long-established services were also eliminated. Classroom sizes in schools have risen again, and whole university faculties and colleges have closed down. Distinguished scientists are fleeing the province, so that every year its capacity to compete in the new technological world is diminished. Transition houses for battered women and children have been "privatized". Victims of racial or sex discrimination must hire lawyers to go to court for redress against discrimination. Support services for the victims of child abuse have disappeared, and so have certain labour rights. With massive unemployment, increasing numbers of British Columbians line up at food banks and soup kitchens, and sleep in church basements. From a guaranteed minimum income under a New Democrat government, the province has moved to reliance on charitable handouts from individuals, churches, and voluntary organizations.

Manitoba

Proving how slow social progress is, the New Democratic Party victory in Manitoba occurred fifty years, almost to the day, after the collapse of the Winnipeg General Strike. Such an historic

149

victory, the second New Democrat provincial government, was modest in its dimensions. Ed Schreyer became premier of a minority government, with 38 per cent of the popular vote. He promptly announced that the government would run a full term, implementing its electoral promises. And it did![4]

Health-care programs were greatly improved, and more options introduced. Home-care services were extended, and non-profit nursing-home care was encouraged. A school dental-care program was introduced. Medicare premiums were first cut in half, then eliminated, to be financed through general revenues. To help seniors and other low-income families remain in their own homes, a program of home repair assistance was instituted. Manitoba legislated a comprehensive landlord/tenant act, including the office of a "rentalsman", or ombudsman, for renters. Young farmers were given assistance to stay on the farm. Producer-controlled marketing boards were encouraged, and cheaper crop insurance was provided. Amenities were improved in the countryside and a new Farm Machinery Act was passed. Manitoba's reform of family property law went the furthest of all the provinces to provide equal sharing of matrimonial property.

Manitoba followed Saskatchewan in establishing public car insurance. Limits on election spending were legislated, and candidates were required to disclose contributions. The requirement that a candidate make a financial deposit upon nomination was abolished. Wire-tapping was outlawed. Royalties and taxes on mining were doubled and the Mineral Resources Corporation was established for exploration. By the time of the 1973 election, pensions were increased and taxes for low-income earners reduced. People earning under $20,000 were paying less in taxes in 1973 than they had in 1969. The government was re-elected with an increase in the popular vote, again showing how slow progress is, of 4 per cent.

The next New Democrat government in Manitoba, after a Conservative interlude, came in 1982, with Howard Pawley as premier. The Pawley example is especially instructive, for with the recession of the early 1980s, the government had less room to manoeuvre. With declining world markets for the province's resources, unemployment shot up. Despite the pressures to cut back government spending, the province invested money in direct job creation.[5]

The Manitoba Jobs Fund was modestly financed, with $200 million in 1983, more money than Conservative provincial governments put into job creation. Immediate jobs were the aim, in what was seen as the first phase of a long-term strategy. Construction projects were undertaken, of schools, community colleges, medical centres, street repairs, museums, and other public property. A special fund for youth unemployment gave wage assistance to businesses, farms, and non-profit organizations to hire young people. A program of new-house construction and old-house renovation was funded. As much as possible, joint projects were encouraged, with the private sector working with the federal and municipal governments. New investment was the result of the program: $60 million by the private sector and $100 million by the other two levels of government. Purchasing power was increased, with spin-off benefits to business, and a decrease in welfare costs to the government.

For all its stress on job creation in small business and in community projects, the Manitoba government has not ignored the "macro" level. Mega projects may risk mega mistakes, but may also stimulate growth generally, give a boost to economically drowsy communities, and encourage technological development. Manitoba has avoided the mistakes of Social Credit in British Columbia in counting wholly on mega projects, and devastating the economy in the course. In 1985 Pawley signed a major hydro export agreement with the United States which is expected to earn billions for the province. The commitment has been made to plough back half of the profits in Manitoba job creation. The requirement that a certain proportion of goods

151

and services for the Limestone project be purchased in the province will stimulate the creation of other jobs.

One last "micro" example will have to suffice to make the point of a judicious mixture of economic strategies. In Manitoba, promises to increase arts funding were kept; Mulroney's similar promise in the 1984 election was followed promptly by a $120-million cut in arts funding. Manitoba's increases, moreover, have gone both to the arm's-length agencies and to the minister's own budget. Again, this is in contrast with the federal government, where all the cutbacks have been directed at the independent agencies, which also have suffered increased government interference in decision-making. The result, for Manitoba, is a thriving arts community. There is new production in theatre, film, and publishing.

Other reforms of the Pawley government include the public financing of elections. Here Manitoba is following the federal example, legislated by a Liberal minority government on New Democrat prodding. In 1985, Manitoba became the second province, after Québec, to legislate equal pay for work of equal value. It has substantially overhauled its native-welfare programs, delegating authority to native communities. The practice of sending native children out of the province for adoption was stopped. Child-care spaces were tripled and women's resource centres funded. A most important reform for women was the institution of "automatic collection" of maintenance payments from their separated or divorced husbands. Here Manitoba has led the country in discovering that 85 per cent of spouses can pay court-ordered maintenance. Other jurisdictions are now following suit. Manitoba also pioneered the practice of treating wife assault like other assaults, for which the police lay charges. This has resulted in such a significant drop in wife abuse that the other provinces and territories are now following Manitoba's lead.

The most dramatic, and contentious, of the NDP's noneconomic reforms has been in language: the re-institution of official bilingualism. This righting of an historic wrong is important for the whole country, and worth retelling. The Conservatives, in 1890, passed the infamous legislation making English the sole official language of Manitoba. French was forbidden in the schools, and police officers were sent into classrooms to enforce the law. Generations of Franco-Manitobans and Métis lost their French heritage. French declined to a "kitchen language" as Francophones were denied an education in their mother tongue. Those who sought civil service jobs, or professional careers, had to compete in their second language. Few overcame this obstacle, and those who did were assimilated into the English-speaking majority.

The NDP was in office in Manitoba while the Supreme Court of Canada was deliberating the constitutionality of the 1890 law. By this time, French-speakers had declined to only 5 per cent of the population. To avoid having to translate ninety years of statutes into French, including those subsequently repealed, the government negotiated a settlement with the Société Franco-Manitobaine. Only a small number of laws would be translated, but services would be provided in French where numbers warranted, not a requirement of the 1890 law. The Conservatives reacted shamefully to this compromise, refusing even to vote on the bill. The legislature's business was held up with unprecedented bell-ringing. Needing a motion to provide it with further funding, the government had to withdraw. The Supreme Court of Canada soon pronounced its decision. As the Pawley government had warned, it ordered the translation of all laws, even those that had been subsequently repealed.

In all three examples of New Democrat provincial administration, the governments have demonstrated high standards of professional competence. In assuming government, the NDP has shown full respect for the principle of an independent public service. This was not always merited, but the NDP has chosen the willing suspension of disbelief over mass firings. Yet, contrary to a popular misconception, there has never been any tendency to build a large bureaucracy.

New Democrat provincial governments have been eminently practical in their dealings with federal governments, both Liberal and Conservative. The Manitoba government, for example, was the first province to sign a communications and culture accord with the federal government. Federal Conservatives and Liberals continue to foster the idea that the New Democratic Party is too extreme or too ideological to be practical; but the facts prove otherwise. Since the days of Tommy Douglas, CCF/NDP governments have had a keen sense of their mandate. They have sought, very practically, to do the best for their people within existing constraints. They all would have liked to go further, but all have respected the right of the people to set the limits.

National Governments

The proof of the pudding is in the eating. We taste that pudding now in other countries, where similar social democratic parties have been in government, two of them for long periods of time. We will begin with Sweden, the country with the longest-lasting social democratic government in the world. Austria will be examined next, as a Central European country with a post-war social democratic government. Finally we will look at one of the new social democracies of the Mediterranean, Greece. None of these countries is similar enough to Canada to serve as a model in any practical sense, yet none is so unlike us as to be wholly irrelevant. All of these three countries are smaller than Canada in population and geography, and none has our wealth of natural resources. In short, they are all countries with more problems to solve than Canada has, and all have rejected the excuse of limited options and have dared to do things differently.

Solidarity in a Cold Climate — Sweden

Swedish social democratic governments have achieved their highly planned economy, high labour force participation, and low unemployment largely through means other than public ownership. The Swedish economy has less public ownership than the French had under decades of conservative governments. Swedish social democracy is not classical nineteenth-century socialism, and purists may be offended. But under social democratic management, Sweden has become a prosperous country, with a high standard of living, an advanced welfare state, an extensive free education system, and some unique measures to promote equality, including equality between the sexes. The country is known for the civility of its political debate. Sweden's private sector is substantial, and her great industrialists live very well indeed. The state provides great social benefits to the middle class, especially in medicare and education. Sweden's unemployment rates are low, less than 2 per cent for decades. Even with the recession of the 1980s, when Canada's unemployment was at the 12 per cent level, Sweden's rate peaked at 4.1 per cent, in September 1983. Average income in Sweden is the second-highest in the industrial world, behind Switzerland and ahead of the United States.

This prosperity is no accident. In the nineteenth century, Sweden was a relatively poor country, slow to industrialize. It suffered the usual crises and recessions of laissez-faire capitalism. Its unemployment in the early 1930s was high, with 200,000 people, or 10 per cent of the labour force, seeking aid in 1932. In the same year, the Swedes elected a social democratic government for the first time. After forty-four years of social democracy there was a conservative interlude from 1976 to 1982. The Social Democrats were then returned to government in 1982 and again elected in 1985. During this time the Social Democratic Party has had a majority on its own for only five years. Otherwise it has had to depend on the

155

support of other parties, sometimes on the left, more often on the right.

Swedish economic planning is consciously based on Keynesian principles, another affront to the pure of mind. Right from its first days in government the decision was made that

> Unemployment and underemployment would not be dealt with through austerity, but through an expansive economic policy with a deficit in the State budget during recession and austerity during boom periods.[6]

The Social Democratic Party of Sweden was founded in 1889. Its members in Parliament went through the apparently universal phase of advocating in opposition the need for social security measures (the old age pension, aid to the unemployed, and the like) for years before these ideas were finally accepted. The first social democratic programs were brought in on a local basis by mutual-aid societies organized by workers. Gradually the municipalities began to contribute financial support, and only much later did the national government participate. The same protests that Canadian Conservatives and Liberals made against government intervention were made by similar-minded politicians and employers in Sweden.

Swedish history took a different course in 1932 when, with unemployment over 22 per cent among unionized workers, five workers were shot during a peaceful demonstration.[7] The voters rejected the old excuses that job creation was impossible and social programs were unaffordable. The new social democratic government they chose immediately began to create jobs through special projects. By 1937 Sweden had passed legislation regularizing its Keynesian policies, permitting deficits in bad years, which would be offset by surpluses in good years. Employment was high in Sweden during the war years, as everywhere, but Sweden did more than other countries to prepare for the post-war readjustment. Its extensive training and retraining programs date from this post-war period.[8]

To this Keynesian demand-stimulation base was added a supply-side labour market policy that is distinctly Swedish. At least as important, and again very Swedish, is the incorporation of an equality principle in basic economic planning. The "solidarity wage" flies in the face of market economics, seeking to level out differences in wages and salaries due to differences in bargaining power of workers in the various sectors. Practically speaking, this means that wages of auto workers are not as high as they would be with ordinary collective bargaining, while workers in weaker industries like food-processing do better than they otherwise would. As a result of this solidarity wage policy, Sweden is one of the few countries in the world where there has been a substantial reduction in the differences between men's and women's wages. This was achieved not through equal pay laws and a complaint system, but by giving, over a period of years, larger increases to the lowest-paid workers, who were disproportionately women.

Swedish economic planning aims at a high level of employment not only for obvious reasons of social democratic principles, but also to maintain purchasing power. Low inflation is another important government goal, and careful attention is given to overall demand for goods and services. Specialized programs for particularly disadvantaged groups ensure them an adequate standard of living, maintaining their purchasing power without overheating the whole economy and causing inflation. Programs for the disabled date back to 1948, and new programs target the new unemployed, youth.

Sweden's unemployment rates are kept artificially low, at less than half the "real rates". In 1970, for example, with an official unemployment rate of 1.5 per cent, there was another 1.8 per cent of the labour force involved in programs of retraining, relief programs, or special programs for the disabled. The "real" rate of unemployment would have been 3.3 per cent. By 1984, unemployment was more serious, with an official rate at 3.1 per cent, and a further 4.1 per cent of the labour force in the various programs, giving a "real" rate of 7.2 per cent. When real unemployment rose, the special programs were considerably expanded in order to keep down the numbers of people on the street looking for work. There are no illusions about the underestimates of Swedish unemployment statistics, but most Swedes would rather be retraining or working on a special project than joining long queues for scarce jobs. Even when the "real" rates are considered, they are much lower than those in Canada, or in Britain under Thatcher, or in the United States under Reagan. Moreover, there is nothing fake about Sweden's *employment* rates, which are high. Labour force participation for the age group 15-64 is 84 per cent in Sweden, compared with 63 per cent in Canada.

The relief projects themselves do useful work. Apart from the usual construction and public-works projects, there is forest conservation, environmental clean-up, and the restoration of cultural landmarks. Housing construction and renovation have been used since the 1930s as job-creation measures as well as to meet housing needs. The latest employment-creation scheme funds "youth teams", targeting the 18-19-year-old population, where unemployment is particularly high. The program guarantees at least a four-hour-a-day job to all youth unable to find regular work, in municipal or church-sponsored projects.

The emphasis on training and retraining reflects the Swedish preoccupation with supply-side economic measures. In the same vein, grants for relocation promote labour mobility. These measures fit logically with the solidarity wage policy so fundamental to the Swedish system. The solidarity wage, by forcing weak enterprises to pay higher wages than in other countries, leads to the failure of some of them. Hence the need for support measures to move labour to more successful enterprises/industries/regions. A substantial state pension plan also promotes labour mobility. With good pension protection, workers are not so fearful of job changes, including major relocations.

Some employment-maintenance projects have not worked, and accordingly they have been discontinued. Subsidies to industries to stockpile unsold products have proved to be ineffective. Financial aid to ailing industries, like textiles, have been largely unsuccessful.

"Co-determination" policies have resulted in at least indirect employment maintenance. Since 1977 there has been a requirement that employers, public and private, negotiate important changes in the workplace with their employees before implementing them. This makes plant closures and major lay-offs more difficult, as does the requirement of longer notice and better severance pay to employees.

Public ownership of industry is lower in Sweden than in many other European countries. Public utilities and public transportation are publicly owned, as is one major bank, and most of the mining, steel, and shipbuilding industries. There is a national enterprise board that owns a variety of companies; but most manufacturing, as well as agriculture, retail sales, commercial services, and tourist facilities, are privately owned. Yet Sweden has an enormous public sector in health, education, research, municipal services, and culture, and Swedes pay the highest taxes in the world for these services. Unlike so many Canadians, Swedes do not believe that the only real jobs are in the private sector. When the private sector is hit by recession and jobs lost, the public sector is deliberately expanded.

The large size of the public-service sector accounts for the high rate of employment of women in Sweden. The female labour force participation rate is close to men's, yet Swedish women continue to work largely in traditional female jobs. Measures to move women into non-traditional jobs exist, but have been scarcely more successful than in Canada.

Employment in the private sector is encouraged through carefully targeted economic planning. Sweden has completely rejected the kind of industrial policies that have been so disastrous for Canada. They have avoided establishing a relatively large number of companies producing an enormous range of articles, and losing economies of scale. Sweden has instead chosen to specialize in a small number of areas, like ball bearings and machine tools. It does not build as many different brands of car, or refrigerator, as Canada does, but those it does produce sell internationally.

Sweden is sixth in the world in her use of research and development, with nearly twice the number of researchers per thousand employees as Canada. As much as 70 per cent of this research is done by private companies, while in Canada only 40 per cent is.

The Social Democratic government of Sweden has promoted equality for women as part of a broader philosophical commitment to social equality. Parental-leave measures are amongst the best in the world, permitting leave to be taken by either parent or shared, at 90 per cent of salary. Of new jobs created with state aid, 40 per cent must be provided for each sex. Women hold more than a quarter of the seats in Parliament. Legal equality was instituted early in Sweden, giving women an equal say in family decisions and the right to retain their original surname. The (established) Church of Sweden was one of the first in the world to ordain women priests, in 1961.

Sweden's social and economic programs were not achieved without a fight. All the programs were contentious when introduced, and some still are. Most, while instituted by the Social Democrats, were continued by the Conservatives and the Liberals during their relatively short periods of government.

An ethic of unions and employers working together to solve economic problems has evolved, even if it is often fraught with difficulties. The first centrally negotiated collective agreement was signed in 1938, and collective bargaining between the national employers' federation and the national union federation has continued ever since. Historically, the government's position has been to remain neutral. Interestingly, this was broken by the Palme government after its 1982 re-election, when it urged the unions to accept lower wage increases in order to combat inflation and aid recovery. What labour lost in accepting restraint is evidently made up for by having a greater voice in government generally.

The union-party connection, described in Chapter 4, is strong. The level of unionization is more than twice that of Canada, 85 per cent of the labour force, to Canada's 39 per cent. Strikes, the sceptic may need to be reminded, are rare. In the 1981-83 period, an average of 19.5 days per thousand workers were lost in strikes, compared with 598 days in Canada.

It is significant that the major new development in Swedish economic policy came from the unions with their proposal of "wage-earner funds".[9] The idea of employee investment funds emerged in the 1960s, initially in response to a distinctively Swedish problem resulting from the solidarity wage. By holding back wages in the most profitable companies, their profits rise. Thus one of the earliest purposes of the wage-earner funds was to cream off these "excess profits". As well, they advance other social democratic goals, such as greater employee involvement in decision-making. More recently they have come to be seen as a means of encouraging savings, to be ploughed into needed capital formation. Although the Social Democratic Party had not adopted the proposal by the 1976 election, the employers' federation made it an election issue.

Undoubtedly there were other reasons the Social Democrats lost the 1976 election, including their policy on nuclear energy, but the employers' fierce attack hurt. Perhaps the employers had read the fine print of the economists' projections: that employees could control their companies in twenty to seventy-five years, depending on the rate of acquisition of the funds.

The Social Democrats also lost the 1979 election, again after a massive attack by the employers. By 1982 the party had adopted a modest version of the wage-earner fund, and won. A referendum was held, the proposal accepted and accordingly legislated. The scheme now in place provides for a slow build-up of the fund, at the rate of 1 per cent a year, but only to 1990. The maximum share that the funds may hold in any one company is 40 per cent. Thus the feared employee take-over of companies will not happen: workers' representation on boards of directors is restricted to 20 per cent. The fund is administered by regional boards, which may invest in new ventures and in companies other than those that generated the money.

The disastrous effects predicted by the employers have not happened. There has been no flight of capital out of the country, and domestic investment actually increased by 15 per cent in the first year of the plan's operation. If the right is now less opposed to the plan, the left is yet far from convinced. Some condemn the wage-earner fund as the brain-child of academic economists; certainly it did not come from the grass roots. Others maintain it diverted attention from other measures that could have been implemented without such an election back-lash.

To round out the picture, let us look briefly at some issues in foreign policy and culture. Sweden is a neutral country, without nuclear weapons but with a substantial army, military conscription, and a conventional arms industry. Clearly tied to the West by history, culture, and economics, Sweden has yet managed to show some independence in foreign policy. It was the first Western country to recognize "red" China. It was strongly critical of American conduct during the Vietnam War. When I spent a sabbatical in Sweden in 1973, the Americans had withdrawn their ambassador in protest against the government's outspoken anti-war position. Sweden's contribution to international aid and development is routinely one of the highest in the world, at .9 per cent to 1 per cent of GNP, or twice the rate of Canada's. Sweden is a strong supporter of the United Nations and its agencies. With Canada now, Sweden is a major participant in UN peace-keeping forces. Sweden was the first country to appoint a minister for disarmament, Alva Myrdal, in 1966.

Finally, Sweden has been innovative in cultural promotion, in circumstances much more difficult than Canada's. With a language spoken only by its 8 million citizens and nobody else, it has devised special measures to promote writing and publishing. For example, Sweden is a pioneer in public lending rights of books. Having attended first to traditional high culture, Sweden is now working at accessibility. There is experimental theatre dealing with workers' concerns, hardly the usual theme of a Bergman film.

Swedes have more opportunity to enjoy cultural activities, family events, sports, and other pursuits, thanks to generous holiday provisions. As is common in countries with social democratic governments, the minimum holiday is one month a year.

In portraying Sweden's success as a social democracy I have underplayed negative criticism, by left and right. Environmentalists condemn the slowness of the government to take their concerns seriously. Social problems continue, and there is still much alcoholism and drunkenness. Efficient and humane as the welfare system is, there are still gaps and problems. The debate continues as to how services can be improved, how new needs can be met, and how people can become more involved in decisions that affect them. Even Social Democrats question the size of the state apparatus, and the tax burden. Some 5 per cent of the population believe that social democracy does not go far enough, and they vote Communist. Inflation is still too high. The Social Democrats have deficit problems as well, although they have been considerably more successful in controlling the deficit than have the other parties.

My final point on Sweden concerns the *durability* of social democratic reforms. The Conservatives and Liberals would not have brought in these measures themselves, but they have learned to accept them. Thus, unemployment remained relatively low in Sweden under the Liberal/Conservative coalition, which did not dare try Thatcherism or Reaganomics.

Social Democracy in Central Europe — Austria

There are many similarities between Austria and Sweden. Both are small, neutral countries that were economically disadvantaged until fairly recently. Like Sweden, Austria has achieved high economic growth and employment, and an advanced welfare state. Similarly, Austria has developed an elaborate economic planning mechanism, based on a "social partnership" between the unions and employers. Yet Austria has developed its structure in quite a different way.[10]

In the 1930s, while Swedish Social Democrats were beginning to build their welfare state and planned economy, rival Austrian groups were fighting each other for control of the state. Social Democrats, and democratic Conservatives and Liberals, all lost as a result, and there was a fascist take-over in 1934. Austria was then occupied by Germany in 1938. Democratic Austrians, of both left and right, had time to reflect on their past tactics while interned in the same concentration camps. They decided to do things differently after the war, and they did. The first welfare state and economic-planning measures in Austria were the product of a coalition government, led by the Social Democrats from 1945 to 1966. For those who survived it, Dachau proved to be a great unifier.

Although a limited old age pension had been instituted in 1936, the creation of a comprehensive social security system dates from this post-war period. Old age pension provisions were extended and medical care and unemployment benefits were established. A massive housing program was undertaken, nearly half of it in the non-profit sector. The education system was fundamentally reformed, to open up access to all income levels. Schools, books, and travel became free. University and colleges ceased to charge fees, and grants were established for students with low incomes. Places are guaranteed to all students who meet the minimum requirement of having passed the preceding level. This access to education is actually one of the major points of contention between the political parties. While the Social Democrats have promoted increased access, the Conservatives consider that educational institutions have been over-extended, and that standards have been lowered as a result. There is, in fact, a surplus of relatively over-educated but underemployed graduates.

Austrian economic planning dates back to the early post-war years, when the country was still under Allied occupation.[11] By 1947 an Economic Commission had been set up, with representatives of the employers, trade unions, and agriculture. This Economic Commission played a major role in drawing up the first wage-and-price agreements that have been the key to the success of the "social partnership" ever since. The next economic-planning organism, established in 1951 as the Economic Directorate, was ruled unconstitutional. Its successor, the Parity Commission for Wages and Prices, is an entirely voluntary arrangement. It is based on a cabinet resolution and an exchange of letters between the principal partners. Originally intended as a provisional measure when it was established in 1957, it has outlasted the political coalition that founded it.

The commission is chaired by the chancellor of the country. The various components of the social partnership are represented in equal numbers, with other ministers and state secretaries. A subcommittee on wages, with equal representation of unions and employers, has an unusual role in the centralized collective-bargaining process. The subcommittee sets the minimum wage for each industry. Individual companies and unions then negotiate particular agreements above this basic minimum. The subcommittee on wages has no power to influence the content of any particular collective agreement, but it may delay negotiations for a wage increase. Thus, a union seeking wage increases must first undertake, although strictly speaking this is voluntary, to seek first the approval of the subcommittee on wages before it begins to bargain. If the subcommittee considers that wages for that enterprise are high enough, it can delay the negotiations. Meanwhile, the old wage structure stands. There is also a subcommittee on prices for key commodities.

Proportional representation extends in Austria to proportional patronage. Quite unlike the case in Canada, members of Opposition parties get their share of appointments to important bodies. The result is a high degree of politicization of professional and community life, but perhaps of a less acrimonious nature. Union leaders, for example, are almost all party members, 80 per cent Social Democrat and 20 per cent Conservative. The civil servants' union is the reverse. Thus, the union, whose members have largely been engaged in implementing Social Democratic policies, has mainly a Conservative membership.

"Co-determination" in enterprises has been provided through a guaranteed one-third of workers' representatives on boards of directors.[12] Two union representatives may demand information on any aspect of the company's affairs. This is a safeguard provision, and in practice the union representatives are not involved in any day-to-day management, nor do they wish to be. Appointment of a worker to the "managing board", as opposed to the board of directors, requires approval by two-thirds of the directors who are not union appointees. Works councils, in enterprises of at least 200 employees, have the power to delay plant shutdowns by four weeks, but cannot stop them. Works councils, more generally, may raise objections to any change in operations that would affect the employees. A mediation structure is in place for the resolution of disputes. The Labour Code governing these relationships, which is considerably more generous to workers than anything in

Canada, was adopted unanimously in 1973. Strikes in Austria are extremely rare.

Broader economic analysis and planning is the work of yet another subcommittee of the Parity Commission, the Advisory Committee for Economic and Social Questions. Again this body is made up of appointees from the various sectors of the social partnership, in this case economic experts. This body worked out plans for the reduction in the work week, from 45 hours in 1970 to 40 hours in 1975. It conducts research into capital markets and long-term pricing trends. Consensus, as before, is required, through a provision that any recommendations affecting a particular sector must be approved by its president before publication.

The Austrian economy is 28 per cent publicly owned; 44 per cent is privately owned, by Austrians, and 28 per cent is foreign-owned. Both the largest and the third-largest banks are state-owned. The largest bank in turn owns a large number of manufacturing enterprises. Public utilities and major means of transportation are publicly owned at one level or another, as is the entire iron and steel industry. The great cultural centres, theatres, and concert and opera halls also belong to the people. In the case of the banks and the iron and steel industry, public ownership came about through circumstances not involving ideology. In the post-war reconstruction it was simply the easiest way of taking over German-held enterprises.

There is a current controversy about the extent of public ownership in the country. The Conservative Volkspartei, characteristically, wants *some* privatization. There are numerous complaints that the publicly owned firms are badly managed. When bad investment decisions are made, state-owned firms are bailed out by government, just as if they were private corporations in Canada! It is argued that social considerations, such as full employment, have had too much influence on economic decisions, and profits not enough. Yet what is a defect, to the Conservatives, is partly responsible for Austria's economic success. The country has survived two recessions with remarkably low unemployment. From a rate of 1.9 per cent in 1980, unemployment peaked at 4.7 per cent in 1985. In Canada the comparable rates were 7.5 per cent in 1980 and up to 11.9 per cent in 1983. Unemployment averaged only 2 per cent in the 1970s, and Austria brought in foreign workers. The "misery index" — the unemployment rate and the inflation rate added together — stayed below 10 per cent in the 1970s, and was sometimes as low as 6 per cent. In Canada, the misery index rose from 9 per cent in 1970 to over 16 per cent in 1974.

As with Sweden, Austria's economic success can be reasonably credited to social democratic planning, and not to extraneous factors. At the break-up of the Austro-Hungarian Empire in 1918, the territory that was left as Austria was poor and small. Experts questioned whether it could survive as a national economy. The young republic certainly needed infusions of foreign loans throughout the 1920s. Thirty-three per cent of the labour force was unemployed in the Depression. The country was still relatively poor in the 1950s. Incomes were catching up, but they still lagged behind EEC averages. Austria depends greatly on trade and suffers the disadvantage of the inordinate influence of a much larger neighbouring economy, that of West Germany. Like Canada, it has the complication of being a federal state. In short, all the obstacles that Canadians face in controlling their own economy Austrians have had also to solve, and then some. The Austrian success shows that a small country with less than one-third Canada's population, and similarly dominated by a powerful neighbouring economy, can yet shape its own destiny.

Socialism in the South — Greece

As we move from northern to southern Europe, the historic trends are reversed. From the early inter-war successes of the

Nordic countries through the post-war example of Austria, we move to the recent elections of social democratic governments in the Mediterranean countries. By the time social democratic parties had come to government in the south, several of the northern countries had actually reverted back to conservative governments. In Portugal, Spain, and Greece, social democratic parties had been all brutally suppressed by right-wing dictators. In each case, liberal democracy was in some sense restored in the 1970s, followed soon after by the election of a social democratic party. Greece's evolution is an especially interesting example, not least for that country's historic role in the development of western democracy.

The merits of Athenian democracy should not be exaggerated, for with the exclusion of women and slaves, probably only 10 per cent of the adult population had the right to vote. Yet the citizens' assemblies developed in Greece are an important source for western-style democracy. The Greeks are still highly political animals. Since the restoration of democracy in the 1970s, election rallies draw crowds of 100,000 people, and voter turn-out is more than 80 per cent of eligible voters.

While the conservative political philosophies of Plato and Aristotle have survived better than those of their radical competition, some of the criticism from this early period has survived. Early condemnations of slavery asserted the fundamental equality of all people, "for," as Antiphon explained, "we all breathe the same air and we all eat with hands." Philemon similarly affirmed, "By nature no one was ever born a slave." Even more to the point for social democracy is the assertion, also from the fifth century B.C., that "equality of wealth is the beginning of freedom, as poverty is the beginning of servitude." Any endeavour to achieve social reform requires the assumption that laws and institutions can be changed, to suit chosen ends. The idea that laws and institutions were not wholly determined by the gods, or written in the stars, was developed in fifth-century-B.C. Athens. This laid the theoretical basis for ongoing

169

political debate as to just what laws and measures were best to solve any particular set of problems.

Solon, in the sixth century B.C., had himself instituted laws to prohibit the selling of citizens into slavery for non-payment of debts. He also restored freedom to some who were "reduced to shameful slavery, and trembled at the caprices of their masters". Thucydides, in *The Peloponnesian Wars*, argued that Athens's superior military strength lay in her democratic institutions. Societies differed not only in geography but in social structure and culture, and these differences had an effect. Democritus described how a sense of pity brought an end to isolation, and encouraged friendship, mutual aid, and harmony amongst the citizens as society was gradually built up. Democritus proposed a number of specific measures to prevent corruption in government, including audits of officials' work at the end of their term. His notion of the social contract, quite unlike that of Hobbes, accorded obligations to the government as well as to the people. The Hippocratics studied public health in addition to tending to private patients, writing papers on the effect of air pollution and water pollution on health. If the nineteenth-century Fabians are more often associated with the use of social research for reform purposes, they have honourable antecedents in ancient Greece.

Yet if the ancient Greeks were the source of so many of the principles of social democracy, their descendants have had little opportunity to put these ideas into practice. For most of their history they have been dominated by military conquerors, from Alexander the Great and the Romans, through the Eastern Empire and the Ottomans, to the Nazis, to mention only the major actors. The latest, now Greek, military dictatorship ended only in 1974, when civilian government was restored. Three elections later, in 1981, a social democratic party, the Pan-Hellenic Socialist Movement (PASOK), was elected to a majority government. It was re-elected in 1985. (PASOK, incidentally, was founded in exile in Toronto and its first

170

meetings were held in the Greek clubs on Danforth Avenue, in Broadview-Greenwood.)

The new government had extraordinary problems to face, problems of economic underdevelopment, inflation at 25 per cent, a business class accustomed to great privileges, and the near-absence of a functioning civil service. At a time when most European countries had a well-developed social security system, Greece had only occupationally organized pensions and medical care, which left large numbers of the population uncovered. The establishment of a social security system, economic development with central planning and incentives, and the creation of an independent foreign policy were all objectives of the new government.[13]

The establishment of a National Health Service was an immediate priority. The strategy adopted was unusual in its emphasis on physician services, while those physicians at the same time were made civil servants. The surplus of doctors under the old private system made the new status acceptable to the doctors, and the shortage of doctors in remote areas prompted a thorough reorganization of medical services. A nation-wide system of health centres is now being established, beginning in the rural areas. These combine doctors' offices with mini-hospitals. A state-run pharmaceutical company has also been established to produce basic drugs and medical products at low cost.

A national pension scheme has been enacted to provide a flat-rate pension. Previously there had been only a highly regressive industry-organized system. Public subsidies were greatest to the better-paid occupations, like doctors, and lowest to the poorly paid. These inequities have not been resolved, but increased taxes on the wealthy have permitted improved pensions at the low end and the flat-rate pension. Taxes on real estate in Greece have been imposed as a progressive form of taxation, and as a means of discouraging the holding of vacant or under-used apartments and houses. Improvements in tax collection mean that some wealthy individuals are paying taxes for the first time. Computers are being used to combat fiscal fraud.

The first PASOK government undertook a major reform of family law, giving Greek women legal equality with men for the first time in history. The previous law had accorded all power in decision-making and responsibility for financial support to the husband. The duty of obedience and all domestic responsibilities fell to the wife. Now each has an equal say in decisions concerning where they will live and how they will educate and care for their children. Women now have the right to retain their own names on marriage. The dowry has been abolished, and with it the husband's right to administer his wife's property and receive debts owed her. Civil marriage has been instituted, and divorce on consent or after four years' separation is now permitted. Adultery is no longer a punishable offence. Divorced wives now have the right to their own medical insurance and pensions. Illegitimate children have been given equal rights with legitimate. Laws have been passed to prohibit sex discrimination in employment and to require equal access to education. Parental leave has been established, including leave for fathers, which cannot be transferred to the mother. Farm wives are now entitled to pensions, health insurance, and maternity benefits. Child-care centres are being provided in rural areas. Overseeing all this activity is a Council for the Equality of the Sexes, which, with a special advisor on equality, reports directly to the prime minister.

In the field of criminal justice, Greece is a pioneer in substituting alternative measures for the imprisonment of non-violent offenders. It is the first country to legislate a ban on the use of torture by the police and the armed forces.

Meagre resources and a surplus population have been Greece's lot since the time of Homer. In ancient times, the founding of colonies was the solution; more recently the solution has been emigration to Toronto, Montreal, New York, or Melbourne. The new government is seeking to reverse this pattern, inviting Greeks to come home, preferably with their savings to invest. Practical encouragement to start new businesses in Greece is given, with favourable terms for loans.

PASOK's economic policy is pragmatic to say the least. The government attempts to give direction to the economy by the establishment of goal-planning. Thus, there is a five-year plan for economic and social development. State-owned industries are few, but joint projects and loan/share arrangements with private companies are preferred. There is a state-owned Industrial and Mining Company, responsible for research as well as extraction. A state international trading company has been established to promote exports of both private and public companies. The Public Power Corporation hopes to achieve energy self-sufficiency through its greater reliance on hydro-electric power and the development of other renewable energy sources. The first Greek-assembled aircraft are under production by a state company. Tourists will be pleased to know that pollution-control measures are being instituted. A subway system is being built in Athens. Tourism is being actively promoted and expanded.

Even so, unemployment remains high, and capital flights are a threat. Inflation has declined from the 25 per cent inherited from the previous government, but it remains high. Unemployment has similarly declined, from 10 per cent to 8 per cent between 1981 and 1984. Economic growth was a modest 2 per cent in 1984, but this was an improvement over the 0 per cent under the previous, conservative, government. Austerity measures have been introduced, resulting in strikes and demonstrations. The budget deficit has been reduced, but to what effect on investment and employment remains to be seen.

Social reforms include de-centralization in many areas. Health centres and schools now have a certain measure of autonomy. Committees for equality have been set up at the local, prefecture, level. Three new universities have been founded, distant from Athens and offering new programs. "Nomarchs councils" have been established, bringing together locally elected mayors and representatives of the central government for consultation.

De-centralization is a primary aim in cultural policy as well. A network of youth centres has been created, with libraries, clubs, and cultural facilities. Local festivals are promoted. The government also has a major cultural-centralization project, the return of the "Elgin Marbles" to Athens from the British Museum. Leading the campaign is the country's high-profile Minister of Culture, Melina Mercouri. Mercouri can take the credit also for a major program of aid to the Greek film industry.

For many political observers, however, foreign policy has attracted the most attention. Greece's goal is to belong to no military bloc, but it does not see this as feasible until all fleets are withdrawn from the Aegean Sea. In the meantime it belongs to the European Economic Community and to NATO. It would like to get rid of its American bases, but it relies on the Americans to prevent Turkish incursions onto its eastern islands. So the bases remain. For now the country pursues more limited goals, such as the recognition of a nuclear-weapons-free zone in the Balkans. It is a participant in the five-nation initiative for nuclear disarmament. Within NATO it has argued for delays in the deployment of Pershing and cruise missiles. Nuclear weapons installed in its own territory by secret agreement under the colonels are being removed.

None of this is to suggest that the government has always chosen the wisest course, making the best use of its scarce economic and political resources. But, as with Sweden and Austria, the government has shown creditable progress in the face of difficult obstacles, in a very short period of time. Greece's achievements are relevant to Canada in that Greece, although a small country far poorer than we are in her resources, is, like us, highly dependent on the good will of the United States.

6

AN ECONOMIC PROGRAM

The party that proposed the solutions for the Depression of the 1930s is now developing its economic program for the end of the century. In the conservative atmosphere of the 1980s, the party has also had to devote much energy to defending present programs. Yet new ideas there are, and how they differ from competing Conservative and Liberal strategies will be shown. For most Canadians, not only the 1,250,000 who are unemployed, unemployment remains the country's top problem to solve. The number of poor people in Canada declined in the 1970s, but began to rise again in the 1980s. We are not in a depression, but 4,000,000 Canadians, of whom more than 1,000,000 are children, were living in poverty in 1986. For many millions of people, then, solving our economic problems, creating enough jobs, and collecting enough taxes to pay for our social programs are absolutely urgent matters.

Industrial Strategy or Free Trade?

The New Democrats' industrial strategy must be considered beside the Conservatives' free-trade proposal as fundamentally opposed approaches to Canada's structural unemployment. Both strategies have lengthy histories. The Conservatives' espousal of the free-trade principle in the 1980s is only the latest form of their traditional remedy of more trade for any recession or depression. It was the Liberals who advocated "reciprocity", Laurier's term for free trade, but long before that the Conservatives had been at least as strong advocates of the policy as an economic panacea.

From the time of George Brown's first, and failed, mission to the United States in 1874, both Liberals and Conservatives have made frequent efforts to negotiate a "reciprocal agreement" on trade. All of these "pilgrimages to Washington" resulted in failure *because the Americans did not find the terms advantageous*. The Liberals were on record for many years as favouring "unrestricted reciprocity" or "commercial union", which we now call free trade. But the idea was not acceptable to the Americans. On the one occasion that the Americans initiated a proposal, in 1911, a provision was included to permit either country to cancel the agreement without notice. Canada rejected it as too unstable. Throughout the history of the issue, the Americans have quite naturally been more concerned about ensuring sufficient markets for their manufactured goods than for Canada's "natural" products.

In a libertarian age it is difficult to be against something called "free trade". Similarly, "enhanced trade" connotes a positive and healthy measure. Opponents seem rigid and ungenerous, wishing to thwart a natural activity that would otherwise flourish. In real life, though, free trade is as illusory as free love, and probably more costly than a free lunch. Canadians themselves are becoming more sceptical of the policy. By early 1986, with the debate barely under way, public support was declining and concern about job losses growing.

Perhaps the main flaw of the free-trade proposal is that it deals with so restricted an area of the problem: if 25-30 per cent of Canada's wealth depends on foreign trade, then 70-75 per cent of it depends on domestic consumption. Even its advocates admit that free trade would cause job losses, which would lead to reduced demand for Canadian goods and services. Yet there is no way that that demand could be replaced by increased sales to the underpaid workers of Third World countries.

The stakes in the free-trade dislocation game are high. For the winners there would be higher incomes, and cheaper goods and services. For the losers, the long-term unemployed, lower prices for imported goods would be little consolation. New jobs in fast-food chains, at the minimum wage, would be a poor substitute for lost jobs, yet the economic trends suggest that this result is the best that could be expected. The Mulroney government had not done any serious sector-by-sector projections when it made the free-trade proposal. The Macdonald Commission, which recommended free trade in 1985, did so on the basis of very little economic analysis. Donald Macdonald himself has since qualified his enthusiasm considerably.

A study conducted of manufacturing in Ontario for 1985 found that most of the nearly 900,000 jobs would be at some risk from a bilateral free-trade agreement with the United States. Nearly a third, or 281,000 jobs, were estimated to be "highly sensitive" to free trade, while 275,000 jobs were rated as "sensitive" to free trade. For 115,000 jobs the risk was unknown, while the 92,000 jobs governed by the present autopact might, or might not, be exempted. This leaves only 107,000 jobs rated as "less sensitive", in industries considered able to adjust to the new conditions of free trade.[1]

Why should the Mulroney government be promoting such a precarious proposition? One may imagine government motives as Machiavellian as fantasy permits. I am partial to the simplistic explanation that Mulroney, in the midst of bank failures, resigning cabinet ministers, and the tuna scandal, wanted to undertake some kind of positive initiative. The timing at least supports that otherwise unsatisfactory explanation. So also does Mulroney's failure to have ever advocated the idea before. He is actually on record from before the 1984 election as an opponent of free trade. In his campaign for the Conservative leadership in 1983, he castigated John Crosbie for favouring it. Free trade with the United States, according to Mulroney then, would be like sleeping with an elephant. "It's terrific until the elephant twitches, and if the elephant rolls over you are a dead man."[2] Canadian firms could not compete with larger-scale American firms "without some kind of protection". Elsewhere, calling free trade "dangerous", Mulroney argued that Canada should consider instead more bilateral arrangements such as the autopact.[3] Michael Wilson, before he became minister of Finance, called free trade "simplistic and naive.... I believe a move at this time to free trade with the United States would only serve to diminish our ability to compete and move to higher levels of productivity."[4] Clearly the Conservatives have no mandate for their current position.

A more sophisticated, and sinister, explanation for the "free trade" position is the Conservative desire to dismantle the Canadian welfare state. A frontal attack would be suicidal, as they discovered when they tried to de-index the old age pension. Free trade instead would provide the pretext for doing the dirty work. The Americans' "level playing field" requirement would bring Canada down to the lowest common denominator: no medicare, unemployment insurance, maternity benefits, regional equalization, or old age pension. The American government has already protested unemployment insurance as an unfair subsidy to Atlantic fishing people. State-run medicare is obviously an advantage to employers, cutting costs to management who would otherwise have to pay higher premiums for private coverage. This reversion to the law of the jungle is what feminists are beginning to call "macho economics", letting the market/jungle do what no person could justify. If true, it is a clever ploy, although there are many barriers yet to free trade's being realized.

Quite apart from its desirability as an option for Canada, the idea that free trade can be a serious possibility is questionable. Free trade assumes the operation of a free market — that is, large numbers of buyers and sellers making offers and settling on the best deal they can negotiate between themselves. Yet most trade between Canada and the United

States is between firms that are not free agents but are either wholly or partially owned by the American trading "partner". Much of what may appear to be international trade is just the ordinary working of the multinational system, in which subsidiaries buy goods and services from their parent company, at inflated prices, and sell their products to it, at deflated prices. Market competition does not determine the price: head office does. A Canadian supplier across the street from an American subsidiary would not be given the contract, even if it beat the parent company's own price. There is no way that free trade could induce a subsidiary to buy the Canadian product, or that of any other competitor, if head office says no. The multinational system itself is the barrier to real competition in trade.

It is hard to see how the Americans could be interested in any agreement that would result in more Canadian sales to them. They already import more from Canada than they sell to us, by $20 billion (Canadian) in 1985, part of an overall trade deficit of $175 billion (Canadian). Clearly, the United States hopes to reduce its trade deficit everywhere. Our trade surplus with the United States, in any event, should not be taken as a healthy sign, for most of it derives from the sale of natural resources, especially non-renewable resources. We have a trade *deficit* with the United States in manufactured goods, a sector that provides far more jobs per investment dollar than does the resource sector. So, in its trading relations with the United States, Canada loses in terms of jobs, and yet it is vulnerable to American retaliation because of the dollar surplus. With the rest of the world Canada has a trade deficit, and surely this is the problem we should be addressing. Pursuing a free-trade agreement with the United States will hardly help us increase our exports to other parts of the world.

The New Democratic Party's task is to show Canadians that there are better alternatives to the law of the jungle and the despairing recourse of "free trade". Rather than shutting

179

ourselves into fortress America, we should be developing our own economy based on our own strengths. New Democrat industrial strategy does just this, and an impressive number of community groups across the country share these ideas. "Canada Unlimited", the 1985 New Democrat Jobs Action Strategy, incorporated an imposing array of job-creation ideas. A remarkably similar thrust has emerged everywhere, for greater local control.

Greatest support was found in single-industry towns that had been hit by plant close-downs. People saw the injustice of letting companies come in, plied with government tax breaks and free services, make their money, and leave. Residents want instead to see the money made in their community reinvested there, to diversify the job base and build the community.

The list of practical recommendations that emerged includes community diversification, funds for single-industry towns, tax credits for job creation, the upgrading of municipal services, housing construction, reforestation and other resource renewal, and Canadian-content and buy-Canadian regulations. All the proposals of the Jobs Action Group were costed and estimates were made of the number of jobs that would be created. In 1985 dollars, the bill came to $6-8 billion. New tax revenues and savings amounted to $5.3-5.8 billion, leaving an estimated deficit for the first year of operation at $1-1.5 billion. With increased tax revenues for the new jobs, that deficit would promptly decline.

A proposal by Citizens for Public Justice is similar in aim to the NDP's, but is bolder in its figures.[5] It calls for $11 billion to be rechannelled directly to job creation and raising incomes of the poor. It would increase taxes for wealthy individuals and corporations to finance these programs, but add nothing to the deficit. CPJ arrived at its $11 billion by quite a different route, using the principle of a "societal tithe", $11 billion being roughly 10 per cent of the federal budget. Again there was a careful costing, and a detailed proposal outlined precisely where the new tax revenues could be found. One-third of the fund ($4.3 billion) would increase incomes of the working poor, the unemployed, and welfare recipients through a guaranteed annual income. The CPJ proposal has the decided merit of stating that the poor need more — not a popular message in the current political climate, but one that urgently needs to be heard. Other elements of the plan include:

$2.2 billion for job training
$1.7 billion for housing
$1.5 billion for energy conservation and local projects
$1.3 billion for child care

There is little point in quibbling over the relative merits of the two proposals. The similarities are great, and both amply demonstrate what could be done. Both show that a sizeable redirection of resources is feasible, that social justice is affordable in Canada. The CPJ proposal makes the additional political point that a substantial measure of social justice could be achieved *without* raising the deficit. As the need for greater government spending in certain areas will be argued later, it is important to be able to show that the money can be found for it.

While the fact of the new conservative wave cannot be denied, neither should its strength be exaggerated. The new right-wing theoreticians are in fashion; certainly they make good attention-getters in the media. Yet they are up against a solid bedrock of Canadian opinion favourable to the welfare state. In 1985 a substantial 89 per cent of Canadians agreed that "people who are poor have a right to an income adequate to live on."[6] Clearly the New Democratic Party's position on a guaranteed annual income and other social-support measures is not out of line with majority Canadian opinion.

The Deficit

Canada has a record high accumulated deficit of $160 billion in 1986, and a further $32 billion is estimated for the 1986-87 fiscal year. The New Democratic Party has been loath to pronounce on this growing deficit for fear of guilt by association: deficit reduction has usually meant job losses and cuts in social programs. During the Depression, Liberal and Conservative governments were both so fearful of increasing the deficit that they let unemployment rise drastically, without putting money into job creation or unemployment insurance. It was the CCF that urged massive, Keynesian-type public spending, to no avail. In fact, the annual deficit never rose above 4 per cent of GNP in the Depression. By comparison, with less unemployment, it is 7 per cent now.

When Canada entered the Second World War, the government suddenly decided it could spend money it did not have. In the worst year of the Depression, with 19 per cent unemployment, the federal deficit was kept to $154 million, whereas in each of the four years from 1942 to 1945 the deficits averaged $2 billion. In 1944, the last full year of the war, the deficit rose to 23 per cent of GNP, and the economy was thriving. Moreover, the economy continued to expand after the war, again indicating that a high deficit is not necessarily the worst thing in the world.

Nevertheless, a large and growing deficit is a burden for a country to bear, limiting its options for the future. Interest has to be paid at the going rate. (The relatively high deficits of the war years cost less, thanks to lower interest rates. Remember 6 per cent loans?) For 1986-87, simply paying the interest on the accumulated deficit costs a staggering $27 billion — and that is without reducing the principal at all. *Canadians spend more on interest on the public debt than on the entire amount allocated to all universal social programs.* As the deficit is still growing, interest charges will be even higher in future years. This means that either taxes will have to be increased, or spending cut, or some combination of both, *simply to keep up with the interest payments.* If interest rates rise significantly,

TABLE 1

FEDERAL REVENUES AND EXPENDITURES, 1986–87

Revenues (in millions)

Personal Income Tax		$ 37,705
Corporate Income Tax		11,675
Unemployment Insurance Contributions		9,437
Sales Tax		11,700
Customs		4,205
Miscellaneous Taxes		6,838
Non-tax revenue		5,715
	Total	$ 87,275

Expenditures (in millions)

All program expenditures		$ 89,365
Public Debt Interest		27,375
	Total	$116,740
	Deficit	$ 29,465

(**Data from the Department of Finance,** *The Fiscal Plan*, 1986, pp. 31, 54)

so will these charges and, logically, the accumulated deficit. New Democrats should make clear their concern that the deficit be reduced, and state why and how. This is not to suggest deficit reduction at any cost. Limits and the reasons for them should be specified.

A deficit is simply the gap between total revenues and expenditures. Whether it occurs because spending is too high or income too low is a matter of opinion. Determining which should be attacked is a matter of economic and political philosophy. The Conservatives are dissimulating here, explaining the high deficit as the result of excessive spending, yet increasing taxes as a remedy.

Table 1 sets out revenues and expenditures for 1986-87, revealing a $29-billion gap. This itself quickly turned out to be an underestimate. In September 1986, Michael Wilson, the Minister of Finance, published a revised estimate of the 1986-

87 deficit, at $32 billion.[7] What is most striking about the revenue figures is the gross disproportion between personal income taxes and corporate taxes, more than a three-to-one ratio. Thirty years ago, by comparison, the two brought in equal amounts of revenue.

The reduction in corporate taxation has been enormous, and most of it has been effected under Liberal governments. The Conservatives continue to shift the burden from corporations to individuals. You will note also, in Table 1, that sales taxes, a regressive type of tax, now bring in as much revenue as corporate taxes. Yet the myth continues of the onerous tax burden corporations must bear!

A quick glance at the figures in Table 1 also shows that the amount of the deficit, at $29 billion, is almost the same as the interest on the public debt. This is an academic point perhaps, but there would not be much of a deficit if that past debt had not been allowed to rise so high.

Uncollected taxes are another important area to consider, the corollary of tax loopholes and the various give-away schemes that have proliferated in recent years. The Auditor General estimated that these amount to $30-50 billion a year, and that it would cost a million dollars simply to come up with a precise figure! Using data published by the Department of Finance, I estimate corporate and investment give-aways for 1981 at $17 billion, and $3.4 billion for individuals. (These are conservative estimates, since data are missing for many items.) Extrapolating the give-away estimates to 1986, this means at least $22.6 billion in corporate exemptions. To the corporate sector we must also add interest on deferred corporate taxes, which now total about $32 billion. This money is used by corporations as investment capital, in effect becoming an interest-free loan from other taxpayers. At commercial rates of interest, 12 per cent, this adds another $3.8 billion to the corporate give-away bundle, for a grand total of $26.5 billion, as shown in Table 2.[8]

TABLE 2
TAX EXEMPTIONS

(in millions)

Benefits to people through non-taxation of:

$1,000 pension income, veterans pension	$ 205
health premiums, U.I. contributions, CPP/QPP	2,770
lotteries, gambling winnings	405
Total	**$3,380**
inflated to 1986$	$5,180

Benefits to investors/corporations through non-taxation of:

RRSP, RPP, RHOSP, MURB	$ 4,110
capital gains	3,352
resource industry	875
miscellaneous investment	6,024
commodity tax	1,415
small-business exemptions	1,325
Total	**$17,101**
inflated to 1986$	$22,672
12% interest on $32 billion deferred corporate taxes	3,840
Total corporate exemptions	**$26,512**

(Data on exemptions, for 1981, taken from the Department of Finance, *Account of the Cost of Selective Tax Measures*; on accumulated deferred taxes, for 1983, from Statistics Canada, *Corporation Taxation Statistics.*)

Remembering that these figures are underestimates, let us go back to the budget table. *Tax concessions to corporations and investors are more than double the amount collected in corporate income taxes*, $26.5 billion given away in tax exemptions compared with $11.7 billion collected. The corporate give-away total, even with this conservative estimate, comes close to the total deficit. In other words, if government were not so generous in its give-aways to corporations and investors, we would not have a deficit problem. Or, if genuine efforts were made to close the loopholes, we could have *more* money to spend on worthy causes, such as improving the social programs, cleaning up the environment, increasing international

185

aid, developing our own productive capacity, and reducing the accumulated deficit. We do have options.

De-mystifying the Budget

Misrepresentation and exaggeration have been key tools of the Conservatives in attacking our social programs. One of the great services the New Democratic Party renders Canadians is budget de-mystification, and I here offer my own version. We begin by tearing apart the "envelope" system, an innovation of the Trudeau government used by both the Liberal and the Conservative parties to obscure real spending priorities. "Social development" is by far the largest of the six "envelopes", with $54 billion, or 47 per cent of all federal expenditures. Yet "social development" includes running the courts, regulatory agencies, the RCMP, and penitentiaries, screening immigrants, translating documents, obtaining legal advice, wire-tapping by the security service, organizing the civil service and Parliament, and providing salaries and limousines for the Governor General and the provincial lieutenant-governors. These expenditures are not the same kettle of fish as the old age pension, family allowance, or welfare benefits most of us would understand as "social development".

The External Affairs envelope similarly mixes apples and oranges, literally grouping together expenditures on champagne for diplomatic receptions and milk powder and wheat for famine victims. The "aid" budget itself is a misnomer, for most of it is tied to purchases from Canadian companies. Export subsidies are aid to the Canadian private sector rather than what we normally understand to be development aid.

To avoid those, and other, misstatements, federal expenditures have been regrouped by function. Who benefits is the prime criterion, rather than which department spends the money. Some departments are split accordingly. Four distinct functions are recognized, apart from payments on the national

TABLE 3
THE FEDERAL BUDGET, 1986–87

(in millions)

1) running the government

—Armed Forces	$11,569	
—External Affairs (excluding aid, export subsidies, and Immigration)	1,301	
—Courts, police, regulation, legal work, prisons	3,261	
—Tax collection & Finance	3,261	
—Other administrative charges	2,446	
—Parliament	207	$22,326

2) improving productive capacity

—Agriculture	$ 1,730	
—Fisheries & Oceans	555	
—Energy, Mines & Resources (excluding Petroleum Incentive Program)	1,001	
—Environment	745	
—Northern Development	150	
—Public Works	1,383	
—Transport	3,464	
—Science & Technology	734	
—Post-secondary education & research	2,747	
—Employment training & placement	144	$12,659

3) benefits for people

Universal Programs:

—Old Age Pension	$ 9,510	
—Family Allowance	2,531	
—Medicare	6,862	$18,903

Selective Programs:

—Unemployment Insurance	$ 2,901	
—Other medical programs	4,539	
—CAP	4,179	
—GIS and Spouse's Allowance	4,171	
—Sports	118	
—Culture	1,251	
—Post Office	65	
—Community job creation	952	

—International aid	479	
—Indian education, welfare	1,628	
—CMHC	1,608	$21,891
4) benefits to the private sector		
—Consumer & Corporate Affairs	$ 229	
—Regional Industrial Expansion	1,329	
—Employment subsidies	598	
—Export subsidies	1,538	
—Petroleum Incentives Program	950	4,647
5) interest on public debt		27,000
Total Federal Expenditures		**$107,432**

(Data from the Department of Finance, *Main Estimates*, Part II, p.1-19)

debt. There is a further $9.3 billion that cannot be allocated by function. This includes reserves for supplementary estimates, loans, and advances. This $9.3 billion added to the total expenditures of $107.4 billion in Table 3 thus comes to the total expenditures of $116.7 in Table 1.

First there are the usual functions of a national government: maintaining the armed services, the RCMP, the courts, prosecutors and regulatory bodies, the Governor General, the lieutenant-governors, Parliament, and embassies, obtaining legal opinions, screening immigrants, hiring, allocating, and training the civil service, collecting taxes and statistics, and translating documents. The total for all these "state maintenance" functions comes to an impressive $22.3 billion, or more than the amount spent on the universal social programs.

In spite of all its talk about restraint, the Conservative government does not look to this promising area for economies. There have even been budget increases here, in National Defence and in the Prime Minister's own office, travel, and entourage expenses. Prime Minister Mulroney has even ordered a new, and enormously expensive, maximum-security penitentiary for his riding. Under the envelope system, this counts as "social development"!

When the Conservatives try to justify cuts in the social programs, they argue that "cuts have to come from somewhere", and play off job creation against the family allowance. Yet this enormous administrative sector could be a prime target. Does the government need to send so many inter-office memos and hire so many lawyers? Would not the money be better spent on education and welfare than on more prosecutors and prisons? As the case for greater spending in the real social-development area is made later, the possible savings in maintaining the government should be remembered.

Improving Canada's productive capacity is the second category in the new reorganized budget. Many of the expenditures here are also of direct benefit to the private sector, and could easily have been grouped there. None the less, the category is a recognition of the need to build the economic base of the country, hence expenditures on agriculture, fisheries and oceans, energy, mines and resources, transport, public works, the environment, science and technology, post-secondary education and research, job placement and training. The sum for these vital functions is a relatively modest $12.6 billion. *The federal government, in other words, spends only half as much in improving our economic capacity as it does in simply maintaining itself.*

Benefits to people — the "social programs" — is the largest category when both the universal and the non-universal programs are considered. At a grand total of $40.8 billion, this is still less than the $54 billion of the "social development envelope". Note also that the much maligned universal programs, at $18.9 billion, cost slightly less than the total for the selective programs, at $21.9 billion. These sums are themselves overestimates, for a number of the items are immediately taxed back, so that the net cost of the programs would be roughly

20 per cent less on these items. This applies to the old age pension, family allowance, and unemployment insurance.

The universal programs include the old age pension, family allowance and medicare. The selective programs include benefits paid directly by the federal government, in the form of unemployment insurance, the guaranteed income supplement and spouse's allowance, and transfer payments to the provinces for welfare, day care, and other health-care costs. As well there is CMHC, half of the Canada Post subsidy (the other half is treated as a subsidy to business), and payments for medical research, sports, health, welfare and education costs for native people, culture, and development aid (less export subsidies).

This is a lot of money, of course, any way you look at it, but this spending is absolutely necessary if we are to maintain decent standards of health and education, enjoy some measure of Canadian culture, and keep the elderly, the unemployed, and single mothers from living in utter destitution. Conservatives, looking for economies in the social programs, tend to substitute selective programs for the universal. They forget that selective programs need large staffs to administer, diverting money from the people who need it to clerks and investigators, prosecutors and tribunals.

The last sector of expenditures is of most benefit to the private sector, in the form of grants to businesses, export subsidies, and half the postal subsidy. The total spent is a mere $4.6 billion, for, as seen above, most of the benefits to the private sector are given by way of tax exemptions or tax deferrals. Here we see a reversal, for benefits to people are paid overwhelmingly by direct means — usually a cheque in the mail — while tax concessions to individuals are relatively modest. This is so contrary to conventional wisdom that perhaps it needs repeating. *Indirect give-aways to corporations, through tax exemptions and deferrals, are greater than federal tax expenditures on the universal programs,* $26.5 billion versus $18.9 billion. Or, whenever corporations say that we cannot afford the universal programs, it must be remembered that the hidden concessions to them are even greater.

Further, the Conservative government is increasingly using public money to provide subsidies to business. Thus, the summer employment program that previously paid for students' jobs in day-care centres, parks, and various community projects now finances private-sector employers. *Direct* subsidies to business are increasing, and the budget is more and more becoming a means of redistribution of income from individuals to corporations.

Lean, Trim Government?

This is not the place to try to duplicate the admirable work of the Auditor General, who, every year, uncovers government misspending in the hundreds of millions of dollars. Only one example will be given here, to show the scale of economies possible. The 1986 budget for the Solicitor General's Department was nearly $2 billion, of which $760 million was allocated to running the penitentiaries.

The Auditor General identified one source of wasted money in Brian Mulroney's having the new penitentiary slated for Drummondville built instead in his riding. Some $15 million of site work would have to be repeated as a result. Further, the economies planned by sharing services with the penitentiary already in operation in Drummondville would be lost, an estimated $3,000,000 annually. These are the economic costs of political interference, and they have been borne by the taxpayer at least since the time of Sir John A. Macdonald, and his massive spending on Kingston Penitentiary in his riding. There are personal costs as well, borne largely by the inmates, their families, and staff. Academics, church leaders, and other criminal-justice advocates all protested the choice of a penitentiary site in a rural area. The necessary trained personnel are not available there, and family visits are made both onerous

191

and expensive. Here the Conservatives are no worse than the last Liberal government, which had a penitentiary built in just as unlikely an area, Renous, also for political purposes.

The Auditor General identified even more serious waste of public funds through administrative negligence or error. This occurs through the department's decision to expand the number of cells and institutions for inmates rated as needing maximum security. It costs roughly $100,000 per inmate more to build at the maximum-security level than at the medium-security, and $15,000 per inmate more each year in operating costs.[9] Thus, if the department overestimates the need for maximum security by 1,000 inmates, it costs the taxpayer $100 million extra in construction costs and $15 million per year in additional operating costs. By the department's own projections, there will be space by 1992 for 659 more inmates in maximum security in Canada than is needed.

In other words, the debate over where the new penitentiary should be built, whether in the Prime Minister's riding or in a Liberal riding, is entirely misplaced. No new maximum-security institution is needed at all. Nor should the last penitentiary, at Renous, have been built.

The penitentiary at Drummondville similarly is a mistake, at enormous cost to the taxpayer. The institution was built to maximum-security specifications, although it houses only medium-security offenders. This occurred because the local people agreed to have a penitentiary in their area only if it were not a maximum-security one. The Solicitor General's Department apparently accepted this condition, and certainly the institution is described as medium-security in subsequent reports to Parliament on the spending estimates. When the local people found out what had been built, they protested, and the department agreed not to send maximum-security offenders to that institution.

Experts outside the department have warned against its proclivity for building maximum-security prisons over medium-security, for many reasons apart from costs. Here more security is not better, but probably worse. As well as being decidedly more unpleasant institutions for staff and inmates, maximum-security institutions are probably more debilitating for inmates, making social adjustment on release more difficult. Great savings could be made in this department, and better services provided, through more careful budgeting. And discussion here is confined only to the use of medium-security prisons over maximum-security ones. The issue of actually reducing the use of prisons in general is another subject entirely.

The Conservative government uses the rhetoric of lean, trim government, but the reality is quite different. Privatization does not necessarily save money. It may even cost the taxpayer more, as in the case of Crown corporations like De Havilland that have been sold at bargain-basement rates, with guarantees of future government loans or purchases.

In the same way, the Conservative government's policy of contracting out services to the private sector is an illusory cost-saver. Contracting out reduces a department's "person-years", which serves the Conservatives' goal of cutting back on the wicked and wasteful public sector. Yet there is no evidence that this has resulted in any actual savings in any department's budget. Wages and salaries may be reduced, but the firm doing the work has administrative costs to pay and a profit to make. In all the cases I have been able to check, the costs to the department were as high by contracting out as by employing staff directly. Ideology, not efficiency, is served.

In some cases the "privatization" object is preposterous. In 1986, for example, parole officers working for the National Parole Board were told that their jobs were being "privatized", although they would continue to earn the same salaries. This was government policy to "help" the private sector, in this case the John Howard Society, a voluntary organization! Demystification of these false economies must continue to be a task for the New Democratic Party.

New Forms of Public Ownership

So far the New Democratic Party is not on record as favouring any particular version of the European "wage-earner funds". It does advocate a variety of forms of social ownership, including employees and municipalities. Let us here consider how the principles of greater community ownership and control, so strongly recommended by the Jobs Action Group, could be developed in this direction. Union support of any such scheme would be crucial. Recognition of the need is growing as the failure of the private sector to produce sufficient jobs becomes more and more painfully clear. Unions no longer have the option of confining their concerns to wage rates and benefits: job security has become a key issue. As unions have to fight roll-backs and lay-offs, the necessity of alternative strategies to promote job creation is increasingly obvious and much in the unions' interest.

Limited state ownership, through Crown corporations, is accepted in Canada but is not a popular demand. A proposal to direct new investment funds to local job creation could have broad appeal. With the promotion of small new enterprises and local control, people need not fear mindless bureaucracy and Leviathan.

Given the extent of differences between Canada and Europe, the European examples can serve only as very rough models. A great deal of discussion would be required in the unions, the NDP, and the community at large to formulate precise proposals suitable for Canada. I expect that there would be considerable support from churches, unions, voluntary organizations, etc., for opportunities to invest in more enlightened enterprises. There are individuals and organizations with money to invest, who do not wish to lose it, but who would accept a modest return on it in support of a good cause. The move to divestment in South Africa indicates this sort of concern.

Some such wage-earner funds/community development/

investment company would operate in a fashion intermediate between a normal commercial enterprise and a non-profit organization. Obviously it could not lose money in the long run or it would collapse. Yet it would not have to make as great a profit as a normal commercial enterprise, for its investors would have chosen it, at least in part, for other social and economic goals. There would have to be some profit goal between a minimum of only keeping up with inflation to a high of some agreed level of real profit. Clearly the lower the profit goal, the greater the attention that could be paid to other social and economic goals. These other social and economic goals similarly would have to be specified and annual reports prepared assessing success in meeting them.

This new intermediate sector of the economy would serve as a cushion against recession. A company operating with a range of goals, not just that of maximizing profits, can survive bad markets longer. It would not be tempted to relocate in an area with cheaper labour and lower labour standards. Inco may close down one of its operations in response to falling world prices, but the unemployment insurance office, the school board, and most other non-profit organizations do not. A productive enterprise in this intermediate sector would not be as secure as a government agency, but it would be more secure than a regular business enterprise, especially a multinational.

Would such an enterprise be viewed as unfair competition with the private sector? Clearly the private sector would have to be convinced that it would not, or at least be persuaded to accept a degree of such competition. The existence of an intermediate sector would be advantageous to the private sector as well, for this cushion effect. Nearly all businesses suffer in a recession, although some are more vulnerable than others. Since unemployed people do not have much money to spend, demand for nearly all goods and services declines. Just as business has come to realize that unemployment insurance and the family allowance help keep up purchasing power in bad times, so it may see that this new economic sector would play a similar stabilizing role in the nation's economy.

Incomes Policy and/or a Social Contract

Trade unions in Canada, for good historical reasons, have opposed legislated ceilings on wage increases, or any incomes policy in general. In the past, incomes policy has meant wage restraint, whatever else it was called. Trudeau's Anti-Inflation Act, supported by the Conservatives, reduced wages while profits rose. The New Democratic Party, as labour's friend in the House, has respected this reluctance even to discuss incomes policy, as well as fighting specific unfair measures. Any freeze imposed would obviously mean the continuation of current inequities.

Yet the party's refusal to articulate any kind of incomes policy is short-sighted. Clearly a social democratic government will have to have some plans for preventing the inflationary spiral of wage demands under conditions of full employment. Refusal to develop an incomes policy only makes sense if the party expects never to be in office or, once there, never to see the economy operating at or near full employment. The Swedish Social Democrats actually promised lower wages in their 1982 election campaign, with increased old age pensions and child-care allowances. In spite of, or because of, this toughness, they were returned to office, after a term out. Swedish voters knew that some such measures were needed, and they trusted the Social Democratic Party to be both tough and fair. They were, and the party was re-elected again in 1985.

There is, in fact, considerable acceptance of the principle of incomes policy in the Canadian population. The Anti-Inflation Act, which the NDP fought so hard, won majority support before it was passed, and support grew after controls were imposed.[10] Surprisingly, perhaps, there was little difference in support between union members and non-members. Most Canadians considered the controls inevitable.

The NDP is the only party that could credibly propose a new and fair social contract to take into account the results of technological change, especially robotics. Thanks to the overall increase in productivity, a shorter working day or week is becoming both possible and desirable. Yet there has been no such reduction in Canada for decades. For parents of small children, a shorter working day or week could make a real difference in the amount of time they could spend at home. For older workers, a shorter work week would permit more time for leisure, travel, or study instead of the shock of compulsory early retirement. For many workers, once the children are grown up, a sabbatical would be affordable and desirable. In short, all kinds of voluntary work-sharing arrangements not currently in effect are possible. Legislation is needed to encourage the provision of a variety of such voluntary measures, and to require companies to offer them under certain circumstances. A shorter work week should be introduced gradually, and the amount of overtime work curtailed. The right of parents of young children to a shorter working day (or week) should be legislated, as a reform in child-care law as much as for the job-creation opportunities it would make possible. Large employers should be induced, or required, to provide for voluntary job-sharing through sabbaticals, and reduced hours of work in the years before retirement. For more physically demanding and unhealthy jobs, earlier ages of retirement should be established. As the country's largest employers, governments should set an example to private business in introducing such reforms to produce new jobs.

New Democrat economic policy today differs from that of the original CCF in being far more eclectic and experimental. The party no longer asserts that any particular theory is correct, proved by science, or revealed by God. Nor is there any suggestion that any particular economic order is inevitable. The unfolding of a predetermined history is simply not believed any more, for too many expectations have been disappointed. Two world wars and a major depression have not brought on the new age. The conditions of present life give even less cause for confidence in any precise prediction.

If now less sure about any particular predictions, Canadian social democrats have more to argue from experience. When the CCF was founded in the early 1930s, European social democrats were just beginning to come into office. Europe has now witnessed half a century of social democratic governments, and there are many positive examples to cite. The Canadian New Democratic Party no longer has to refer to purely hypothetical alternatives. The measures it proposes have been tried in other countries. Economic growth is higher, and unemployment lower, where social democratic governments have held office. High standards of health care, education, and social services have been attained, with a high degree of personal liberty, thriving political debate, and civility.

The Voluntary Sector

A distinctive feature of Canadian society is the strength and vitality of its voluntary organizations. They are active in direct service, public education, and the advocacy of new programs and policies. Government recognizes the importance of their contribution by consulting them — with increasing frequency — and funding them — although with decreasing generosity. Voluntary organizations of a charitable or an educational nature receive indirect government support by being able to issue receipts to contributors for income tax deductions. Groups that actively lobby for change are excluded, however, as being political. The government then turns around and offers them support by a different means, through grants. Virtually all federal departments have some kind of grant system for voluntary organizations active in their field. Thus, ironically, government funds its own lobbyists. Groups duly apply, stating their lobbying proposals to justify their planned expenditures. The government then evaluates groups on the success of their programs!

There are two basic faults in this system. First, the amount of money allocated to the voluntary sector is too low, so that groups have to spend an inordinate amount of time and energy in raising money through other means as well as from government. Second, government ties the hands of advocacy groups by not permitting them to give tax deductions for donations. The grotesque anomaly of the government's deciding how much support its lobbyists will receive compounds the irony.

In the arts, for example, the Department of Communications funds its major lobbyist, the Canadian Conference of the Arts, as well as many of the smaller advocacy groups. Individual grants range from a low of $3,500 to a high of $115,000. In a reversal of the singing-for-your-supper practice, government pays for dinners for which the organization provides the audience, and the minister is the guest speaker. A quite different approach to funding is clearly needed, and so is more support. The New Democratic Party has supported greater funding, and better methods of providing it, through such measures as a tax credit. My own proposal goes somewhat further than party policy. People would decide which advocacy organizations they wish to support, and the government's role would be confined to the bookkeeping. A certain amount of support would be specified, perhaps as a percentage of GNP or of the federal budget. The voluntary sector could then look forward to support as a matter of course, instead of having to make new applications to the government every year. By this arrangement, Canadians themselves would decide the amount of funding for each group, by filling out their tax return. Each adult resident would be allocated a certain sum to be directed to the organizations of his or her choice. The organizations themselves would have to be registered in the same way that charities now are, except that advocacy work should not bar them from such registration. Any person not choosing to allocate the specified sum would forfeit it.

Voluntary organizations would have to make their pitch directly to the general public rather than file grant applications with the government. Small groups might combine to share the proceeds, as charities do now for United Appeal drives. This proposed method would be far simpler to administer than the present system. It would make some bureaucrats' jobs unnecessary. Most importantly, it would put control — of a small area of expenditures — in the hands of those who should have that control: the public.

7
NOT BY BREAD ALONE

Elections are not necessarily, if ever, won on the basis of core economic strategy. Tommy Douglas ran his first election campaign as a series of lectures on social and economic structure, complete with charts. He lost, and never tried that again. The New Democratic Party cannot neglect economic strategy, but it cannot rely on it as a major vote-winner. Most people are more interested in issues that have a more immediate impact on them, like gasoline prices, pornography at the corner store, day-care places, extra billing, and even tobacco smoke in the workplace. The new "yuppie" voters, often the sons and daughters of blue-collar workers, trade unionists, and traditional NDP supporters, have also to be considered.

Health

The party that brought Canada medicare is now proposing the de-institutionalization of the health-care system. Canada's medicare system is excellent by world standards, but there are gaps and inconsistencies. The most expensive services — doctors and hospitals — are the most accessible, but more coverage of home care and preventive services is needed. The system's partiality to institutions over other services results in higher costs, without necessarily giving patients the best care possible. Hospitals cost approximately $90,000 per bed to build and $100 a day to operate. Yet the patient may prefer to be at home aided by a visiting nurse. More such options should be available, including nurse practitioners, home support services, home birthing, and community health clinics. The beauty of this proposal is that a better range of services would actually cost less money. Canadians could have more of what they want, be healthier, and save money.

New Democrat health-care policy is already moving in this direction. The Ontario party made home care a concern in the 1985 provincial election. New Democrat governments in Saskatchewan and Manitoba have both pioneered such services. The federal caucus proposed amendments to the Canada Health Act to give it greater flexibility. Joint federal/provincial funding for these services, as for other medical items, is needed throughout the country. The same federal funding should be provided for these important services as is now available for hospitals and doctors' services.

The drama of open-heart surgery and organ transplants should not distract us from the real issues of *health* care. Preventive measures and good nutrition will save more lives than any foreseeable improvements in actual medical technology. Since the great infectious diseases have been beaten, the big killers are tobacco, booze, and the debris of a high-tech "civilization" in dioxins and nuclear wastes. As public-health threats they require different kinds of control than viruses — vaccination does not work — but they are not beyond our present reach.

In September 1986 Brian Mulroney announced that Canada suffered the same "epidemic" of drug use as the United States. He was even prepared to follow President Reagan in establishing compulsory urine tests for federal public servants. Unfortunately, he had in mind only the use of illegal drugs, not the more lethal legal drugs: tobacco (35,000 Canadians a year) and alcohol (12,000 Canadians a year).

Tobacco is the most flagrant cause of unnecessary deaths, including an estimated thousand per year who are not themselves smokers but who are forced to breathe secondary smoke. Canadians are more likely to be killed by someone else's cigarette smoke than by murder. Tobacco users pay $3 billion a year to governments in taxes, but cost their fellow taxpayers more than $8 billion in additional medicare costs, fire losses, and so forth. Multinational tobacco companies are permitted to make great profits, and society at large foots the bill for the consequences. Surely this is a problem on which a social democratic party should have something to say!

The Canadian public is ready for action on this issue. Most smokers themselves would like to quit. Many recognize the secondary-smoke problem, and support better protection for non-smokers at work and in public places. The "right to smoke" has been replaced by the "right to clean air". No one, except the tobacco companies, is pleased that the average age of first-time smokers has dropped to twelve years. Everybody is offended by tobacco advertisements blatantly appealing to young people. What is needed is a comprehensive program to discourage all tobacco use, and protect the non-smoking majority from the side effects until the habit — not the addict — dies. The right to a smoke-free workplace should be legislated. So should the public's right to travel, shop, or visit Parliament and their MP without danger to their health from tobacco smoke. Tobacco advertising should be phased out, including sports and cultural sponsorships. Money the federal Department of Agriculture now spends on encouraging tobacco farming should go to crop substitution. The Agriculture department's periodical, *The Lighter*, should be put out. Export subsidies to Canadian producers selling surplus tobacco to Third World countries should not be permitted. Tax money from cigarette sales should go into advertising against the habit, and programs for prevention and quitting, as well as for crop substitution, should be devised.

The federal caucus actually has adopted a comprehensive tobacco control policy, but support for it is mixed. This is an issue on which provincial action is needed as well, but no provincial party or caucus has yet shown any leadership.

So long as smokers are not vilified, but understood as victims of addiction, measures to protect non-smokers need not offend the one-third of the population that now inconveniences and irritates its fellows. Twenty per cent of Canadians suffer from conditions aggravated by tobacco smoke, from cystic fibrosis, emphysema, and heart conditions to wearing contact lenses. The party that fights for occupational health and safety should also combat the major pollutant at the workplace.

My own experience of working on the issue is that it is popular. It consistently draws more and better correspondence than traditional New Democrat subjects. The people who respond, moreover, are the party's natural constituency: old age pensioners unable to use inter-city buses because they are smoky, and workers out of a job because they can only work in a smoke-free environment. Smoking is more prevalent among blue-collar workers than among white-collar, which means that the need for protection is greater yet for non-smoking workers.

Alcohol-related diseases come second on the list of preventable health problems. They have received a great deal of attention, but government policy has consistently focussed more on difficult and expensive cures than on prevention. The one great social experiment regarding prevention, of course, was prohibition. Contrary to what is generally believed, prohibition in Canada as a public-health measure was a great success. Consumption declined, and with it, alcohol-related diseases and deaths. It was the lucrative black market, making organized crime a growth industry, that made prohibition such a failure.

Prohibition would hardly be a feasible strategy today, but other, vigorous, preventive measures should be undertaken. For a start, there should be a complete ban on alcohol advertising and promotion. More effective enforcement, and not just stiffer penalties, should be developed to curtail drunk driving. For alcohol use, as for tobacco, the issue is one of quality of life and not just one of statistics. Better preventive methods would reduce health-care costs, save lives, and spare many families incalculable suffering.

Women

The New Democratic Party has great credibility on women's issues and is building on this strength. The party already recognizes the need to do more for "traditional" women, full-time homemakers. Its work on equal pay for work of equal value, affirmative action, maintenance, and child care is strong. Yet for a large number of Canadian women these reforms will have little impact.

The chief reason for the poverty of elderly widows in Canada is the lack of a pension for homemakers. Like all persons over sixty-five years of age, homemakers receive the basic old age pension, and many are eligible as well for the income-tested guaranteed income supplement. Otherwise they depend on their late husbands' incomes. Elderly widows are likely to be poor, since most employer-sponsored schemes offer no survivor's benefit. For those that do, the amount is usually set at 50 per cent or 60 per cent of the wage earner's pension. Divorced homemakers are normally ineligible, and a widowed homemaker loses the pension if she remarries. Even the survivor's benefit under the CPP/QPP is only 60 per cent of the full pension, while if the wage earner is the survivor, the pension remains at 100 per cent. For a divorced spouse, the best that can be expected is 50 per cent of the earning spouse's pension, pro-rated according to the number of years of the marriage.

The New Democrat approach to pension reform for women has been to rely on improving the level of CPP/QPP benefits, and then splitting the pension in half. If the CPP/QPP were doubled, this would mean considerably better pensions for homemakers, assuming no divorce, especially for those whose husbands earned comfortable or high incomes. Since approximately one-third of Canadian marriages today end in divorce, a large number of women would still be left badly provided for. *All* women should be included in the CPP/QPP, *in their own names*. A homemakers' pension would recognize the importance of work done in the home. Pensions for women, as for men, should be a recognition of contribution, and not a mark of financial dependency.

The present pension-splitting approach is unfair also in being a regressive measure, forcing lower-paid workers to pay for benefits received largely by the better-paid. By not requiring married earners to pay additional contributions for the survivor's benefit, unmarried workers are in effect paying this subsidy. The real losers are unmarried women, who are generally underpaid in the work force to begin with, and who lose 15 per cent of their pensions to subsidize survivor's benefits for the spouses of their better-paid male colleagues. Any reform to increase survivor's benefits would *increase* the subsidies, and thus the unfairness. The better answer is to provide adequate pensions for both the employee and the homemaker spouse, with contributions charged to all those who can afford to pay them. The only subsidies should be to those who cannot afford to pay, as single-parent homemakers. These people are now excluded from the Canada/Quebec Pension Plan altogether.

There is broad support in Canadian society for homemakers to be included in the CPP/QPP. A 1982 survey showed 77 per cent of Canadians in favour of the reform. By 1986, support had increased to 82 per cent and is probably still rising. The NDP continues to oppose this measure, on the grounds that the Canadian Labour Congress is opposed to it, one of the few progressive measures the CLC does not support. Yet here both the CLC and the NDP are out of touch with most of their membership. The same survey that showed 77 per cent of Canadians supporting the homemakers showed an even higher proportion — 79 per cent — in households with a union member than in non-union households at 75 per cent.

When the New Democratic Party recommends systematic pension-splitting for all pensions, it is recognizing the equal contribution of both spouses to the family. This position is consistent with the new family-property laws of the provinces, which consider the contribution of unpaid services in child care and housekeeping the equivalent of earning a wage or salary. The next logical step is the equalizing of incomes during the couple's working years as well as on retirement. This would mean that the homemaker spouse would have an income on which she, or he, could depend. The sharing of financial decision-making would become the norm. The homemaker spouse would no longer be a dependant, and both spouses would share in the financial benefits of their partnership, as both would contribute to their creation. The vows in the marriage service could even become, partially, realizable. "With all my worldly goods I thee endow" was always fictional, but "half my pay cheque will be thine alone" could actually happen.

For a party committed to a greater measure of equality, this proposal has obvious merit. Whether or not the public is ready is obviously a matter to investigate. Many couples already practise some form of income-sharing. In cases where both partners have a job, normally the wife is paid much less, and normally she does most of the housekeeping and child-care work at home. Income-splitting means recognition of her additional unpaid work in the home, which permits her husband to give more time to his career. With pension-splitting to become the rule on retirement, couples will have to work out ways of managing their joint income. Why should they not start earlier, or why should wives have to wait until they are sixty-five to get recognition for their work?

In its policies on child care, the New Democratic Party advocates a range of possible choices, all of which assume that responsibility should be shared by the parents and the community. In 1970, the Royal Commission on the Status of Women concluded that mothers should have the option of looking after their children at home, regardless of their financial circumstances. The New Democratic Party has made the same recommendation. To make this option possible would require a number of changes in present social policy. Community child-care services would have to be extended and improved. More options for parents to share child care in the home must also be provided. The right of both parents of young children to a shorter work week should be legislated, one point raised in the previous chapter. A homemakers' pension and income-splitting would facilitate the care-at-home choice.

Again, surveys show strong public approval for publicly supported child care along the lines proposed by New Democrats. A study commissioned by the Canadian Union of Public Employees found that the most preferred option by far, with 61 per cent support, was to fund child-care centres run by voluntary non-profit organizations. Only 16 per cent of Canadians wanted child-care centres to be run directly by government, while the least popular option, at 13 per cent, was for privately run centres that are run for profit. A hefty 75 per cent of Canadians today rate child care as an important issue for government. The Conservatives' reluctance to make child care a higher priority, and to ensure its adequate funding, demonstrates that it is out of touch with what Canadians want.[1]

Poverty and Homelessness

Shameful as is the poverty of elderly women in Canada, there are men and women of all ages who are worse off. Following a long period of government inattention to affordable housing, the recession has created a new group of urban homeless. Some are former psychiatric patients, released from large, impersonal institutions, who have nowhere to go. Others are alcoholics. Some are normal working adults who have lost their jobs and have run out of unemployment insurance. Some are young people who have never found that first job. A growing number are women. For all of them the "welfare state" does not provide help. Temporary shelters, food banks, and soup kitchens keep most of them alive. Some agencies provide counselling, group support, and practical help to commence a job search. But, fundamentally, overnight hostels and food depots are a condemnation of us all. That they exist also in a province run by a New Democrat government, Manitoba, is more shameful still. This unhappy fact also suggests the difficulty of attacking the problem at only one level of government. Clearly, co-operation between all three levels is necessary.

Many of the social security measures proposed by the New Democratic Party would reduce the number of people living in poverty. These programs include a guaranteed annual income, an old age pension at age sixty for the unemployed, and a vigorous program to build affordable housing. Now is the time for the party to go further, and launch a direct campaign against homelessness. From the beginning, the party has declared decent housing a *right* for all. Party policy needs no changing, but the issue should be given higher priority.

The housing problem would be relatively easy to solve. The number of homeless is not large, and the money required to house them is wholly manageable. This is, after all, Canada in the late 1980s, not Europe after the Second World War. The federal government already spends far more with its tax giveaways on housing for the wealthy than an entire program would require.

That a problem so solvable is not a serious item on the political agenda tells us something about the broader political climate in Canada. We are not as mean as Mrs. Thatcher's Britain and we do not have the deterioration of Reagan's America, not even pro-rated one-tenth. Nevertheless, Reaganomics and Thatcherism have made justice and decency bad politics. Doing something for people who cannot help themselves does not seem "sensible" at the present. Good public policy, it is said, is stimulating investment. When there is enough investor confidence, the economy will expand again, and the unemployed find work. Yet the market will never build enough low-cost housing when there is more money to be made in luxury condominiums.

Politically the problem is that the poorest people do not form organizations, lobby, or even vote. For a party to take up their cause requires great commitment. The churches and voluntary organizations that now serve Canada's most destitute citizens are becoming politically more astute. They are not only making moral pronouncements, but they are beginning to lobby. The New Democratic Party has natural allies here for such a campaign.

This is not to suggest that the party will be rewarded at the polls for its efforts, although that is just barely possible. It should take up the cause because it is right to do so, in the same way that the party has taken up other seemingly hopeless causes in the past. Health care was a private responsibility in the past, meaning that if you could not afford it you had to do without, or take what charity would provide. Housing for all should be regarded in precisely the same way. It should become as unthinkable for a poor person to sleep on the street as it now is for a poor person to be denied a hospital bed. And, comparatively speaking, the housing problem of today is easier to solve than establishing medicare was several decades ago.

Criminal Justice

Curiously the CCF/NDP has never been as radical on matters of criminal justice as it has been on economic justice. As well, in its early years the CCF was not sceptical enough of the possibility of rehabilitating criminals. As a result, with the best of intentions it ended up supporting repressive measures it should not have. For example, in the prison classification system in Saskatchewan there were more categories of woman prisoner than there were actual women prisoners! On the other hand, the party's stance on civil liberties has always been good, thus moderating its tendency to intervention for the subject's own good.

The party has been slow to understand the community's response to law and order, and has been outmanoeuvred by the Conservatives as a result. There is a "law and order" current in Canada, although never so extreme as in Britain or the United States. People are fearful of "rising crime", although crime, to the best of our knowledge, is not rising. People worry about "violence in the streets", although they are at greater risk of physical attack from someone they know than from a stranger. These fears are one of the unhappy effects of watching television — especially American television. Some people think we have crime in the American style, and at American rates; most fortunately do not.

The party that has fought so hard for individual rights must now develop a better understanding of collective rights and devise policy to ensure them. This is not to advocate abandoning its traditional respect for due process and civil liberties, which are now well guaranteed by the Charter of Rights, and usually well enforced by the courts. It is simply to say that those battles have been largely won and new concerns have arisen.

Individual rights are now being cited in attacks on collective rights. The recent attacks on unions, for example, are based on the individual's "right" not to pay dues to a union. If these attacks are successful, unions could be confined to a narrow economic role, and unable to take up broader issues of social and economic justice. Churches are afraid that they could be required to perform homosexual marriage ceremonies if the state recognizes an individual right to equal services without discrimination. Clearly collectivities like churches and unions are part of our social fabric, and their rights need to be protected as well.

Victims' rights have not been sufficiently heeded. Pornography is a threat to people's right to security, and to women's rights to equality with men. Communities feel unable to control their own law enforcement, and they want more say in how they are policed. Drunk drivers kill more people every year than do murderers, and the public's demand for a clamp-down is entirely reasonable. The New Democratic Party should treat these as serious and legitimate concerns and not look down on their proponents as lacking in commitment to civil liberties.

The Canadian criminal justice system is grossly over-built. There are literally too many prisons, and the system is badly deficient in preventive measures and low-key methods of dealing with crime. Since maximum-security institutions are so enormously expensive, a reduction in their use could free up money for more effective methods of crime control. As with medicare, a better justice system would have the additional merit of costing less. The party could even advocate greater *privatization* of the criminal justice system. Where punishment is the object, the state has the responsibility to administer it. Where treatment and help rather than control are required, a good case can be made for greater involvement of the voluntary agencies.

Canadians are not a particularly punitive people. It is true that a majority want to bring back capital punishment, but most people would insist on so many safeguards that it would scarcely if ever be used. People are badly misinformed as to the nature and extent of crime and the punishments typically meted out to offenders. Most Canadians think that punishments are much lighter than they in fact are. Asked if penalties should be tougher, they say yes. Asked what the punishment should be for a particular crime, most will choose one lighter than what the courts usually hand out. Most Canadians support considerably less use of prisons.[2]

The party has given some leadership to the fight against pornography, but in my view it could do more. Evidence of the effect of violent pornography in encouraging violence against women and children is growing. There is even increasing evidence of a similar effect from non-violent, merely degrading, pornography. The women's movement is now persuasively arguing that pornography is an abuse of women's right to equality. Women who are portrayed as abject, servile sluts, revelling in their degradation, are patently not men's equals. Yet there is still, among some party members, a greater commitment to the right of pornographers to free expression than to the right of their victims to security and dignity. The Charter of Rights guarantees not only freedom of expression but also the right to life and security of the person, and equal rights to men and women. Where choices have to be made, the party should be strong and clear that people's right to physical security, and women's right to equality, must take precedence over the pornographer's "right" to sell abusive material.

Concern for victims of crime is a major new area for reform in the criminal justice system. The New Democrat government in Manitoba has led in introducing measures where the provinces have jurisdiction, but federal legislation is needed as well. Criminal Code changes are required to facilitate compensation for victims.

The party should support measures for reducing punishments and the excessive use of the courts for minor matters. This applies especially to northern communities, where the over-use of jails, particularly for natives, has been routine. In policing, training and research in crime prevention, and keeping the peace, need to be stressed.

Drunk driving should be attacked comprehensively, with a ban on alcohol advertising, rather than just the threat of higher penalties. Communities, through their representatives, should be consulted on their priorities for policing.

The most radical new approach to criminal justice has come from the churches. Prison abolition is undoubtedly too radical a goal for any political party, but many of the other reconciliation proposals would be eminently feasible. A few experiments are under way in Canada, although these are confined to the less serious offenders. The approach has the merit of making a complete break with the traditional retribution model. As Gandhi pointed out, the product of "an eye for an eye and a tooth for a tooth" is a world of blind, toothless people. Measures for compensation for the victim and reconciliation between victim and offender could achieve real security. People would feel safer knowing that the criminal in question would not continue to commit crimes. Punishment alone cannot achieve that security. The restoration of harmony in a community must be the object.

While the New Democratic Party has been by far the best defender of individual rights — especially when it has hurt to do so — the Conservatives have lately managed to appear as the great defenders of individualism. In an era of "me first" and "looking out for Number 1", the rhetoric of individualism can score points. Yet Conservatives and Liberals have tended to have a poor understanding of the relation of the individual to society. Both would see us as isolated atoms on a vast frontier. Both Conservatives and Liberals see freedom as individual opportunity in the absence of social restraint. For social democrats this is impossible. Even the people on the farthest frontiers had their suppliers, traded with others, and were sometimes rescued by the Indians from starvation and disease. On the Canadian frontier they also had a police force. The lone frontiersman was always a myth, and is even less credible today.

The very evolution of the word "freedom" supports the social democratic understanding of community. In English, German, and Dutch, "freedom", "free", "frei", and "frij" come from the same roots as "friend", "Freund", and "vriend". *The free person is the one with friends, not the person with no ties at all.* The case is even stronger with the Latin roots, where "libido" and "liberty" share a common origin. The pouring out of love makes

214

for liberty; independence and isolation do not. New Democrats should here challenge the Conservatives' fraudulent claims.

It is no coincidence that the countries with many years of social democratic governments enjoy low rates of crime, especially of violent crime. High crime rates are the natural corollary of other values, when cut-throat competition becomes just that. Yet there is a real risk that the Conservatives will try to ride to another election victory on a law-and-order tide. Especially if unemployment and the deficit remain high, the government may be tempted to assume the role of defenders of law and order. In the summer of 1986 they stooped to recalling Parliament to pass a bill on mandatory supervision of ex-inmates, in the guise of keeping the streets safe for law-abiding citizens. Mulroney followed Ronald Reagan in making an "epidemic" out of drug abuse and even suggested the possibility of compulsory urine tests for public servants. A debate on capital punishment might be seen as a convenient vote-getter, especially if the Conservatives continue to look bad as economic managers, or scandals continue to raise doubts about the Prime Minister's honesty and integrity.

Cultural Policy

The New Democratic Party has considerable credibility in cultural policy — and not just owing to the prodigious cutbacks, mistakes, interference, and general shortsightedness of the other two parties in the arts. The New Democratic Party is the only party in Canada to have articulated a comprehensive cultural policy. Specifically the party supports adequate funding for the CBC, sufficient funding that commercials can be gradually phased out of television, and second channels, English and French, can be opened. To keep the CBC from being so vulnerable to political pressure, its funding should be fixed as a percentage of the federal budget; the Fowler Commission recommended 1 per cent some years ago. The NDP has long supported increased funding for the Canada Council as the main agency for support of writing, composing, and the visual arts.

None of this is unrealistic, and in fact all of it makes good economic sense. Since arts expenditures are such a small part of the federal budget, even a doubling of the present funding is entirely practicable. Since arts expenditures create jobs at six times the rate of investment in manufacturing, the money can also be justified as the most effective economic stimulus. Happily, opinion surveys show there is strong public support for increased arts expenditures.

Peace and Disarmament

The New Democratic Party has been a conscientious and lucid voice for peace and nuclear disarmament in the House of Commons and in public forums across the country wherever the issues are raised. In so far as Canada has maintained an independent stance in foreign policy, distancing itself from the United States, the party deserves much of the credit. External Affairs critic Pauline Jewett has done distinguished service in raising the critical questions and pointing to a better way.

Peace groups in the community play an important role, but their very credibility is affected by what is said, and not said, in Parliament. Without the New Democrats raising issues in Question Period, peace and disarmament would have little public profile. Without the New Democrat members of committee ensuring that disarmament experts and peace advocates are invited to hearings, the debate would be one-sided indeed. While the Liberals are in opposition, they play more of a peace advocacy role than when in government, but this should not fool anyone. The Liberals set up the "defence sharing" agreements with the United States under which cruise missile components are manufactured in Canada. It was the Liberals who approved cruise testing. Their current opposition to the

216

NOT BY BREAD ALONE

American Star Wars program is suspect and opportunistic. So too is the Conservatives' rejection of official participation in Star Wars while allowing participation by the back door.

If the NDP is to be faulted for its work on peace and disarmament, it can only be for not giving the issues more prominence. Unfortunately, virtuous foreign policy has never been a great vote-getter in Canada, but I believe that in this case the risk has to be taken. Where the issues are so important, the party must do what it can to inform the public and encourage greater involvement. There is doubtless some potential for votes, for the number of people concerned about peace and disarmament is growing, but most are still voting for the old-line parties. Attracting such people away from their bad habits of voting Liberal and Conservative will not be easy, but the effort must be made.

The party's anti-NATO and anti-NORAD positions, of course, do not have majority support in the population, but the common ground between NDP policy and public opinion is probably much greater than is thought. It is Mulroney's excessive deference to the Americans that is out of step with Canadians' aspirations for greater independence in foreign policy. According to a study commissioned by External Affairs,[3] more than two-thirds (69 per cent) of Canadians agree that Canada should pursue its own independent policies, even if this leads to certain problems in our relations with the United States. More than three-quarters (79 per cent) want a higher priority given the efforts to maintain the peace between East and West, and to reduce the level of armaments. Almost as many Canadians (76 per cent) agree also that the arms race is a product of competition between two powerful countries, not of ideology. Reagan's view of world affairs has little credence in Canada.

The Environment

New Democrats deserve an easier conscience on environmental

questions than do Conservatives or Liberals, but only to a degree. The plain truth is that the party's commitment to jobs and growth makes it sometimes cavalier on environmental issues. The party does not take political donations from corporations that pollute, or from those that do not, for that matter. Nor is it tied by ideology to defending the corporate sector. It has, then, a potential for being a friend of the earth, and of future generations, in a way no other party has. Neither trees nor future generations vote, of course, and people threatened by job losses in environmentally sensitive areas do. The result is that the NDP has been a voice for the environment up to a point, but it could be saying more.

Alex Macdonald, former New Democrat Attorney General of British Columbia, has pointed out how successfully Social Credit used the party's environmentalist conscience against it for votes. He is amongst those who think the party does too much on environmental issues. Indeed, in his most delightful book of advice to a young social democrat, *My Dear Legs*, he chides environmentalists as "romantics" who put ecosystems ahead of "the only creature that can look before and after".[4] Yet Canadians are becoming increasingly environmentally conscious. Their views on the causes of, and solutions to, pollution increasingly resemble the New Democratic Party's own. Two-thirds (67 per cent) believe that acid rain is largely the fault of American corporations. Neither the Conservatives nor the Liberals deny this, but both downplay this key point. As many as 81 per cent of Canadians consider that we are "losing control over the quality of our environment".[5]

The differences between the NDP and the other parties on the domestic use of nuclear power are significant. The Liberal government of Ontario in 1986, after Chernobyl and against NDP advice, decided to go ahead with construction of the Darlington nuclear plant. Its grounds were that so much money had already been spent on it, a justification that could be used equally well for not taking thalidomide off the market! Conservative and Liberal politicians responded to the Chernobyl disaster with fast, even glib, denials that anything like it could ever happen in Canada. The similarities in design and safety precautions between Canadian and Soviet plants were ignored. The New Democrat reaction was more thoughtful. The federal caucus set up a public inquiry on the subject, including consideration of a totally non-nuclear future for the country.

Social democratic parties ignore the environment issue at their peril. If the New Democratic Party does not take up environment issues seriously, it risks competition from the new Green Party. A Green Party has been established federally, and has begun to run candidates. As yet it has not been a threat to the NDP, but one suspects that the few votes it does get so far come from disgruntled New Democrats. The Green Party has done devastating damage to the Social Democratic Party of West Germany, but then no party deserved it more. The Swedish Social Democrats were outflanked by the Liberal Party on nuclear policy, but learned their lesson faster than the West Germans. (Sweden is now committed to phasing out all nuclear plants.) In Austria the Social Democratic government has held up the opening of a nuclear-power generator at the insistence of its *Liberal* coalition partner.

The conflict between industrial development and the environment involves profound differences in conception of what is right for a community, as well as differences in interests. Obviously, in the long run, there are limits to growth. At some point, societies will have to learn how to function without GNP increasing every year. Political parties will have to develop appeals to voters based on goals other than expansion. The question is when, and perhaps the NDP can only pray, with St. Augustine, "God make me pure, but not yet."

Within the party there is at least the potential for the Green debate, and a Green Caucus. The party can play the educational role in the country on environment issues that it has played historically on the social programs and civil rights. New

Democrats already work with environmental groups, bringing their concerns to Parliament and their advocates to committee. The more the party does this, the better. Moreover, if the NDP does not, no one will, for the Green approach by itself is too narrow. The issues of peace and disarmament, the environment, and social justice must be dealt with in an integrated way. Environmentalists themselves have become increasingly aware that their concerns cannot be met while the arms race and the quest for ever higher profits go on. Environmentalists with a social conscience realize the unfairness of zero GNP growth for those people with unmet material needs. If gains for the poor cannot be met through such growth, then questions of distribution of income and wealth again become pertinent. Thus, concerns for the environment, peace, the economic order, and social justice all converge, and dovetail on social democracy.

International Affairs

In discussing peace and nuclear disarmament in Chapter 3, I have already made the point that the party must continue to argue its case, educate the public, and hope to encourage people concerned with these issues to vote accordingly. Other important areas of foreign policy are human rights and Third World development. The party's record as an advocate of human rights, especially in Latin America, is admirable. It has even had some success in keeping Canada's policy distinctive from that of the United States. It must continue to be a voice for these countries, and become a more vigorous advocate for them. Canada, for example, has all too often been silent on American use of the International Monetary Fund to further its own political objectives. Canada ignominiously followed the United States in banning imports of Nicaraguan beef, one of the few opportunities that impoverished country had to earn foreign exchange. If the NDP will not voice these concerns in Parliament, who will?

The New Democratic Party continues to work for decent development aid policy. Under the Liberals the Canadian International Development Agency began the policy of requiring that 80 per cent of aid money be spent on Canadian purchases. A promise to allow developing countries to bid on Canadian aid projects was subsequently made, but not acted on. This "tied aid" policy has been continued under the Conservatives, despite concerted pressure from the churches and voluntary aid agencies. The Conservatives have gone even further — cancelling previously announced increases in aid and diverting more funds to the promotion of Canadian business. The new Export Development Program means that the poorest countries will be excluded because they cannot afford the Canadian purchases required. Nor will this "aid to business" approach be successful in promoting Canadian exports in the long run. Other countries, with Thatcher's Britain leading the way, have shown that companies that cannot compete abroad without government subsidies cannot compete with them either. The disadvantage to the recipient country only begins with the 20 per cent higher costs incurred through having to buy the "donor's" products. Projects selected to benefit Canadian business happen to be in sectors that skew development in the wrong direction. Countries that need to improve agriculture are encouraged instead to buy equipment for urban electrification or telecommunications. Countries with a labour surplus are "given" labour-saving devices. Major aid experts now go so far as to say that Canadian aid is adding to the problem, not helping in the solution.

Canadians like to think they are generous in international aid, and the Conservatives should not get away so easily with their cuts. Social democratic countries, like Sweden, have maintained higher levels of aid even with the recession. That Canada should further reduce its modest assistance, which is now below 0.7 per cent of GNP, is reprehensible. As to the number of votes to be gained on human-rights and development issues, I would not care to guess. There are at least as many, I suspect, as there are in protesting interest-rate rises and plant shut-downs, always after the fact.

The New Democrat position on development aid, in fact, has strong public support. As many as 81 per cent of Canadians consider it to be a moral responsibility to help other countries. Nearly as many, 72 per cent, support the party's position, and that of voluntary organizations, that aid should not be tied to purchases from Canadian businesses. Only 12 per cent of Canadians share the Conservative and Liberal goal of increased sales of Canadian goods as a proper motive for aid. These data, incidentally, were collected in a study commissioned by the Department of External Affairs itself.[6]

Graft and Sleaze

New Democrats in government have been remarkably efficient, thrifty, and honest. Contrary to the conventional wisdom, it is the Liberals and Conservatives who are the big spenders — on executive jets, public-relations consultants, advertising contracts, and cushy jobs for their friends. None of this is appreciated by the public, which is not so cynical as to have stopped caring. The Conservatives and the Liberals like to accuse the New Democrats of not being any different, but of merely lacking opportunity. The provincial record suggests otherwise. The government of Tommy Douglas could not be bought, nor could those of Woodrow Lloyd, Alan Blakeney, Ed Schreyer, Dave Barrett, or Howard Pawley. In Ontario the NDP made cleaning up patronage appointments a condition of its support for a Liberal government in 1985. In British Columbia the NDP's Disclosure Act has enabled some control of ministerial conflict-of-interest situations. In Saskatchewan the CCF introduced fair purchasing procedures by government, with a strict system of tendering. In fairness it must be said that since the New Democratic Party accepts no political donations from corporations, it can have hardly anything to gain from a system of graft.

The NDP has more to gain than any other party by clean elections with low expenses. Specifically, a political reform package should include

— lowered limits on spending by the parties
— full disclosure of party spending between elections as well as during
— a ban on corporate donations to any party
— a ban on donations from outside Canada
— a ceiling on individual donations

Tendering for government contracts should be routine. In line with what people think is current practice, but is not, the tendering system should be extended to all but inconsequential amounts. The New Democratic Party could set an example by undertaking, on election, to reduce government advertising substantially, say to a quarter of the current level.

Regarding government appointments to boards and commissions, a completely new system is needed. Not all existing boards are useful and some could be eliminated completely. The system should be de-politicized as far as possible. Qualifications for the positions should be publicly stated, and organizations in the area concerned should be invited to nominate candidates. A government is entitled to appoint people with policy views consistent with its intentions, but this need not require that board members hold a party card. A substantial proportion of the appointments should go to people with no political affiliation. The government party could reasonably be given half of the political appointments, the remainder going to the opposition parties on the basis of popular vote. Appointments should, in addition, reflect regional and language balance, and include both sexes in proportion.

Such a reform package would not be a guaranteed vote-winner. Yet I believe that Canadians really do not like corruption and patronage, and they would prefer a better alternative. For the New Democratic Party to become the credible alternative requires that it be specific about what it would and would not do in government. Its good record in office will influence no one so long as the party does not talk about it.

The policies discussed in these last two chapters hardly exhaust the list. They are not necessarily the best choices. Some obviously reflect personal priorities. Yet the list as a whole does respect a vital principle, of a judicious array of concerns from traditional to trendy, sometimes leading the way, and sometimes reflecting strong majority opinion. A civil-libertarian party like the NDP will always defend unpopular causes, from nude Doukhobors in the 1930s to gays and lesbians in the armed forces in the 1980s. The party could not, and should not, give up its civil-liberties principles, but it must be careful not to become, or appear to be, a party only for deviants. A party that defends prisoners must also remember that guards have rights, as do prisoners' victims and their families. In defending prostitutes' rights to freedom of expression, it must also remember other people's rights to peace and quiet on their streets. So, in taking up unpopular causes it must be careful to balance them with mainstream issues. If not always with the "moral majority", the party must not be, or seem to be, a moral nonentity.

Party Strategy and Style

The NDP is not a party "*comme les autres*". It has a democratic structure and an active membership. Policy is determined democratically at biennial conventions by votes after debate, and in between conventions by elected councils. The party's support comes from the grass roots in a way that no other party can claim. There is, in short, much good to be preserved whenever changes are contemplated.

Many of the things the party needs to do to break the 20

per cent barrier in federal elections will cost money. Thus new and better fund-raising tactics have become an important part of party strategy. For example, the party is experimenting with mass-mailing techniques, so far with only modest success. In my view it should continue these mailings, but with greater attention to content. The party began in the 1970s to adopt dinners as a major means of fund-raising. Here it is following the example of the old-line parties too closely for the taste of many stalwarts. The price for these events had reached $100 a plate by the early 1980s. Although this is still well below the usual Conservative and Liberal dinner prices, it is prohibitive to most members. Anniversaries (such as Ed Broadbent's tenth as leader) and general tributes (Tommy and Irma Douglas were persuaded to lend their names to one dinner) are all used to persuade the faithful to buy a ticket. Much the same people go to each, and the menu rarely changes.

Surely the party can do better. The anti-free-trade coalition, for example, put on a splendid show at Massey Hall in 1986, with wicked imitations of Brian Mulroney and Ronald Reagan. Political satire not only cheers up the believers but can be good missionary work as well.

In a period when few people will turn out to conventional public meetings or "educationals", other means of bringing people together have to be devised. Such events must be low-cost and relatively easy to organize. Ideally, successful ideas would be repeated, so that a habit of going to certain events at predictable times would be developed among those interested. The Ontario party did one year try a spring festival, which was a good idea, but it scheduled it too early in the year when the weather was rainy and cold. A better idea might be a midsummer celebration held on the longest day of the year. Our pagan ancestors used the solstice to burn bonfires all night and otherwise frolic. The Christians then took it over for the feast of St. John the Baptist, and the *indépendantistes* laid claim to it as a national day in Québec. Surely the NDP as the environmental party has as good a claim on the day, or is it too secular to take on an ancient religious rite?

The New Democratic Party could do more to celebrate its own history and heroes as well. The birthplaces of the founders and sites of important events should be marked and visited. People who will not go to classrooms to learn history or policy may be willing to learn of them in other ways. John Sewell's walks about Toronto during the 1979 mayoralty campaign were an excellent way of demonstrating his concerns for neighbour-hoods. They were immensely popular, attracting up to a thousand people per walk. Similarly, a feminist bus tour of Toronto, sponsored by the National Action Committee, visited the sites of early suffragette struggles. In any area of Canada, a bus or a walking tour could be a significant means of raising consciousness. People need to know their history, yet little social history is taught in the schools. By taking people to the places themselves, our past can be made visible. The buildings, street corners, churches, parks, and clubs important to the party's history have a story to tell; it is up to the party to tell it.

It is even more essential for the NDP than it is for the other parties to reach out to youth. The party cannot depend as much as the old-time parties do on parents' passing on their party loyalty to their children. Not only are there fewer New Democrat parents to begin with, but the rate of children accepting parental party identification is less strong in the NDP. Of course, the party would still be condemned to zero growth even if all the children of its supporters were to become New Democrats. Yet the party cannot even count on the *status quo*; it has to win its supporters afresh, even the children of long-time party faithful.

The New Democratic Party abolished separate clubs for young people in 1973, on the illogical grounds that since the voting age had dropped to eighteen years, youth groups were somehow no longer needed. The Conservatives and the Liberals have been organizing massively on university and college campuses.

The NDP is now beginning to work towards re-establishing their own groups for young people.

While the party needs more money, not all the reforms suggested would be costly. Volunteers, who are fundamental to the party's organizational work, could be far better used in the area of policy development. People with expertise do in fact volunteer their services all the time, but there is currently no way to integrate them. One possible solution would be the formation of a "researchers' auxiliary" to the NDP. Its purpose would be policy development and debate, with no official status. Paid staff would continue to do their work as usual. Local riding associations would continue to develop policy resolutions for convention or council as in the past. The researchers' auxiliary would meet on occasion for the presentation of papers, workshops, or general discussions. Caucus members and research staff could take part as they wished. Caucus members might ask researchers to work on a specific problem in their area of responsibility, and meet with them for discussion. The auxiliary could hold conferences or "think tank" sessions on particular subjects. Good ideas they developed would find their way into the party. Party members could take them back to their own riding association or to a policy convention of the party. MPs might take them up in question period or develop a private member's bill from them.

Along with the development of new policy, the party must distribute more information about its existing programs and its past history. A researchers' auxiliary could be a means of commissioning writers to these ends and of getting them together with publishers. In their capacities as university teachers and researchers, historians and political scientists have done some excellent work. Sizeable gaps, however, remain in the record. There is no collection of the works of J. S. Woodsworth, despite the importance of his thought to the development of the party and the country. There is no readily available work on the successes of the CCF/NDP provincially.

There is some good material on Saskatchewan, but it is now out of date. There is no comprehensive work on the party's contribution at the federal level. Yet it is conceivable that if more people knew of the accomplishments of the party, more people would vote for it.

As became clear in Chapter 4, every successful social democratic party has had some kind of national press supporting it and promulgating its analysis of the world. This is without exception. Long the victim of editorial putdowns and general short shrift in the conservative press, the NDP would dearly love to have its own paper. On occasion, arguments can be heard that the party should forgo an election and spend the funds instead to buy a newspaper. The reality is that even in countries with strong parties and larger populations than Canada's, social democratic papers have folded. Starting one now, under the restriction of increasing dependence on commercial advertisers, would be impossible.

Just possible, however, is a more modest goal than a daily newspaper: a Sunday tabloid. To reach its target audience, such a paper would have to have a popular nervy style, report on entertainment and sports, if not also the occult, and include advice to the lovelorn, gourmets, and dieters. A social democratic message may be more complicated than a conservative one, but it can be conveyed in short sentences and a basic vocabulary. Cartoons can poke fun without being racist. Editorials can call for peace instead of arms. Hard-hitting columnists can strike their blows at bank profits instead of at welfare recipients. Community and co-operation can be the theme of human-interest stories. Investigative journalists can reveal the sordid facts of corporate crime instead of arousing fear of crime on the streets.

To pay for such a paper (to be named *The Eclipse*?) would require some ingenuity, but the attempt should be made. Presumably some advertising, if less than that for existing conservative papers, could help to support it. Support from the unions would be crucial, for no other sector of society has the membership or the organization on the scale necessary. Possibly some help would come also from voluntary organizations wanting access to a broad cross-section of the public. For the unions, a popular Sunday paper could be a major channel of communication with its own members. Unions also need to get their message out to a broader public, and they, like the party, cannot count on either sympathetic or thorough coverage in the conservative papers.

Party strategy in recent years has been to focus on "priority ridings", the thirty or so incumbent seats, and the ten to forty best prospects — ridings previously held or where the party has come close. It is only in these 40-70 ridings that the party has any real presence at all. In the other 210-240 ridings, few voters have ever seen a New Democrat canvasser at the door, or received any literature seriously attempting to explain party policy.

Up to a point this concentration on a small number of ridings is necessary. If the party spread its efforts equally across all ridings, it would risk winning none of them. In the long run, however, such a narrowing of focus is self-defeating, for it does not foster growth. Campaign efforts, as well, often seem ill-directed from the point of view of growth. The literature typically features, as do Conservative and Liberal brochures, the local candidate's name, face, family, and dog. His, or her, accomplishments as a hockey coach or a library board member bring no one to a social democratic understanding of society. Probably the same candidate will not run again, and the local organization is back to square one at the next election.

There never seems to be a time to present the NDP as a party with a different approach to life. During an election, time is too short to do "educational work". The candidate as family member, pictured with dog and party leader, is featured. But this appeal does not build committed supporters in the public. Come the next election there are no new New Democrat

THE PARTY THAT CHANGED CANADA

supporters in the riding, only another fresh young candidate, now perhaps with lacrosse stick and cat, to sell to the voters.

Voting studies show us that the New Democratic Party has not done as well as the other parties, especially the Liberals, in developing long-term commitment to it.[7] Far fewer people identify with the party than vote for it in any particular election. For example, 13 per cent of those surveyed identified themselves with the party in 1979, although 18 per cent had voted for it. In the 1980 election the proportions were 15 per cent identifying with and 20 per cent voting for the party. For the Liberals, on the other hand, more people identified with the party than voted for it in both those elections. Even in ridings held by the NDP, more voters identify with the Conservative Party than with the NDP. In short, the party gets many of its votes in spite of party identification, not because of it.

This gives a certain justification to the practice of emphasizing the local candidate over party philosophy. Yet if this were the only lesson to be learned, the party ought to be paying far *more* attention to candidate selection and preparation, as much as it does to policy development. Currently the party seems to get the worst of both worlds, leaving candidate selection to the most haphazard of methods, and then ignoring the party in favour of the candidate in the actual election campaign. Yet if New Democrats have not done as well as would be desirable in building party identification, this is not a disaster. Most Canadian voters, 63 per cent, are "flexible partisans", meaning that they identify with a party but do not necessarily vote for it. In 1974, 1979, and 1980, for example, only 44 per cent of voters chose the same party in all three elections. The New Democratic Party can, and does, raid votes from the other parties.

As to whether this, or any other, combination of policy positions and strategies will attract enough voters to bring the New Democratic Party to government is an unanswerable question. The fact that the party has remained a third party federally this long is discouraging, as are certain economic trends that have damaged social democratic parties all over the world. The loss of manufacturing jobs means ever greater problems of organizing labour support. The de-skilling and contracting-out of jobs make it hard for the party to urge realistically that workers take control of their lives. So do the powerlessness and vulnerability promulgated by the mass media, especially television. Even so, as argued earlier, social democratic parties have made it to government in other countries in circumstances more difficult than those faced by the New Democratic Party.

Yet there is a most encouraging trend in the rise of a new generation of Christians, Catholic and Protestant, who are re-examining the gospel for its implications in social and economic life. The term "social gospel" is seldom used and few claim to be "Christian socialists". Catholics refer to the "preferential option for the poor", and both they and the Protestants have been powerfully influenced by the "liberation theology" of Latin America. Whatever name is invoked, however, it is clear that the same concerns are being raised as at the turn of the century: responsibility for one's neighbour, and indeed towards one's enemies, and stewardship of the land.

For the New Democratic Party this new movement of the spirit must be deeply encouraging. It means co-workers in common struggles, and probably some votes. As well as bringing practical aid, it presents the NDP with a theoretical challenge. The impact of Latin American experience, where inequalities are so great, has meant a sharper posing of the issue of equality as a social goal. These radical Christians are raising anew the age-old questions about equality, peace, nature, and community. Some of them would make the New Democratic Party, including the Left Caucus, look revisionist and tame.

Other trends are also favourable to the party. Young people do not have the same prejudices against the party that their parents and grandparents had, so every wave of new voters will help. There is growing concern in the areas in which the party has credibility: women's equality, foreign control of the economy, peace, nuclear disarmament, and the environment. In short, the pool of potential supporters is growing. The party's stands in these areas are far closer to majority opinion than those of either the Liberals or the Conservatives. Obviously the party must persuade Canadians to vote as they think, not, as of old, praying that the kingdom come, but voting that it not.

8

THE NEW JERUSALEM, OR POLITICS BY POLLING?

If the New Democratic Party is to form a federal government in Canada, it must gain strength in all regions of the country, but especially where it has historically been weakest: in Québec and Atlantic Canada. Its prospects in these two regions are the first subject of this chapter.

The failures of the CCF/NDP in Québec are a source of deep embarrassment. The party there has never elected a federal member, and only once, in 1944, was a provincial member elected, in Rouyn-Noranda. It is not easy to be the only representative of your party in a legislature. Grant Notley bore the isolation, and taunts, heroically for years in Alberta. The first CCF member in Québec, unfortunately, could not endure, and he defected to the Liberals.

When the NDP ran 90 candidates for 121 seats in the 1985 Québec provincial election, this was considered a major achievement in itself, for a provincial wing of the party had only just been formed. Its popular vote of 1.4 per cent was disappointing, although the party outstripped the other minor parties, including the Conservatives. The Néo-Démocrate leader, Jean-Paul Harney, did somewhat better than the provincial average, with 8 per cent of the vote in his Quebec City riding. The Québec Federation of Labour did not endorse the party, but at least it refrained from endorsing the Parti Québécois. The Québec Federation of Labour had endorsed the founding of the federal NDP, although this never led to active support. Here the party has to make up for lost ground.

The Catholic Church in the 1940s was openly hostile to the party, denouncing it from the pulpit and in bishops' letters to the faithful about godless materialism. In other parts of the country, the Catholic vote for the New Democratic Party is now roughly the same as the Protestant vote, and it is difficult to see why it should lag so far behind in Québec. One might expect New Democrat voting to be *higher* among socially conscious Catholics, of whom Québec has a goodly share.

Recent Catholic discussions on social and economic questions have been vague on specifics and, of course, do not endorse any particular party. Yet church teachings are perfectly clear, stressing social responsibility for one another, co-operation rather than competition, and the priority of human needs over higher profits for the few. All of these coincide with New Democrat principles, and share common origins in the Gospel. The Church's teachings on peace, nuclear disarmament, and international aid are again similar to the NDP's, and far from those of both the old-line parties. The Church does not publicly admit to these similarities, but this does nothing to lessen any of them. Common ground is increasingly noticed by commentators, partisan and academic, religious and secular. Perhaps one day the similarities will be generally recognized as a shared commitment to justice and social purpose.

The party's old centralization policies can no longer be the barrier to a higher Québec vote, for these have gone the way of the Saskatchewan box factory and the Regina Manifesto. The CCF's insensitivity to provincial rights should not be minimized as an historic factor. For the best of practical reasons the CCF urged federal action on a host of problems under provincial jurisdiction. It seemed incomprehensible in the Depression that provincial rights could be a higher object than legislating unemployment insurance, the eight-hour day, and employment centres. The party did eventually come to an understanding of the need to respect Québec's distinctive character. By the time of the founding of the New Democratic Party the "*deux nations*" concept was written into the constitution. The party early endorsed bilingualism and a provision that permitted Québec's opting out of federal programs without financial penalty.

New Democrat economic understanding has changed over the decades in response to changed economic conditions. Centralized economic planning is no longer necessary or desirable. The party's economic strategy stresses local control. Where public ownership is considered desirable, provincial and municipal ownership are amongst the options, as is co-operative ownership.

With the defeat of the Parti Québécois in 1985 the political scene in Québec has opened up considerably. Under Pierre-Marc Johnson the PQ has moved to the right, and the independence issue has been pushed to the back. Johnson himself actively recruited Conservatives to run as candidates. He had considered joining the Conservative Party in the event that René Lévesque would not step down as leader. The PQ-Conservative alliance for the 1985 election was obvious to all, and was only half-heartedly denied by Mulroney. Is it not a little suspicious that the Conservative Party, which won 50 per cent of the popular vote in Québec in 1984 federally, could do no better than 1 per cent in 1985 provincially?

The PQ swing to the right, even before Pierre-Marc Johnson's replacing Lévesque, is even more to the point. The party has always been an uneasy alliance of left-wing and right-wing nationalists, and the 1980s recession brought out the PQ's most conservative tendencies. The result is that, in the late 1980s, Québec has two parties offering the new conservatism. Yet the population has become accustomed to a high standard of progressive government.

The Parti Québécois in government reflected both its social democratic and its Liberal origins. Some members had been CCF or NDP supporters before joining the PQ. Those who had

235

not were still more prone to advocate state intervention than the Liberals or the Conservatives would in other parts of the country. Not only was the result creative, effective government, but the PQ managed to surprise even its supporters by its capacity to govern well. All those professors and poets proved to be practical and competent! Québec's legislation on labour, human rights, and women's equality was the most advanced in Canada. The Quebec Pension Plan was expanded to cover homemakers caring for children under seven, while the Ontario government's use of its veto power to block such a reform retarded its adoption in the rest of the country for years. The PQ government instituted an excellent system of community health centres. It also made the first serious attempt to accommodate immigrants of neither French nor English origin. Economically its performance was good, relying on a mixture of the old and the new: energy exports, mega projects, and the promotion of specialized manufacturing. The party's second victory, in 1981, was clearly due to its overall effectiveness and progressiveness as a government, and not to its policy on sovereignty association.

In its last term of office the Parti Québécois managed to alienate *all* of the groups most important to its success: labour, social democrats, feminists, and nationalists. It abandoned its pro-labour stance, dealing harshly with its own public servants. It toned down its previously activist Human Rights Commission. It reversed several important progressive measures for women. Its economic pronouncements began to mimic the rhetoric of Mulroney and Reagan. Then the issue of sovereignty association was completely put aside. The result is that there is a substantial number of committed, experienced activists in Québec with no place to call home. Their social views overlap considerably with those of the New Democrats. Indeed, they are the same people who, in other provinces, joined the party and brought it to power. Those still in the PQ are putting on a brave front, but one wonders how long they can maintain it. Can the Parti Québécois satisfy those members as a party in which social democratic views may at least be *expressed*, when those views are so evidently unwelcome?

One wonders, too, how long organized labour can be content to be so disunited. By 1985 there were labour leaders variously supporting the Liberal Party, the Conservative Party, and the Parti Québécois. It is possible that all are wrong in their endorsements, but they cannot all be right! In European countries the trend has been to a coalescing of the unions around a social democratic party. Québec labour has much to gain by making a political alliance with the New Democratic Party, and the party is ready for it. The opinion polls already suggest that such a move has begun. In 1986 the party was at its highest point of popularity ever achieved in Québec, between 25 per cent and 32 per cent, behind the Liberals but ahead of the Conservatives. This compares dramatically with 9 per cent in the 1984 election.

Atlantic Canada

The fragile economy of Atlantic Canada since Confederation has made for one of the greatest ironies in Canadian politics. In 1984 Atlantic Canada voted massively for the Conservative Party, which promptly began to dismantle the economic-support programs on which the Atlantic provinces, more than any other region, depend. The heavy-water plant at Glace Bay was closed despite explicit election promises to the contrary. Transfer payments to the provinces were reduced, and so were income-security programs like family allowance. The Conservative strategy was to strengthen the private sector, as the "engine of growth" *in a region with virtually no private sector.* Conservative MPs from the region themselves have admitted as much. Wanting to be re-elected, they have fought these Draconian measures, in caucus if not publicly. Hardly closet socialists, these politicians have yet been forced to develop a more pragmatic approach to politics. Jobs are jobs, and if the public sector will create them, take them.

Common sense suggests that a party that emphasizes job creation, and would devote both public and private resources to furthering that aim, should attract political support. Yet the New Democratic Party so far has made only sporadic breakthroughs, and has not been able to follow them up as a governing party. The N.S. Labour Party elected four members to the House of Assembly in 1920, but the party collapsed three years later. The CCF actually became the Official Opposition in 1945, albeit with only 14 per cent of the popular vote, and two seats. There were four Cape Breton New Democrats in the Nova Scotia House in the 1970s. Again defeat came from within, this time from a break-away faction. Federal members have been elected in Cape Breton and in Corner Brook, Newfoundland, but have been subsequently defeated.

Altogether the CCF/NDP roots go back a long time in Atlantic Canada, but they never seemed to spread. There were Maritimers at the founding convention of the CCF. The first union to affiliate with the party was in Cape Breton, brought in by MP Clarie Gillis. The co-operative movement of Antigonish stimulated social thought similar to that of the CCF/NDP. It is no coincidence that the first CCF MP, Clarie Gillis, was a Catholic involved in that movement. So was the first New Democrat MP, a Catholic priest named Andy Hogan. The first provincial members were also from Cape Breton.

There is reason to hope for a dramatic change in Atlantic Canada and there are some signs of it in opinion surveys. By 1986 the polls were showing 23 per cent New Democrat support for the region, a near doubling of the 12 per cent in the 1984 federal election. The party is strongest in Nova Scotia, with three mainland members in the provincial House and the possibility now of a comeback in Cape Breton. The party's popular vote in the 1984 provincial election was 16 per cent. The leader, Alexa McDonough, was the only woman member, and the only New Democrat in the House during her first term.

She is recognized by friend and foe alike as an effective and constructive Opposition leader. In Newfoundland only the party leader, Peter Fenwick, has a seat. The party won 14 per cent of the popular vote in the provincial election of 1985. In New Brunswick the lone New Democrat member was joined briefly by a second, who subsequently went over to the Liberals. The New Democrat popular vote in New Brunswick was 10 per cent.

Politics by Polling

The gains in the polls that the New Democrats have made since the 1984 election have prompted a new wave of speculation in the media and optimism in the party. Political commentators talk about a three-way split in the next election. The party that has done so much to change Canada may yet be elected. Some party enthusiasts see the light glimmering on the horizon. Others view the results as only another blip, a false oasis, a mirage. Who is right?

On the optimistic side, the increases are substantial — five percentage points or more — and have been sustained for a fair period of time. Blips do not usually last so long. Yet a regional breakdown reveals some bad news with the good, as the table below shows. The poll, for which 1,972 persons were interviewed in May and June 1986, is typical, neither the best nor the worst results for the party in this period.

	NEW DEMOCRAT SUPPORT	
	1984 Election (%)	1986 Poll (%)
Canada	19	24
West	28	26
Ontario	21	22
Québec	9	25
Atlantic	12	23

Most remarkable, indeed unprecedented, is the similarity of support across the country. New Democrat voting intentions in Atlantic Canada, at 23 per cent, are only just under the national average of 24 per cent, while in Québec, at 25 per cent, they are only just over it. In both cases, the 1986 support marks a great improvement, a near tripling of support in Québec, from 9 per cent in the 1984 election, and a near doubling in Atlantic Canada, from 12 per cent. New Democratic support is up only one percentage point in Ontario, while it is actually down two percentage points in the West. The Québec and Atlantic gains, in other words, mask losses in the party's traditional base of support in the West.

A cynic might further wonder why the party is not doing even better, given the popularity of its leader, and the general disenchantment with Brian Mulroney and John Turner. A pessimist with a good memory might even worry about *déjà vu*. When the CCF moved ahead of the Conservatives and Liberals back in 1943, it was massively attacked by business interests and the media, and its programs were stolen by Mackenzie King. The same crude campaign is unlikely, for it would not work today. But a more sophisticated, and more subtle, attack is indeed possible, and the Conservatives, at least, have the money for it. The Toronto *Globe and Mail* was prompted by the polls to publish an editorial against the NDP, complete with specious accusations of its favouring a $36-billion deficit and of being "economically isolationist".[1] The only party policy of which the paper approved, tax reform, was misrepresented. According to the *Globe and Mail*, it was the Conservatives who put tax reform on the economic agenda, and the NDP only "appears to share" in it!

Wholesale theft of New Democrat policy by the Conservatives is unlikely. Brian Mulroney might purloin New Democrat rhetoric — he does seem fond of the word "compassion" — but scarcely its policy. It is even doubtful if there will be serious tax reform, the one area in which there is at least a similarity in announced intentions. Otherwise, the policy difference between the two parties is too great.

Speculation aside, some hard facts are clear enough. The New Democratic Party is not advancing in a significant part of the country, the four western provinces and Ontario, which together make up the majority of the Canadian population. More to the point, the NDP is not gaining support in the areas that know it best, Saskatchewan, Manitoba, British Columbia, and Ontario. Welcome as the new support is, the party will have to face that reality, bring back its old friends, and find more like them in the West and in Ontario. It will accordingly have to re-examine, not its fundamental beliefs, but its choice of priorities and the means by which it conveys its message.

With this in mind let us consider a few unpleasant facts before concluding. The NDP is too often the bearer of bad news. Its message to the 80 per cent of voters who do not support it is that they have made a mistake. It seeks to convince Canadians that the Conservative and Liberal parties are not acting in their best interests. Indeed, these parties have done serious damage to the country. Yet most Canadians are not all that dissatisfied with their lot. Wages and salaries have not been keeping up with inflation, but the losses have been in the order of 1 per cent per year. For the 90 per cent of the labour force who are employed, life is now materially better than it was ten years ago. In a 20-to-30-year period, material circumstances have improved considerably for most families.

Studies show Canadians to be a contented people. A major 1985 life-styles survey found that 80 per cent were "very satisfied with the way things are going with my life" — perhaps the same 80 per cent who vote Conservative and Liberal?[2] The same study found that 74 per cent of Canadians rated their family income as "enough to satisfy all our important desires". There are hardly the makings of a revolution here! A similar proportion allowed that they were "much happier now than

241

ever before". Two-thirds (67 per cent) expected that their family income would be "a lot higher" in five years' time. Such contentment poses a considerable challenge to the New Democrats, who continue to tell people that they are worse off than they realize.

When the polls showed New Democrat support falling in 1982, a special hard-hitting brochure was distributed in a door-to-door canvass to fight back. The Ontario NDP's version, in large, bold print, accused:

PIERRE TRUDEAU AND THE LIBERALS HAVE TAKEN A LOT AWAY FROM YOU. BRIAN MULRO-NEY AND THE CONSERVATIVES WANT TO TAKE A LOT MORE.

Neither message was believed. By that time, Canadians had become hostile to Trudeau, but not for what he had taken away from them. That Mulroney would raise their taxes and de-index "the sacred trust" was not credible. People then were prepared to take Mulroney's word that "together we can be better". Canadians have since learned to be more sceptical about Mulroney, but this has not sent them to the New Democratic Party.

The cheerful Canadian poses a real problem for the party. The 80 per cent who are contented with their lot do not want to be told it will be getting worse. Conditions have changed radically from the time of the party's founding. In the Depression, virtually everybody was hurt, suffering everything from minor business losses to major losses of job, home, farm, and business, and even utter destitution. The party's message then was of hope, of a new society free of injustice and want. It proclaimed this message with the confidence of a sure scientific discovery or a received truth.

The focus on economic self-interest holds another risk, in making the Conservatives' case for them. When social democratic theory was formulated in the nineteenth century, there was little alternative to collective action for the person seeking a better life. Upward mobility, and emigration, might improve one's lot materially, but neither course got you to the top of your own society. Class barriers were enormous, and the nobility was still effectively a caste into which one had to be born. Today, upward mobility is more than a remote possibility for Canadians, if not as frequent as commonly believed. Brian Mulroney can cite his humble origins in Baie Comeau and invite others to follow him on the path to success, via the Conservative Party. Not everyone can become prime minister, of course, but who would tell any particular aspirant not to hope? Thus, even to the dissatisfied 20 per cent, the Conservatives have a message to compete with the New Democrats' to go it alone rather than work for a better life for all. To the 80 per cent who are satisfied, it can warn them not to risk change.

Paradoxically, it might be in the party's self-interest to promote altruism more, and self-interest less. Those people who feel they are better off now than they were ten years ago may yet have some anxiety for their children and grandchildren. Those complacent about their material well-being may have concerns about peace and disarmament, the environment, and social justice. As the survey data cited in the previous chapter show, Canadians do have a highly moral approach to many issues. On aid to the Third World, the universal social programs, the threat of nuclear arms, and environmental hazards, a good majority are on the side of the angels. It is the Conservatives and the Liberals who are out of step with the great majority of "bleeding-heart", "do-good" voters.

It is true that capitalism has survived, if considerably modified, far better than expected in the 1930s. Yet it is not at all clear that our present version of it can survive, or we survive it. The problem is simple enough. Capitalism requires ever greater profits, which depend on increasing production and

243

sales. The result is the gradual depletion of the earth's resources, and environmental pollution. The necessity of growth, and the physical limits to it, are so far unsolved problems in our economic system. Planned economies in social democratic countries have done *somewhat* better in improving material conditions without inordinate growth. In Austria, for example, there have been annual increments in GNP without population growth, which have led to greater prosperity per capita. Social democratic countries have also been somewhat better on environmental issues, but this is only to say that they have been lesser offenders than Britain, West Germany, and the United States. The basic problem of scarce resources and physical limits to growth remains.

Political theorist Charles Taylor, among others, is raising the right questions, in looking at "the cult of production" and the "endless propensity to consume":

> We cannot hope to change this propensity without our understanding of it, and we cannot hope to build a socialist society, one founded on more humane priorities, or one in which endless production would not be an end in itself, unless we can bring our urge to consume back into sane proportions.[3]

Taylor offers a plausible explanation for inordinate consumption in the individual's loss of control in the production process. For the average person today, the only way to have a sense of control is to consume.

Yet the socialist tradition is "woefully inadequate" to the task of finding a different foundation for technological society. I agree. It is also perfectly clear that the best chance for dealing with the challenge is through the social democratic parties; whatever else their faults, they at least are not bound, as are the old-line parties, to the corporations and their thirst for profits. Fundamental to the social democratic tradition is the ethic of making the economy serve the people, not the other way around.

Social democratic parties, including the New Democratic Party, have a long way to go in coming up with a viable alternative, but the work has begun.

In Canada we have the added advantage of a native tradition, with profoundly different values, and a far better record on stewardship than anyone who has arrived in the country since. Not so well known is the fact that the native peoples had achieved a high standard of living at the same time. Thus, respect for the environment need not require life that is brutish and short. Native culture stresses respect for the land and other creatures, co-operation, and shared responsibility, all good social democratic values.

The New Jerusalem

If contented Canadians pose a challenge to the New Democratic Party, so do its more idealistic, and increasingly frustrated, members. When the CCF was formed, it offered no less than the vision of a new society to a desperate people. Now it discusses such matters as a 1 per cent increase in the federal sales tax, consumers' rights, severance pay, and the right of pornographers to free expression. Public car insurance has proved to be a good thing, but is hardly the stuff of the New Jerusalem. In 1984 in Canada, obesity and not malnutrition is a medical problem. The under-nourished are more likely to be anorexic teen-agers, whose lives may be empty, but whose refrigerators are full.

The fact is that many of the party's original goals have been achieved. The present struggle revolves around minor improvements where there are gaps, and against setbacks when a government ostensibly wants to save money. On unemployment insurance, for example, the party is seeking better benefits, questions the waiting period, and fights rule changes that make certain claimants ineligible. All these are important matters, of course, but none are as difficult as the fight in the 1930s

245

to establish a system at all. Ideology is far from dead, but the debates are undeniably tamer.

Must it ever be so? Is the party condemned to fighting for ever more minor concessions on behalf of ever more obscure claimants? I think not. I would argue that we live in truly revolutionary times, with problems even greater to face than those of the Depression or the two world wars. If the disparities between rich and poor in Canada are less problematic now than then, those in the world at large are greater. The possibility of nuclear war threatens all life on the planet. Should we escape a nuclear winter we might yet face the prospect of the "greenhouse effect", the melting of the polar icecap, and the flooding of every coastal city in the world. Or we might be overtaken by a peaceful version of nuclear winter, the ozone catastrophe, caused by insufficient light breaking through the atmosphere to enable photosynthesis.

The experts tell us that millions of premature deaths have already occurred through low-level radiation from uranium mining and processing, nuclear-power stations, and nuclear-test explosions. Meanwhile, the pace of technological change outpaces societal adjustment to it. The leisure society so confidently predicted for all is a reality for very few. Instead, technological change has meant de-skilling, lower wages and salaries, early lay-offs, and an insecure future for millions of people. Poverty remains the lot of over 4 million Canadians.

Canadians can, of course, turn aside from this, and other similar doom-and-gloom scenarios. The greenhouse and ozone scares may prove to be only science fiction. The poor nations may continue to accept their lot. We can justify our uranium mining and processing on the grounds that if we did not, someone else would. We can hope that Pickering, Bruce, Darlington, and Point Lepreau neither blow up nor melt down, and maybe they won't. We can excuse ourselves with the thought that even if we cleaned up all our pollution, there would still be plenty left in the world.

246

Yet Canadians are not an inward-looking lot. Many indeed are very internationally minded, and most have a keen conscience pricking them. Only one party has a message directed to that population, and a plan for it to work toward a more co-operative world. Only the New Democratic Party has a message to those who still follow the gleam.

In proclaiming that message, New Democrats must remain aware of their double existence, as activists in a movement and as members of a party. The party has always existed on both levels and must continue to do so, balancing long-term concerns with short-term ones, education with vote-getting, changing the climate of opinion and electing members to legislatures. As a movement it must work with those who share its concerns for peace, justice, and sanity in the world. It must work both with the older, established movements, especially organized labour, and with the newer organizations of feminists, environmentalists, and peacemakers. It must convince activists in all these groups that their struggle is fundamentally political. Only with a government committed to the same goals will there be fundamental, and lasting, change. The occasional victories of lobbyists, achieved when government bows reluctantly to public opinion, will never be safe. They risk being very token gestures indeed.

There is even some reasonable prospect that activists in these causes will come to see that the New Democratic Party is the only party for them. A century ago, trade unionists were content to go cap-in-hand to the government of the day, with rational arguments as to need. It took decades before they became convinced of the futility of lobbying a party profoundly unsympathetic to their concerns, and closely linked to opposing interests. This process may well continue, as activists become aware of the need for political change, and commit themselves and their organizations to work with a party that shares their concerns.

Tommy Douglas, who could make his point succinctly, used to electioneer with the challenge:

Give us 70 seats and we'll turn Parliament upside down.
Give us 170 seats and we'll turn Canada right side up.

We are aware now more than ever that setting Canada to rights will require changes throughout the world. A safe environment cannot be achieved in any one country alone, nor can any country live in security while the rest of the world is in turmoil. The struggle for peace, justice, and environmental sanity is an international one. Yet only through a social democratic government, I believe, can Canada even begin to play the global role that it should. The New Democratic Party wants Canada to take on that larger task, to set Canada right side up, and to join with like-minded people the world over in the struggle for a safe environment, peace, and justice.

NOTES

Chapter 1

1. J. S. Woodsworth, *My Neighbor* (Toronto: University of Toronto Press, second edition, 1972), p. 20.
2. Gregory Vlastos, *Christian Faith and Democracy* (New York: Hazen, 1939), pp. 22, 23.
3. R. B. Y. Scott and Gregory Vlastos, *Towards the Christian Revolution* (Chicago: Willott, Clark, 1936), p. 23.
4. William Irvine, *Can a Christian Vote for Capitalism?* (Ottawa: Labour Publishing, 1935), p. 17.
5. Salem Bland, *The New Christianity* (Toronto: University of Toronto Press, second edition, 1973), p. 18.
6. Irvine, *Can a Christian Vote for Capitalism?*, p. 26.
7. Scott and Vlastos, *Towards the Christian Revolution*, p. 23.
8. Woodsworth, *My Neighbor*, p. 212.
9. Irvine, *Can a Christian Vote for Capitalism?*, p. 28.
10. Richard Allen, *The Social Passion* (Toronto: University of Toronto Press, 1973), p. 73f.
11. T. C. Douglas, *The Making of a Socialist* (Edmonton: University of Alberta Press, 1984), p. 82.
12. David Lewis and Frank Scott, *Make This YOUR Canada* (Toronto: Central Canada Publishing, 1943), p. vi.
13. *Ibid.*, pp. 155, 145.
14. Reginald Whitaker, "Hot Nights in Napanee", in *The Canadian Forum*, vol. 66, Aug./Sept., 1986, p. 32.
15. The *Montreal Star*, March 28, 1944, p. 10.
16. The *Globe and Mail*, January 1, 1944, p. 3.

17. David Lewis, *The Good Fight* (Toronto: Macmillan, 1981), p. 310.
18. The *Ottawa Journal*, January 12, 1944.
19. Pauline Jewett, from a paper given at an annual meeting of the Canadian Political Science Association, Montreal, 1961.

Chapter 2

1. T. C. Douglas, Speech, 1945.
2. *Hansard* (Senate), June 8, 1926, pp. 160-1.
3. *Ibid.*, p. 181.
4. Grace MacInnis, *J. S. Woodsworth* (Toronto: Macmillan of Canada, 1953), Chapter 15; and Morden Lazarus, *The Pension Story* (Ottawa: Canadian Labour Congress, 1980).
5. *Hansard* (Senate), March 13, 1927, p. 133.
6. *Hansard* (Senate), March 23, 1927, p. 151.
7. *Hansard*, July 27, 1944, p. 5486.
8. *Hansard*, July 31, 1944, p. 5677.
9. *Hansard*, July 27, 1944, p. 5471.
10. *Ottawa Journal*, August 10, 1944, p. 3.
11. *Hansard*, July 27, 1944, p. 5487.
12. *Hansard*, July 28, 1944, p. 5545.
13. *Hansard*, July 27, 1944, p. 5486.
14. *Hansard* (Senate), August 10, 1944, p. 423.
15. *Hansard*, July 31, 1944, p. 5676.
16. *Hansard*, July 28, 1944, p. 5540.
17. *Hansard*, July 31, 1944, p. 5670.
18. *Ibid.*, p. 5705.
19. J. S. Woodsworth, "Unemployment", in *The Canadian Forum*, 1921, p. 201.
20. *Hansard*, March 14, 1922, p. 87.
21. *Hansard*, April 24, 1922, p. 1070.
22. *Hansard*, March 14, 1922, p. 85.
23. *Hansard*, May 14, 1923, p. 2725.
24. *Ibid.*, p. 2721.
25. *Ibid.*
26. *Hansard*, January 21, 1935, p. 52.
27. *Ibid.*, p. 55.

28. *Hansard*, January 17, 1935, p. 3.
29. *Hansard*, January 18, 1937, p. 46.
30. *Hansard*, February 25, 1936, p. 515.
31. *Hansard*, January 18, 1937, p. 46.
32. *Hansard*, April 24, 1922, p. 1073.
33. Royal Commission on Industrial Relations, *Report*, 1919, p. 25.
34. *Hansard*, February 24, 1930, p. 38.
35. *Hansard*, August 29, 1931, p. 1095.
36. *Hansard*, November 22, 1932, p. 1452.
37. *Report of the Standing Committee on Banking and Commerce*, 1943, p. 130.
38. *Ibid.*, p. 128.
39. *Hansard*, June 26, 1925, p. 4973.
40. Kenneth McNaught, *A Prophet in Politics* (Toronto: University of Toronto Press, 1959), p. 237.
41. *Ibid.*, p. 245.
42. Walter D. Young, *The Anatomy of a Party* (Toronto: University of Toronto Press, 1969), p. 8.
43. *Hansard*, February 20, 1936, p. 377.
44. *Ibid.*, p. 378.
45. *Ibid.*, p. 380.
46. *Hansard*, February 5, 1942, p. 342.
47. *Hansard*, July 2, 1942, p. 3878.
48. *Hansard*, June 30, 1943, p. 4208.
49. *Hansard*, June 10, 1942, p. 3224.
50. *Hansard*, June 30, 1943, p. 4207.
51. *Ibid.*, p. 4208.
52. *Ibid.*, p. 4212.
53. *Ibid.*, p. 4210.
54. *Hansard*, April 9, 1946, p. 701.
55. *Hansard*, April 22, 1947, p. 2313.
56. *Ibid.*, p. 2317.
57. *Ibid.*, p. 2322.
58. *Ibid.*, p. 2320.
59. *Saskatchewan Debates*, March 19, 1947, p. 982.
60. *Ibid.*, March 21, 1947, p. 1041.
61. *Ibid.*, March 19, 1947, p. 993.
62. *Ibid.*, p. 1006, and March 21, 1947, p. 1063.

63. *Hansard*, March 21, 1947, p. 1067.
64. *Ibid.*, p. 1068.
65. *Ibid.*, pp. 1051, 1053.
66. *Ibid.*, p. 1050.
67. *Ibid.*, p. 1052.
68. *Ibid.*, p. 1053.
69. Regina *Leader-Post*, March 18, 1947.
70. *Saskatchewan Debates*, March 26, 1947, p. 1091.
71. Saskatoon *Star-Phoenix*, March 20, 1947.
72. *Ibid.*, March 29, 1947.
73. *Hansard*, April 9, 1946, p. 698.
74. *Hansard*, May 2, 1946, p. 1128.
75. *Leader-Post*, November 9, 1944.
76. *Ibid.*, October 31, 1944.
77. *Ibid.*, November 13, 1944.
78. *Moose Jaw Times-Herald*, November 13, 1944.
79. *Leader-Post*, October 31, 1944.
80. *Ibid.*, November 11, 1944.
81. *Ibid.*, November 9, 1944.
82. *Ibid.*, November 17, 1944.
83. *Ibid.*
84. *Leader-Post*, November 9, 1944.
85. *Ibid.*, March 27, 1947.
86. *Ibid.*, November 11, 1944.
87. *Ibid.*, February 13, 1947.
88. *Hansard*, March 20, 1924, p. 522.
89. MacInnis, *J. S. Woodsworth*, p. 235.
90. *Hansard*, July 12, 1947, p. 5528.
91. *Ibid.*, p. 5532.
92. Robin F. Badgley and Samuel Wolfe, *Doctors' Strike* (Toronto: Macmillan of Canada, 1967), p. 26.
93. Saskatoon *Star-Phoenix*, June 4, 1960, p. 9.
94. Toronto *Telegram*, April 27, 1960.
95. Reginald W. Bibby, *Anglitrends*, Study for the Anglican Diocese of Toronto (Toronto, 1986), p. 28.
96. Mackenzie King Diaries, August 9, 1943 (Ottawa: Public Archives Canada).

97. *Ibid.*, September 26, 1943 (Ottawa: Public Archives Canada).
98. *Ibid.*, June 22, 1944.
99. *Ibid.*, October 15, 1943.
100. *Ibid.*, September 21, 1943.
101. *Ibid.*, January 24, 1944.
102. *Ibid.*, February 11, 1947.

Chapter 3

1. Walter D. Young, *The Anatomy of a Party: The National CCF* (Toronto: University of Toronto Press, 1969), p. 197ff.
2. *Ibid.*, p. 186.
3. *Ibid.*, p. 185.
4. Alan Whitehorn, "The New Democratic Party in Convention", in George Perlin, ed., *Party Democracy in Canada* (Toronto: Prentice-Hall, 1987).
5. Gerald L. Caplan, *The Dilemma of Canadian Socialism* (Toronto: McClelland and Stewart, 1973), p. 200.
6. Young, *The Anatomy of a Party*, p. 289.
7. *Ibid.*, p. 179.
8. Jane Jenson, "Party Loyalty in Canada", *Canadian Journal of Political Science*, vol. 8, 1975, pp. 543-53.
9. Neil Compton, "The Mass Media", in Michael Oliver, ed., *Social Purpose for Canada* (Toronto: University of Toronto Press, 1961), pp. 70-3.
10. Robert A. Hackett, "For a Socialist Perspective on the News Media", *Studies in Political Economy*, vol. 19, 1986, p. 149.
11. *Ibid.*, p. 150.
12. George Gerbner et al., "TV Violence", *Journal of Communications*, Profile No. 8, 1977, pp. 171-89, and Profile No. 9, 1978, pp. 176-207.
13. *Ibid.*, Profile No. 10, 1979, pp. 177-96.
14. John Carson and Frank J. Porporino, "Redirecting Corrections", *Policy Options*, March 1986, pp. 3-5. On the "rising crime" misperception, see also Lynn McDonald, *The Sociology of Law and Order* (Toronto: Methuen, 1979).

15. Tannis MacBeth-Williams, *The Impact of Television: A Natural Experiment in Three Communities* (Orlando, Florida: Academic Press, 1986).
16. Anthony N. Doob and Glenn E. Macdonald, "Television Viewing and the Fear of Victimization", *Journal of Personality and Social Psychology*, vol. 37, 1978, pp. 170-9.
17. Morris Wolfe, *Jolts* (Toronto: Lorimer, 1986), p. 101.
18. Margaret Atwood, *Survival* (Toronto: Anansi, 1972), p. 34.
19. Wolfe, *Jolts*, p. 121.

Chapter 4

1. George Sayers Bain and Robert Price, *Profiles of Union Growth* (Oxford: Blackwell, 1980), International Labour Organization, *The Trade Union Situation in Norway* (Geneva, 1984).
2. Anton Pelinka, *Social Democratic Parties in Europe* (New York: Praeger, 1983).
3. William E. Paterson and Alastair H. Thomas, eds., *Social Democratic Parties in Western Europe* (London: Croom Helm, 1974).
4. Peter Gourevitch et al., *Unions and Economic Crisis* (London: Allen & Unwin, 1984), vol. 2.
5. Vincent E. McHale, ed., *Political Parties of Europe* (Westport, Conn.: Greenwood, 1983), vol. 2.
6. Margaret Stewart, *Trade Unions in Europe* (Epping: Gower, 1974).
7. McHale, ed., *Political Parties of Europe*, vol. 2.
8. Bain and Price, *Profiles of Union Growth*.
9. David Butler and Gareth Butler, *British Political Facts* (Hailsham: Dod's, sixth edition, 1986); and McHale, ed., *Political Parties of Europe*, vol. 2.
10. McHale, ed., *Political Parties of Europe*, vol. 1.
11. *Ibid.*
12. U.S. Department of Labor, *International Labor Profiles* (Detroit: Grand River Books, 1980).
13. McHale, ed., *Political Parties of Europe*, vol. 1; and André Kédros, *Les Socialistes au Pouvoir* (Paris: Plon, 1986).
14. Pelinka, *Social Democratic Parties in Europe*.
15. Stewart, *Trade Unions in Europe*.

16. McHale, ed., *Political Parties of Europe*, vol. 1.
17. *Ibid.*, vol. 2.
18. *Ibid.*
19. L. F. Crisp, *The Australian Federal Labour Party* (Sydney: Hale & Iremonger, 1978); and Australian Information Service, "Fact Sheet on Australia: 1983 Election Results".
20. Bain and Price, *Profiles of Union Growth.*
21. Richard Mulgan, *Democracy and Power in New Zealand* (Auckland: Oxford University Press, 1984); and Leslie Lipson, *The Politics of Equality* (Chicago: University of Chicago Press, 1948); *New Zealand Labour Party Journal*, vol. 2, no. 2, 1966.
22. *New Zealand Official Year Book.*
23. Bain and Price, *Profiles of Union Growth.*
24. Doris French, *Faith, Sweat and Politics* (Toronto: McClelland and Stewart, 1963), p. 144.
25. Gad Horowitz, *Canadian Labour in Politics* (Toronto: University of Toronto Press, 1968); Desmond Morton, *Social Democracy in Canada* (Toronto: Samuel Stevens, Hakkert, second edition, 1977), Chapter 1.

Chapter 5

1. C. H. Higginbotham, *Off the Record: The CCF in Saskatchewan* (Toronto: McClelland and Stewart, 1968); and Desmond Morton, *Social Democracy in Canada* (Toronto: Samuel Stevens, Hakkert, second edition, 1977).
2. George Cadbury, "Planning in Saskatchewan", in Laurier La-Pierre, ed., *Essays on the Left* (Toronto: McClelland and Stewart, 1971).
3. Unpublished information on the programs courtesy of former ministers Dennis Cocke and Alex Macdonald and of former MLA Rosemary Brown.
4. Morton, *Social Democracy in Canada.* Further unpublished information courtesy of the Hon. Muriel Smith, the Hon. Eugene Kostyra, and Bill Blaikie, MP.
5. Government of Manitoba, "Manitoba Jobs Fund", Winnipeg, 1983.
6. Mats Forsberg, *The Evolution of Social Welfare Policy in Sweden* (The Swedish Institute, 1984), p. 31.

7. Martin Linton, *The Swedish Road to Socialism* (London: The Fabian Society, 1985), No. 503.
8. Bo Jangenäs, *The Swedish Approach to Labor Market Policy* (The Swedish Institute, 1985).
9. Rudolf Meidner, *Employee Investment Funds* (London: Allen & Unwin, 1978).
10. Franz Grössl, *The Political System in Austria* (Vienna: Federal Press Service, 1984).
11. *The Rational Approach to Labour and Industry* (Vienna: Federal Press Service, 1984); and Sven W. Arndt, ed., *The Political Economy of Austria* (Washington: American Enterprise Institute for Public Policy Research, 1982).
12. Franz Grössl, ed., *Labour Code* (Vienna: Federal Press Service, 1983).
13. André Kédros, *Les Socialistes au Pouvoir* (Paris: Plon, 1986).

Chapter 6

1. Ministry of Industry, Trade and Technology, "Assessment of Direct Employment Effects of Freer Trade for Ontario's Manufacturing Industries" (Toronto, 1985).
2. *Globe and Mail*, June 3, 1983.
3. *London Free Press*, June 1, 1983.
4. *Toronto Star*, May 31, 1983.
5. Brief, Citizens for Public Justice, Toronto, 1986.
6. Reginald W. Bibby, *Anglitrends*, Study for the Anglican Diocese of Toronto (Toronto, 1986), p. 28.
7. Department of Finance, Communiqué, September 18, 1986.
8. For a similar analysis, see Lukin Robinson, "Budget Politics", *Canadian Forum*, vol. 66, November 1986.
9. A "most conservative" estimate is made of $32,000 per inmate in the Report of the Auditor General of Canada to the House of Commons, Ottawa, 1986. Based on the spending estimates themselves, however, the difference is $132,000 per inmate.
10. F. J. Fletcher and R. J. Drummond, "Attitude Trends 1960-1978", *Institute for Research in Public Policy*, No. 4, 1979.

Chapter 7

1. Canadian Union of Public Employees, "Survey of Public Opinion", June 1986.
2. Anthony N. Doob and Julian Roberts, *Crime: Some Views of the Canadian Public* (Centre of Criminology, University of Toronto, 1982); and "Sentencing", Department of Justice, Ottawa, 1983.
3. Department of External Affairs, Decima survey on foreign policy, 1985.
4. Alex Macdonald, *My Dear Legs* (Vancouver: New Star, 1985), p. 157.
5. Needham and Harper, "Lifestyle and Product Use", Toronto, 1985.
6. The Decima survey on foreign policy, 1985.
7. Jane Jenson, "Party Loyalty in Canada", *Canadian Journal of Political Science*, vol. 8, 1975, pp. 543-53.

Chapter 8

1. *Globe and Mail*, September 18, 1986.
2. Needham and Harper, "Lifestyle and Product Use", Toronto, 1985.
3. Charles Taylor, "The Agony of Economic Man", in Laurier LaPierre, ed., *Essays on the Left* (Toronto: McClelland and Stewart, 1971), p. 229.

NOTE ON SOURCES

A number of the sources cited in the Notes are unpublished or now out-of-print materials not readily available to the general reader. Fortunately, however, there are also many good sources on the New Democratic Party that are in print and accessible. These are all fully noted in the Notes.

For the reader interested in pursuing the subject further, I would recommend the following reading list:

On the social gospel movement and the formation of the CCF:

Allen, Richard, *The Social Gospel in Canada*. Ottawa: National Museums of Canada, 1973.

———, *The Social Passion*. Toronto: University of Toronto Press, 1973.

Bland, Salem, *The New Christianity*. Toronto: University of Toronto Press, second edition, 1973.

Brennan, J. William, ed., *Building the Co-operative Commonwealth*. Regina: Plains Research Center, 1984.

Caplan, Gerald L., *The Dilemma of Canadian Socialism*. Toronto: McClelland and Stewart, 1973.

Coldwell, M. J., *Canadian Progressives on the March*. New York: League for Industrial Democracy, undated.

Crysdale, Stewart. *The Industrial Stuggle and Protestant Ethics in Canada*. Toronto: Ryerson Press, 1961.

Douglas, T. C., *The Making of a Socialist*. Edmonton: University of Alberta Press, 1984.

French, Doris, *Faith, Sweat and Politics*. Toronto: McClelland and Stewart, 1963.

258

Horn, Michiel, *The League for Social Reconstruction*. Toronto: University of Toronto Press, 1980.

Irvine, William, *The Farmers in Politics*. Toronto: McClelland and Stewart, 1920.

Lewis, David, *The Good Fight*. Toronto: Macmillan of Canada, 1981.

———— and Frank Scott, *Make This YOUR Canada*. Toronto: Central Canada Publishing, 1943.

Lipset, S. M., *Agrarian Socialism*. Berkeley: University of California Press, 1959.

McHenry, Dean E., *The Third Force in Canada*. Berkeley: University of California Press, 1960.

MacInnis, Grace, *J. S. Woodsworth*. Toronto: Macmillan of Canada, 1953.

McNaught, Kenneth, *A Prophet in Politics*. Toronto: University of Toronto Press, 1959.

Mardiros, Anthony, *William Irvine*. Toronto: Lorimer, 1979.

Penner, Norman, *The Canadian Left*. Scarborough, Ont.: Prentice-Hall, 1977.

Scott, R. B. Y., and Gregory Vlastos, *Towards the Christian Revolution*. Chicago: Willott, Clark, 1936.

Vlastos, Gregory, *Christian Faith and Democracy*. New York: Hazen, 1939.

Shackleton, Doris French, *Tommy Douglas*. Toronto: McClelland and Stewart, 1975.

Young, Walter D., *The Anatomy of a Party: The National CCF*. Toronto: University of Toronto Press, 1969.

Major sources on the formation and early history of the New Democratic Party are:

Knowles, Stanley, *The New Party*. Toronto: McClelland and Stewart, 1961.

LaPierre, Laurier, ed., *Essays on the Left*. Toronto: McClelland and Stewart, 1971.

Morton, Desmond, *Social Democracy in Canada*. Toronto: Samuel Stevens, Hakkert, second edition, 1977.

Oliver, Michael, ed., *Social Purpose for Canada*. Toronto: University of Toronto Press, 1961.

INDEX